THIS EXAM KIT COMES WITH
FREE ONLINE ACCESS
TO EXTRA RESOURCES AIMED AT HELPING YOU PASS YOUR EXAMS

IN ADDITION TO THE OFFICIAL QUESTIONS AND ANSWERS IN THIS BOOK, GO ONLINE AND EN-gage WITH:

- An iPaper version of the Exam Kit
- Articles including Key Examinable Areas
- Material updates
- Latest Official ACCA exam questions
- Extra question assistance using the Signpost icon
- Timed Questions with an online tutor debrief using the Clock icon

And you can access all of these extra resources anytime, anywhere using your EN-gage account.

How to access your online resources

If you are a Kaplan Financial tuition, full-time or distance learning student

You will already have an EN-gage account and these extra resources will be available to you online. You do not need to register again, as this process was completed when you enrolled. If having problems accessing online materials, please ask your course administrator.

If you purchased through Kaplan Flexible Learning or via the Kaplan Publishing website

You will automatically receive an e-mail invitation to EN-gage online. Please register your details using this e-mail to gain access to your content. If you do not receive the e-mail or book content, please contact our Technical Support team at engage@twinsystems.com.

If you are already a registered EN-gage user

Go to www.EN-gage.co.uk and log in. Select the 'add a book' feature and enter the ISBN number of this book and the unique pass key at the bottom of this card. Then click 'finished' or 'add another book'. You may add as many books as you have purchased from this screen.

If you are a new EN-gage user

Register at www.EN-gage.co.uk and click on the link contained in the e-mail we sent you to activate your account. Then select the 'add a book' feature, enter the ISBN number of this book and the unique pass key at the bottom of this card. Then click 'finished' or 'add another book'.

Your Code and Information

This code can only be used once for the registration of one book online. This registration will expire when the final sittings for the examinations covered by this book have taken place. Please allow one hour from the time you submitted your book details for us to process your request.

EN-gage

pcE5-Ueo0-S6T2-F3Tg

Please be aware that this code is case-sensitive and you will need to include the dashes within the passcode, but not when entering the ISBN. For further technical support, please visit www.EN-gage.co.uk

For technical support, please visit www.EN-gage.co.uk

Professional Examinations

Paper F5

Performance Management

EXAM KIT

KAPLAN

PUBLISHING

British Library Cataloguing-in-Publication Data

A catalogue record for this book is available from the British Library.

Published by:

Kaplan Publishing UK

Unit 2 The Business Centre

Molly Millar's Lane

Wokingham

Berkshire

RG41 2QZ

ISBN: 978-1-84710-989-7

© Kaplan Financial Limited, 2010

Printed in the UK by CPI William Clowes Beccles NR34 7TL

Acknowledgements

The past ACCA examination questions are the copyright of the Association of Chartered Certified Accountants. The original answers to the questions from June 1994 onwards were produced by the examiners themselves and have been adapted by Kaplan Publishing.

We are grateful to the Chartered Institute of Management Accountants and the Institute of Chartered Accountants in England and Wales for permission to reproduce past examination questions. The answers have been prepared by Kaplan Publishing.

CONTENTS

Section

Key features in this edition

In addition to providing a wide ranging bank of real past exam questions, we have also included in this edition:

- An analysis of all of the recent new syllabus examination papers.

- Paper specific information and advice on exam technique.

- Our recommended approach to make your revision for this particular subject as effective as possible.

  This includes step by step guidance on how best to use our Kaplan material (Complete text, pocket notes and exam kit) at this stage in your studies.

- Enhanced tutorial answers packed with specific key answer tips, technical tutorial notes and exam technique tips from our experienced tutors.

- Complementary online resources including full tutor debriefs and question assistance to point you in the right direction when you get stuck.

December 2009 – Real examination questions with enhanced tutorial answers

The real December 2009 exam questions with enhanced "walk through answers" and full "tutor debriefs" is available on Kaplan EN-gage at:

www.EN-gage.co.uk

You will find a wealth of other resources to help you with your studies on the following sites:

www.EN-gage.co.uk

www.**acca**global.com/students/

INDEX TO QUESTIONS AND ANSWERS

INTRODUCTION

The style of current Paper F5 exam questions are different to old syllabus Paper 2.4 questions. In addition, the structure of the F5 exam was changed for exams from June 2009 onwards. Before June 2009 the exam contained four compulsory questions worth 25 marks each. The exam now contains five compulsory questions worth 20 marks each.

Accordingly, many of the old ACCA questions within this kit have been adapted to reflect the new style and structure. If changed in any way from the original version, this is indicated in the end column of the index below with the mark *(A)*.

Note that the majority of the questions within the kit are past ACCA exam questions, the more recent questions (from 2005) are labelled as such in the index.

The pilot paper is included at the end of the kit.

KEY TO THE INDEX

PAPER ENHANCEMENTS

We have added the following enhancements to the answers in this exam kit:

Key answer tips

Most answers include key answer tips to help your understanding of each question.

Tutorial note

Most answers include more tutorial notes to explain some of the technical points in detail.

Top tutor tips

For selected questions, we "walk through the answer" giving guidance on how to approach the questions with helpful 'tips from a top tutor', together with technical tutor notes.

These answers are indicated with the "footsteps" icon in the index.

ONLINE ENHANCEMENTS

 Timed question with Online tutor debrief

For selected questions, we recommend that they are to be completed in full exam conditions (i.e. properly timed in a closed book environment).

In addition to the examiner's technical answer, enhanced with key answer tips and tutorial notes in this exam kit, online you can find an answer debrief by a top tutor that:

- works through the question in full

- points out how to approach the question

- how to ensure that the easy marks are obtained as quickly as possible, and

- emphasises how to tackle exam questions and exam technique.

These questions are indicated with the "clock" icon in the index.

 Online question assistance

Have you ever looked at a question and not know where to start, or got stuck part way through?

For selected questions, we have produced "Online question assistance" offering different levels of guidance, such as:

- ensuring that you understand the question requirements fully, highlighting key terms and the meaning of the verbs used

- how to read the question proactively, with knowledge of the requirements, to identify the topic areas covered

- assessing the detail content of the question body, pointing out key information and explaining why it is important

- help in devising a plan of attack

With this assistance, you should then be able to attempt your answer confident that you know what is expected of you.

These questions are indicated with the "signpost" icon in the index.

Online question enhancements and answer debriefs will be available from Spring 2010 on Kaplan EN-gage at:

www.EN-gage.co.uk

SPECIALIST COST AND MANAGEMENT ACCOUNTING TECHNIQUES

DECISION MAKING TECHNIQUES

BUDGETING

STANDARD COSTING AND VARIANCE ANALYSIS

PERFORMANCE MEASUREMENT AND CONTROL

ANALYSIS OF PAST PAPERS

The table below summarises the key topics that have been tested in the new syllabus examinations to date.

Note that the references are to the number of the question in this edition of the exam kit, but the Pilot Paper is produced in its original form at the end of the kit and therefore these questions have retained their original numbering in the paper itself.

	Jun 08	Dec 08	Jun 09	Dec 09	Jun 10
Specialist cost and management accounting techniques					
ABC	Q3				Q1
Target costing					
Lifecycle costing		Q7			
Throughput accounting			Q9		
Decision making techniques					
Key factor analysis					
Linear programming	Q14				Q3
Pricing				Q5	
Relevant costing			Q15	Q5	
Uncertainty and risk		Q23	Q24		
Budgeting					
Budgeting		Q7	Q24		
Forecasting		Q7, Q30		Q3	
Learning curves		Q30		Q2	
Standard costing and variance analysis					
Standard costing		Q7			
Basic variances	Q40		Q37		Q1, Q2
Labour idle time	Q40				
Mix and yield			Q37	Q1	
Planning and operational					
Performance measurement and control					
Performance measurement	Q55	Q48	Q56	Q1,Q4	Q2, Q5
ROI/ RI		Q48			
Transfer pricing					Q4
Not for profit organisations					

KAPLAN PUBLISHING

EXAM TECHNIQUE

- Use the allocated **15 minutes reading and planning time** at the beginning of the exam:
    - read the questions and examination requirements carefully, and
    - begin planning your answers.

    See the Paper Specific Information for advice on how to use this time for this paper.

- **Divide the time** you spend on questions in proportion to the marks on offer:
    - there are 1.8 minutes available per mark in the examination
    - within that, try to allow time at the end of each question to review your answer and address any obvious issues

    Whatever happens, always keep your eye on the clock and **do not over run on any part of any question!**

- Spend the last **five minutes** of the examination:
    - reading through your answers, and
    - **making any additions or corrections**.

- If you **get completely stuck** with a question:
    - leave space in your answer book, and
    - **return to it later.**

- Stick to the question and **tailor your answer** to what you are asked.
    - pay particular attention to the verbs in the question.

- If you do not understand what a question is asking, **state your assumptions**.

    Even if you do not answer in precisely the way the examiner hoped, you should be given some credit, if your assumptions are reasonable.

- You should do everything you can to make things easy for the marker.

    The marker will find it easier to identify the points you have made if your **answers are legible**.

- **Written questions**:

    Your answer should have:
    - a clear structure
    - a brief introduction, a main section and a conclusion.

    Be concise.

    It is better to write a little about a lot of different points than a great deal about one or two points.

- **Computations**:

    It is essential to include all your workings in your answers.

    Many computational questions can be answered using a standard step by step approach.

    e.g. ABC computations, linear programming and variance calculations.

    Be sure you know these steps before the exam and practice answering a range of questions using the same step by step approach.

- **Reports, memos and other documents**:

    Some questions ask you to present your answer in the form of a report, a memo, a letter or other document.

    Make sure that you use the correct format – there could be easy marks to gain here.

PAPER SPECIFIC INFORMATION

THE EXAM

FORMAT OF THE EXAM

Number of marks

5 compulsory questions worth 20 marks each.   100

There will be a mixture of written requirements (40-50%) and computational requirements (50–60%).

Total time allowed: 3 hours plus 15 minutes reading and planning time.

Note that:

- All syllabus areas will be examined.

- The exam may contain one question from each syllabus area. However, some exam questions have examined more than one syllabus area in the same question.

- Questions will be based around a short scenario. It is important to refer back to this scenario when answering the question.

PASS MARK

The pass mark for all ACCA Qualification examination papers is 50%.

READING AND PLANNING TIME

Remember that all three hour paper based examinations have an additional 15 minutes reading and planning time.

ACCA GUIDANCE

ACCA guidance on the use of this time is as follows:

This additional time is allowed at the beginning of the examination to allow candidates to read the questions and to begin planning their answers before they start to write in their answer books.

This time should be used to ensure that all the information and, in particular, the exam requirements are properly read and understood.

During this time, candidates may only annotate their question paper. They may not write anything in their answer booklets until told to do so by the invigilator.

KAPLAN GUIDANCE

As all questions are compulsory, there are no decisions to be made about choice of questions, other than in which order you would like to tackle them.

Therefore, in relation to F5, we recommend that you take the following approach with your reading and planning time:

- **Skim through the whole paper**, assessing the level of difficulty of each question.

- **Write down** on the question paper next to the mark allocation **the amount of time you should spend on each part.** Do this for each part of every question.

- **Decide the order** in which you think you will attempt each question:

  This is a personal choice and you have time on the revision phase to try out different approaches, for example, if you sit mock exams.

  A common approach is to tackle the question you think is the easiest and you are most comfortable with first.

  Psychologists believe that you usually perform at your best on the second and third question you attempt, once you have settled into the exam, so not tackling the most difficult question first may be advisable.

  It is usual however that students tackle their least favourite topic and/or the most difficult question in their opinion last.

  Whatever you approach, you must make sure that you leave enough time to attempt all questions fully and be very strict with yourself in timing each question.

- **For each question** in turn, read the requirements and then the detail of the question carefully.

  Always read the requirement first as this enables you to **focus on the detail of the question with the specific task in mind.**

  For computational questions:

  Highlight key numbers / information and key words in the question, scribble notes to yourself on the question paper to remember key points in your answer.

  Jot down proformas required if applicable.

  For written questions:

  Take notice of the format required (e.g. letter, memo, notes) and identify the recipient of the answer . You need to do this to judge the level of financial sophistication required in your answer and whether the use of a formal reply or informal bullet points would be satisfactory.

  Plan your beginning, middle and end and the key areas to be addressed and your use of titles and sub-titles to enhance your answer.

  For all questions:

  Spot the easy marks to be gained in a question and parts which can be performed independently of the rest of the question. For example, a definition of a variance or an explanation of the steps carried out in target costing.

  Make sure that you do these parts first when you tackle the question.

> Don't go overboard in terms of planning time on any one question – you need a good measure of the whole paper and a plan for all of the questions at the end of the 15 minutes.
>
> By covering all questions you can often help yourself as you may find that facts in one question may remind you of things you should put into your answer relating to a different question.

- With your plan of attack in mind, **start answering your chosen question** with your plan to hand, as soon as you are allowed to start.

 Always keep your eye on the clock and do not over run on any part of any question!

DETAILED SYLLABUS

The detailed syllabus and study guide written by the ACCA can be found at:

www.**acca**global.com/students/

KAPLAN'S RECOMMENDED REVISION APPROACH

QUESTION PRACTICE IS THE KEY TO SUCCESS

Success in professional examinations relies upon you acquiring a firm grasp of the required knowledge at the tuition phase. In order to be able to do the questions, knowledge is essential.

However, the difference between success and failure often hinges on your exam technique on the day and making the most of the revision phase of your studies.

The **Kaplan complete text** is the starting point, designed to provide the underpinning knowledge to tackle all questions. However, in the revision phase, pouring over text books is not the answer.

Kaplan Online fixed tests help you consolidate your knowledge and understanding and are a useful tool to check whether you can remember key topic areas.

Kaplan pocket notes are designed to help you quickly revise a topic area, however you then need to practice questions. There is a need to progress to full exam standard questions as soon as possible, and to tie your exam technique and technical knowledge together.

The importance of question practice cannot be over-emphasised.

The recommended approach below is designed by expert tutors in the field, in conjunction with their knowledge of the examiner and their recent real exams.

The approach taken for the fundamental papers is to revise by topic area. However, with the professional stage papers, a multi topic approach is required to answer the scenario based questions.

You need to practice as many questions as possible in the time you have left.

OUR AIM

Our aim is to get you to the stage where you can attempt exam standard questions confidently, to time, in a closed book environment, with no supplementary help (i.e. to simulate the real examination experience).

Practising your exam technique on real past examination questions, in timed conditions, is also vitally important for you to assess your progress and identify areas of weakness that may need more attention in the final run up to the examination.

In order to achieve this we recognise that initially you may feel the need to practice some questions with open book help and exceed the required time.

The approach below shows you which questions you should use to build up to coping with exam standard question practice, and references to the sources of information available should you need to revisit a topic area in more detail.

Remember that in the real examination, all you have to do is:

- attempt all questions required by the exam

- only spend the allotted time on each question, and

- get them at least 50% right!

Try and practice this approach on every question you attempt from now to the real exam.

EXAMINER COMMENTS

We have included the examiners comments to the specific new syllabus examination questions in this kit for you to see the main pitfalls that students fall into with regard to technical content.

However, too many times in the general section of the report, the examiner comments that students had failed due to:

- "not answering the question"

- "a poor understanding of why something is done, not just how it is done"

- "simply writing out numbers from the question. Candidates must understand what the numbers tell them about business performance"

- "a lack of common business sense" and

- "ignoring clues in the question".

Good exam technique is vital.

THE KAPLAN PAPER F5 REVISION PLAN

Stage 1: Assess areas of strengths and weaknesses

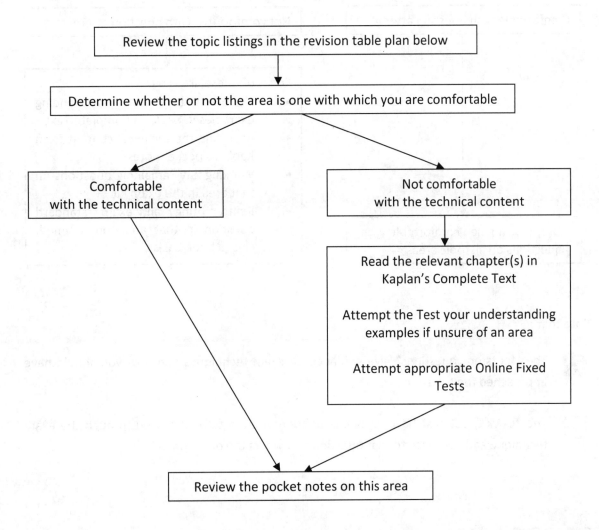

Stage 2: Practice questions

Follow the order of revision of topics as recommended in the revision table plan below and attempt the questions in the order suggested.

Try to avoid referring to text books and notes and the model answer until you have completed your attempt.

Try to answer the question in the allotted time.

Review your attempt with the model answer and assess how much of the answer you achieved in the allocated exam time.

Fill in the self-assessment box below and decide on your best course of action.

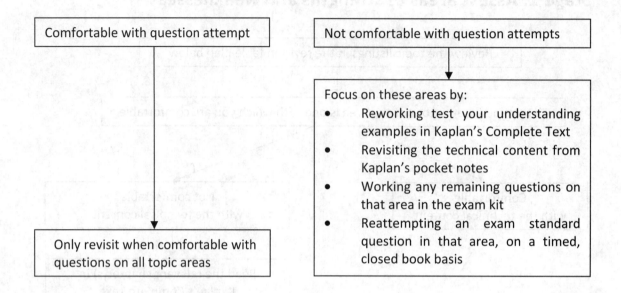

| Comfortable with question attempt | Not comfortable with question attempts |

Focus on these areas by:
- Reworking test your understanding examples in Kaplan's Complete Text
- Revisiting the technical content from Kaplan's pocket notes
- Working any remaining questions on that area in the exam kit
- Reattempting an exam standard question in that area, on a timed, closed book basis

Only revisit when comfortable with questions on all topic areas

Note that :

 The "footsteps questions" give guidance on exam techniques and how you should have approached the question.

 The "clock questions" have an online debrief where a tutor talks you through the exam technique and approach to that question and works the question in full.

Stage 3: Final pre-exam revision

We recommend that you **attempt at least one three hour mock examination** containing a set of previously unseen exam standard questions.

It is important that you get a feel for the breadth of coverage of a real exam without advanced knowledge of the topic areas covered – just as you will expect to see on the real exam day.

Ideally this mock should be sat in timed, closed book, real exam conditions and could be:

- a mock examination offered by your tuition provider, and/or

- the pilot paper in the back of this exam kit, and/or

- the last real examination paper (available shortly afterwards on Kaplan EN-gage with "enhanced walk through answers" and a full "tutor debrief").

THE DETAILED REVISION PLAN

Topic	Complete Text Chapter	Pocket note Chapter	Questions to attempt	Tutor guidance	Date attempted	Self assessment
Specialist cost and management accounting techniques						
– ABC	1	1	2 3 4 1 (pilot paper)	This is a key costing technique. Make sure that you can calculate the cost per unit using the five step approach. Be ready to explain the reasons for the development of ABC, the pros and cons of ABC and the implications of ABC. Successful completion of the recommended questions should reassure you that you would be able to tackle an ABC question in the exam.		
– Target costing	1	1	8	This is an excellent question on target costing. It is important that you can calculate the total cost and the cost gap and that you are able to discuss the process of target costing as well as recommending methods for closing the cost gap. Exam questions may also ask for a discussion of the implications of target costing or of the use of target costing in the service industry.		
– Lifecycle costing	1	1	6	This is a relatively straightforward technique but it is still important to practice at least one question to ensure you have the required knowledge.		

– Environmental Management accounting	1	11	This is a good written question on EMA. It is important that you can explain what is meant by EMA and that you understand how it should be used. Make sure that you reference your points back to the scenario.
– Throughput accounting	1	9 10	Two good questions covering the different calculations and written areas that could be examined on throughout accounting. This is a more difficult costing technique and it is therefore important to complete these questions before the exam.
Decision making techniques			
– Linear programming	2	16 17	Two excellent questions on linear programming. In addition to the six step approach, the examiner is likely to examine some peripheral areas such as shadow prices, slack or linear programming assumptions.
– Pricing	3	22	A good question on pricing that mixes calculations with written parts.

KAPLAN PUBLISHING

Relevant costing	4	4	This is a difficult area but a methodical approach to answering questions, i.e. setting up a summary of relevant cash flows with separate workings referenced in, should help when answering these questions. If you are not sure about a particular number, take a guess and move on. The aim is not to get the question 100% correct but to get through the question in time and to score a pass in the question.
		18	
		19	
Uncertainty and risk	5	5	The calculations are important here but you must also be prepared to discuss the various methods of managing risk. Some of the terms, e.g. minimax regret, make this area appear difficult but the underlying concepts are relatively straightforward.
		28	
		31	
Budgeting			
Budgeting	6 and 7	6 and 7	Do not overlook this area. Knowledge of the written areas of budgeting can help you to score relatively easy marks in the exam. The simple budgeting calculations should not cause you too many problems.
		32	
		33	
Learning curves	8	8	Two excellent questions on learning curves and are representative of what you should expect in the exam. Be prepared to discuss the reservations with the learning curve.
		36	
		37	

Standard costing and variance analysis

– Basic variances and idle time	9	9	44	A key question on variances. This is a typical exam question and requires a discussion of a number of pre-calculated variances as well as the calculation of a number of additional variances. It is important that you practice these calculations in order to ensure that you can complete the calculations to time in the exam.
– Mix and yield	10	10	45	The pilot paper question requires an in depth discussion and calculation of mix and yield variances and is good preparation for the exam.
– Planning and operational	10	10	51	Q51 is representative of the type of question that may come up on this area.

Performance measurement and control

– Performance measurement	11	11	57	There are a large number of questions on this area but these three questions are representative of what may come up in the real exam. It is important that you can assess the financial and non-financial performance of a business. Do not simply copy numbers from the scenario but discuss the implications of the numbers.
– ROI/ RI	12	12	55	It is important that you can calculate the ROI and RI but you must also be able to discuss the pros and cons of each of these methods.

KAPLAN PUBLISHING

– Transfer pricing	12	12	59	A difficult question on transfer pricing requiring an in depth understanding of the information contained in the scenario.
– Not for profit organisations	13	13	66 67	Two in depth questions on not for profit organisations but these will serve as excellent preparation for any exam question on this area.

Note that not all of the questions are referred to in the programme above. We have recommended a large number of exam standard questions and successful completion of these should reassure you that you have a good grounding of all of the key topics and are well prepared for the exam.

The remaining questions are available in the kit for extra practice for those who require more question on some areas.

FORMULAE

Learning curve

$Y = ax^b$

Where y   = average cost per batch

        a   = cost of first batch

        x   = total number of batches produced

        b   = learning factor (log LR/log 2)

        LR   = the learning rate as a decimal

Regression analysis

$y = a + bx$

$$b = \frac{n\sum xy - \sum x \sum y}{n\sum x^2 - (\sum x)^2}$$

$$a = \frac{\sum y}{n} - \frac{b\sum x}{n}$$

$$r = \frac{n\sum xy - \sum x \sum y}{\sqrt{(n\sum x^2 - (\sum x)^2)(n\sum y^2 - (\sum y)^2)}}$$

Demand curve

$P = a - bQ$

$$b = \frac{\text{Change in price}}{\text{Change in quantity}}$$

a = price when $Q = 0$

KAPLAN PUBLISHING

Section 1

PRACTICE QUESTIONS

SPECIALIST COST AND MANAGEMENT ACCOUNTING TECHNIQUES

1 ABC

(a) Discuss the conditions under which the introduction of ABC is likely to be most effective, paying particular attention to:

- product mix
- the significance of overheads and the ABC method of charging costs
- the availability of information collection procedures and resources, and
- other appropriate factors. **(12 marks)**

(b) Explain why ABC might lead to a more accurate assessment of management performance than absorption costing. **(8 marks)**

(Total: 20 marks)

2 BRICK BY BRICK (JUNE 10 EXAM)

Brick by Brick (BBB) is a building business that provides a range of building services to the public. Recently they have been asked to quote for garage conversions (GC) and extensions to properties (EX) and have found that they are winning fewer GC contracts than expected.

BBB has a policy to price all jobs at budgeted total cost plus 50%. Overheads are currently absorbed on a labour hour basis. BBB thinks that a switch to activity based costing (ABC) to absorb overheads would reduce the cost associated to GC and hence make them more competitive.

You are provided with the following data:

Overhead category	Annual overheads $	Activity driver	Total number of activities per year
Supervisors	90,000	Site visits	500
Planners	70,000	Planning documents	250
Property related	240,000	Labour hours	40,000
	———		
Total	400,000		
	———		

A typical GC costs $3,500 in materials and takes 300 labour hours to complete. A GC requires only one site visit by a supervisor and needs only one planning document to be raised. The typical EX costs $8,000 in materials and takes 500 hours to complete. An EX requires six site visits and five planning documents. In all cases labour is paid $15 per hour.

Required:

(a) Calculate the cost and quoted price of a GC and of an EX using labour hours to absorb the overheads. (5 marks)

(b) Calculate the cost and the quoted price of a GC and of an EX using ABC to absorb the overheads. (5 marks)

(c) Assuming that the cost of a GC falls by nearly 7% and the price of an EX rises by about 2% as a result of the change to ABC, suggest possible pricing strategies for the two products that BBB sells and suggest two reasons other than high prices for the current poor sales of the GC. (6 marks)

(d) One BBB manager has suggested that only marginal cost should be included in budget cost calculations as this would avoid the need for arbitrary overhead allocations to products. Briefly discuss this point of view and comment on the implication for the amount of mark-up that would be applied to budget costs when producing quotes for jobs. (4 marks)

(Total: 20 marks)

3   JOLA PUBLISHING CO (JUNE 08 EXAM)

Jola Publishing Co publishes two forms of book.

The company publishes a children's book (CB), which is sold in large quantities to government controlled schools. The book is produced in only four large production runs but goes through frequent government inspections and quality assurance checks.

The paper used is strong, designed to resist the damage that can be caused by the young children it is produced for. The book has only a few words and relies on pictures to convey meaning.

The second book is a comprehensive technical journal (TJ). It is produced in monthly production runs, 12 times a year. The paper used is of relatively poor quality and is not subject to any governmental controls and consequently only a small number of inspections are carried out. The TJ uses far more machine hours than the CB in its production.

The directors are concerned about the performance of the two books and are wondering what the impact would be of a switch to an activity based costing (ABC) approach to accounting for overheads. They currently use absorption costing, based on machine hours for all overhead calculations. They have accurately produced an analysis for the accounting year just completed as follows:

	CB	TJ
	$ per unit	$ per unit
Direct production costs:		
Paper	0.75	0.08
Printing ink	1.45	4.47
Machine costs	1.15	1.95
Overheads	2.30	3.95
Total cost	5.65	10.45
Selling price	9.05	13.85
Margin	3.40	3.40

The main overheads involved are:

Overhead	% of total overhead	Activity driver
Property costs	75.0%	Machine hours
Quality control	23.0%	Number of inspections
Production set up costs	2.0%	Number of set ups

If the overheads above were re-allocated under ABC principles then the results would be that the overhead allocation to CB would be $0.05 higher and the overhead allocated to TJ would be $0.30 lower than previously.

Required:

(a) **Explain why the overhead allocations have changed in the way indicated above.**

(7 marks)

The directors are keen to introduce ABC for the coming year and have provided the following cost and selling price data:

1   The paper used costs $2 per kg for a CB but the TJ paper costs only $1 per kg. The CB uses 400g of paper for each book, four times as much as the TJ uses.

2   Printing ink costs $30 per litre. The CB uses one third of the printing ink of the larger TJ. The TJ uses 150ml of printing ink per book.

3   The CB needs six minutes of machine time to produce each book, whereas the TJ needs 10 minutes per book. The machines cost $12 per hour to run.

4   The sales prices are to be $9.30 for the CB and $14.00 for the TJ.

As mentioned above there are three main overheads, the data for these are:

Overhead	Annual cost for the coming year ($)
Property costs	2,160,000
Quality control	668,000
Production set up costs	52,000
Total	2,880,000

The CB will be inspected on 180 occasions next year, whereas the TJ will be inspected just 20 times.

Jola Publishing will produce its annual output of 1,000,000 CBs in four production runs and approximately 10,000 TJs per month in each of 12 production runs.

Required:

(b) **Calculate the cost per unit and the margin for the CB and the TJ using machine hours to absorb the overheads.** **(5 marks)**

(c) **Calculate the cost per unit and the margin for the CB and the TJ using activity based costing principles to absorb the overheads.** **(8 marks)**

(Total: 20 marks)

Note: The original question, as written by the examiner also had the following requirement for 4 marks:

Briefly explain the implementation problems often experienced when ABC is first introduced.

4 ABKABER PLC

Abkaber plc assembles three types of motorcycle at the same factory: the 50cc Sunshine; the 250cc Roadster and the 1000cc Fireball. It sells the motorcycles throughout the world. In response to market pressures Abkaber plc has invested heavily in new manufacturing technology in recent years and, as a result, has significantly reduced the size of its workforce.

Historically, the company has allocated all overhead costs using total direct labour hours, but is now considering introducing Activity Based Costing (ABC). Abkaber plc's accountant has produced the following analysis.

	Annual output (units)	Annual direct labour hours	Selling price ($ per unit)	Raw material cost ($ per unit)
Sunshine	2,000	200,000	4,000	400
Roadster	1,600	220,000	6,000	600
Fireball	400	80,000	8,000	900

The three cost drivers that generate overheads are:

- Deliveries to retailers – the number of deliveries of motorcycles to retail showrooms

- Set-ups – the number of times the assembly line process is re-set to accommodate a production run of a different type of motorcycle

- Purchase orders – the number of purchase orders.

The annual cost driver volumes relating to each activity and for each type of motorcycle are as follows:

	Number of deliveries to retailers	Number of set-ups	Number of purchase orders
Sunshine	100	35	400
Roadster	80	40	300
Fireball	70	25	100

The annual overhead costs relating to these activities are as follows:

	$
Deliveries to retailers	2,400,000
Set-up costs	6,000,000
Purchase orders	3,600,000

All direct labour is paid at $5 per hour. The company holds no inventories.

At a board meeting there was some concern over the introduction of activity based costing.

The finance director argued: 'I very much doubt whether selling the Fireball is viable but I am not convinced that activity based costing would tell us any more than the use of labour hours in assessing the viability of each product.'

The marketing director argued: 'I am in the process of negotiating a major new contract with a motorcycle rental company for the Sunshine model. For such a big order they will not pay our normal prices but we need to at least cover our incremental costs. I am not convinced that activity based costing would achieve this as it merely averages costs for our entire production'.

The managing director argued: 'I believe that activity based costing would be an improvement but it still has its problems. For instance if we carry out an activity many times surely we get better at it and costs fall rather than remain constant. Similarly, some costs are fixed and do not vary either with labour hours or any other cost driver.'

The chairman argued: 'I cannot see the problem. The overall profit for the company is the same no matter which method of allocating overheads we use. It seems to make no difference to me.'

Required:

(a)   Calculate the total profit on each of Abkaber plc's three types of product using each of the following methods to attribute overheads:

(i)   the existing method based upon labour hours

(ii)   activity based costing.   **(13 marks)**

(b)   Explain the implications of activity based costing for Abkaber plc, and is so doing evaluate the issues raised by each of the directors   **(8 marks)**

(Total: 20 marks)

 Online question assistance

5   LIFECYCLE COSTING

'Companies operating in an advanced manufacturing environment are finding that about 90% of a product's life cycle cost is determined by decisions made early in the cycle. Management accounting systems should therefore be developed that aid the planning and control of product life-cycle costs and monitor spending at the early stages of the life cycle.'

Required:

Having regard to the above statement:

(a)   explain the nature of the product life cycle concept and its impact on businesses operating in an advanced manufacturing environment   **(7 marks)**

(b)   explain life cycle costing and state what distinguishes it from more traditional management accounting practices   **(9 marks)**

(c)   explain briefly the concept of activity based management and TWO benefits that its adoption could bring for a business.   **(4 marks)**

(Total: 20 marks)

6 MANPAC

SY Company, a manufacturer of computer games, has developed a new game called the MANPAC. This is an interactive 3D game and is the first of its kind to be introduced to the market. SY Company is due to launch the MANPAC in time for the peak selling season.

Traditionally SY Company has priced its games based on standard manufacturing cost plus selling and administration cost plus a profit margin. However, the management team of SY Company has recently attended a computer games conference where everyone was talking about life cycle costing, target costing and market-based pricing approaches. The team has returned from the conference and would like more details on the topics they heard about and how they could have been applied to the MANPAC.

Required:

As management accountant of SY Company:

(a) Discuss how the following techniques could have been applied to MANPAC:
   - life cycle costing
   - target costing. **(8 marks)**

(b) Evaluate the market-based pricing strategies that should have been considered for the launch of the MANPAC and recommend a strategy that should have been chosen. **(6 marks)**

(c) Explain briefly each stage in the product life cycle of the MANPAC and consider ONE issue that the management team will need to consider at each stage **(6 marks)**

(Total: 20 marks)

7 WARGRIN (DEC 08 EXAM)

Wargrin designs, develops and sells many PC games. Games have a short lifecycle lasting around three years only. Performance of the games is measured by reference to the profits made in each of the expected three years of popularity. Wargrin accepts a net profit of 35% of turnover as reasonable. A rate of contribution (sales price less variable cost) of 75% is also considered acceptable.

Wargrin has a large centralised development department which carries out all the design work before it passes the completed game to the sales and distribution department to market and distribute the product.

Wargrin has developed a brand new game called Stealth and this has the following budgeted performance figures.

The selling price of Stealth will be a constant $30 per game. Analysis of the costs show that at a volume of 10,000 units a total cost of $130,000 is expected. However at a volume of 14,000 units a total cost of $150,000 is expected. If volumes exceed 15,000 units the fixed costs will increase by 50%.

Stealth's budgeted volumes are as follows:

	Year 1	Year 2	Year 3
Sales volume	8,000 units	16,000 units	4,000 units

In addition, marketing costs for Stealth will be $60,000 in year one and $40,000 in year two. Design and development costs are all incurred before the game is launched and has cost $300,000 for Stealth. These costs are written off to the income statement as incurred (i.e. before year 1 above).

Required:

(a)   Explain the principles behind lifecycle costing and briefly state why Wargrin in particular should consider these lifecycle principles.   **(4 marks)**

(b)   Produce the budgeted results for the game 'Stealth' and briefly assess the game's expected performance, taking into account the whole lifecycle of the game.

(9 marks)

(c)   Explain why incremental budgeting is a common method of budgeting and outline the main problems with such an approach.   **(7 marks)**

(Total: 20 marks)

Note: The original question, as written by the examiner, also had the following requirement for 6 marks:

Discuss the extent to which a meaningful standard cost can be set for games produced by Wargrin. You should consider each of the cost classifications mentioned above.

---

8   EDWARD CO (DEC 07 EXAM)

Edward Limited assembles and sells many types of radio. It is considering extending its product range to include digital radios. These radios produce a better sound quality than traditional radios and have a large number of potential additional features not possible with the previous technologies (station scanning, more choice, one touch tuning, station identification text and song identification text etc).

A radio is produced by assembly workers assembling a variety of components. Production overheads are currently absorbed into product costs on an assembly labour hour basis.

Edward Limited is considering a target costing approach for its new digital radio product.

Required:

(a)   Briefly describe the target costing process that Edward Limited should undertake.

(3 marks)

(b)   Explain the benefits to Edward Limited of adopting a target costing approach at such an early stage in the product development process.   **(4 marks)**

A selling price of $44 has been set in order to compete with a similar radio on the market that has comparable features to Edward Limited's intended product. The board have agreed that the acceptable margin (after allowing for all production costs) should be 20%.

Cost information for the new radio is as follows:

Component 1 (Circuit board) – these are bought in and cost $4.10 each. They are bought in batches of 4,000 and additional delivery costs are $2,400 per batch.

Component 2 (Wiring) – in an ideal situation 25 cm of wiring is needed for each completed radio. However, there is some waste involved in the process as wire is occasionally cut to the wrong length or is damaged in the assembly process. Edward Limited estimates that 2% of the purchased wire is lost in the assembly process. Wire costs $0.50 per metre to buy.

Other material – other materials cost $8.10 per radio.

Assembly labour – these are skilled people who are difficult to recruit and retain. Edward Limited has more staff of this type than needed but is prepared to carry this extra cost in return for the security it gives the business. It takes 30 minutes to assemble a radio and the assembly workers are paid $12.60 per hour. It is estimated that 10% of hours paid to the assembly workers is for idle time.

Production Overheads – recent historic cost analysis has revealed the following production overhead data:

	Total production overhead ($)	Total assembly labour hours
Month 1	620,000	19,000
Month 2	700,000	23,000

Fixed production overheads are absorbed on an assembly hour basis based on normal annual activity levels. In a typical year 240,000 assembly hours will be worked by Edward Limited.

Required:

(c)   Calculate the expected cost per unit for the radio and identify any cost gap that might exist.   **(13 marks)**

(Total: 20 marks)

> **Note:** The original question also had the following requirement for 5 marks:
>
> **Assuming a cost gap was identified in the process, outline possible steps Edward Limited could take to reduce this gap.**

Walk in the footsteps of a top tutor

For tips on approaching the question, work through the boxed notes in order.

Once each requirement has been completed review the answer detail. Use this approach to reading and answering the question when tackling other questions.

> **(2) New product**

> **(1)** Start by reading each requirement and allocating time (1.8 mins per mark). Now read back through the question. Make notes or annotate the question whilst reading.

Edward Limited assembles and sells many types of radio. It is considering extending its product range to include digital radios. These radios produce a better sound quality than traditional radios and have a large number of potential additional features not possible with the previous technologies (station scanning, more choice, one touch tuning, station identification text and song identification text etc).

A radio is produced by assembly workers assembling a variety of components. Production overheads are currently absorbed into product costs on an assembly labour hour basis.

> **(3)** Traditional absorption costing

Edward Limited is considering a target costing approach for its new digital radio product.

> **(4) New costing approach being considered**

Required:

(a) Briefly describe the target costing process that Edward Limited should undertake. **(3 marks)**

(b) Explain the benefits to Edward Limited of adopting a target costing approach at such an early stage in the product development process. **(4 marks)**

> (5) Now answer parts (a) – (b). See separate notes at end of question.

A selling price of $44 has been set in order to compete with a similar radio on the market that has comparable features to Edward Limited's intended product. The board have agreed that the acceptable margin (after allowing for all production costs) should be 20%.

> (7) This is the target selling price and margin. Calculate target cost using this info.

> (8) Include this cost.

Cost information for the new radio is as follows:

Component 1 (Circuit board) – these are bought in and cost $4.10 each. They a bought in batches of 4,000 and additional delivery costs are $2,400 per batch.

> (9) Spread this cost over the number of batches

Component 2 (Wiring) – in an ideal situation 25 cm of wiring is needed for ea completed radio. However, there is some waste involved in the process as wire is occasionally cut to the wrong length or is damaged in the assembly process. Edward Limited estimates that 2% of the purchased wire is lost in the assembly process. Wire costs $0.50 per metre to buy.

> (10) Adjust usage for loss.

Other material – other materials cost $8.10 per radio.

> (11) Include these costs.

Assembly labour – these are skilled people who are difficult to recruit and retain. Edward Limited has more staff of this type than needed but is prepared to carry this extra cost in return for the security it gives the business. It takes 30 minutes to assemble a radio and the assembly workers are paid $12.60 per hour. It is estimated that 10% of hours paid to the assembly workers is for idle time.

> (12) Adjust hours for idle time.

Production Overheads – recent historic cost analysis has revealed the following production overhead data:

	Total production Overhead ($)	Total assembly labour hours
Month 1	620,000	19,000
Month 2	700,000	23,000

> (13) A mix of fixed and variable costs. Use hi-low to separate.

(6) Now read this requirement and allocate time. Read back through the remainder of the question, making notes or annotating the question in the same way as before.

Fixed production overheads are absorbed on an assembly hour basis based on normal annual activity levels. In a typical year 240,000 assembly hours will be worked by Edward Limited.

(14) Use to calculate the OAR.

(15) Now answer part (c). Set up a summary of costs with separate workings where required

Required:

(c) **Calculate the expected cost per unit for the radio and identify any cost gap that might exist.** **(13 marks)**

(Total: 20 marks)

Notes

- This is only a short scenario and so it should not take long to read and annotate the question. That should leave plenty of time to plan and write up the answer to requirements (a) – (c).

- Requirement (a) is worth 3 marks. Aim for 3–4 concise points. Brainstorm the key points first. Headings could be used for each key stage of the target costing process.

- Requirement (b) is worth 4 marks so aim to brainstorm 4 benefits first. A succinct explanation is all that is required and therefore 7 minutes should enough time to plan and write up the answer. Separate each of the benefits using individual paragraphs or headings. Make sure the actual requirement is answered, i.e. do not talk about general benefits of target costing.

---

9 YAM CO (JUNE 09 EXAM)

 Timed question with Online tutor debrief

Yam Co is involved in the processing of sheet metal into products A, B and C using three processes, pressing, stretching and rolling. Like many businesses Yam faces tough price competition in what is a mature world market.

The factory has 50 production lines each of which contain the three processes: Raw material for the sheet metal is first pressed then stretched and finally rolled. The processing capacity varies for each process and the factory manager has provided the following data:

Processing time per metre in hours

	Product A	Product B	Product C
Pressing	0.50	0.50	0.40
Stretching	0.25	0.40	0.25
Rolling	0.40	0.25	0.25

The factory operates for 18 hours each day for five days per week. It is closed for only two weeks of the year for holidays when maintenance is carried out. On average one hour of labour is needed for each of the 225,000 hours of factory time. Labour is paid $10 per hour.

The raw materials cost per metre is $3.00 for product A, $2.50 for product B and $1.80 for product C. Other factory costs (excluding labour and raw materials) are $18,000,000 per year. Selling prices per metre are $70 for product A, $60 for product B and $27 for product C.

Yam carries very little inventory.

Required:

(a) Identify the bottleneck process and briefly explain why this process is described as a 'bottleneck'.   (3 marks)

(b) Calculate the throughput accounting ratio (TPAR) for each product assuming that the bottleneck process is fully utilised.   (8 marks)

(c) Assuming that the TPAR of product C is less than 1:

(i)   Explain how Yam could improve the TPAR of product C.   (4 marks)

(ii) Briefly discuss whether this supports the suggestion to cease the production of product C and briefly outline three other factors that Yam should consider before a cessation decision is taken.   (5 marks)

(Total: 20 marks)

 Calculate your allowed time, allocate the time to the separate parts.....................

---

10   FLOPRO PLC

(a) Flopro plc makes and sells two products A and B, each of which passes through the same automated production operations. The following estimated information is available for period 1:

(i)
Product unit data:	A	B
Direct material cost ($)	2	40
Variable production overhead cost ($)	28	4
Overall hours per product unit (hours)	0.25	0.15

(ii) Production/sales of products A and B are 120,000 units and 45,000 units with selling prices per unit $60 and $70 respectively.

(iii) Maximum demand for each product is 20% above the estimated sales levels.

(iv) Total fixed production overhead cost is $1,470,000. This is absorbed at an average rate per hour based on the estimated production levels.

Required:

Using net profit as the decision measure, show why the management of Flopro plc argues that it is indifferent on financial grounds as to the mix of products A and B which should be produced and sold.   (5 marks)

(b) One of the production operations has a maximum capacity of 3,075 hours which has been identified as a bottleneck which limits the overall production/sales of products A and B. The bottleneck hours required per product unit for products A and B are 0.02 and 0.015 respectively.

Flopro plc has decided to determine the profit maximising mix of products A and B based on the Throughput Accounting principle of maximising the throughput return per production hour of the bottleneck resources. This may be measured as throughput return per production hour = (selling price − material cost)/bottleneck hours per unit.

Required:

(i) Calculate the mix (units) of products A and B which will maximise net profit and the value of that net profit. **(8 marks)**

(ii) Calculate the throughput ratio for product B which is calculated as: throughput return per hour of bottleneck resource for product B/overall total cost per hour of bottleneck resource. **(3 marks)**

(iii) Comment on the interpretation of throughput accounting ratios and their use as a control device. You should refer to the ratio for product B in your answer. **(4 marks)**

(Total: 20 marks)

11 ENVIRONMENTAL MANAGEMENT ACCOUNTING

FXT is a pharmaceutical company trying to decide whether to continue with the production of one of its drugs. On economic grounds, the decision to continue manufacture is marginal; However, in the light or recent high–profile corporate scandals linked to environmental disasters, FTX is particularly anxious to make an informed decision based mainly on the environmental effects of continued production.

Following up on a review of its operations and various reports from its Operations Director, FXT's management accountant has identified the company's main environmental costs as follows:

1 Waste disposal

2 Water consumption

3 Energy consumption

4 Transport and travel

Required:

(a) Explain how the costs listed above arise and what control measures could be implemented by FXT in order to manage them. **(10 marks)**

(b) Briefly describe four management accounting techniques for the identification and allocation of environmental costs. **(10 marks)**

(Total: 20 marks)

12 CHOCOLATES ARE FOREVER (CAF)

CAF Ltd produces a single large item of confectionary, Product S, that is sold for $12 per unit. You have been provided with the following information about the 'S' for the forthcoming year:

Sales   6,000 units

Variable costs $7 per unit

CAF's overheads are budgeted to amount to $20,000. CAF's Financial Director has asked you to prepare some documents for a presentation to the Board of Directors.

Required:

(a)   Calculate, and briefly explain the significance of, CAF'S breakeven point and margin of safety, expressed as a percentage.   **(4 marks)**

(b)   Based on CAF's information above, construct and explain the purpose of the three following charts:

1   A breakeven chart;

2   A contribution graph;

3   A profit – volume chart.

                                                                                    (12 marks)

(c)   Briefly outline the limitations of breakeven analysis.   **(4 marks)**

                                                                                    (Total: 20 marks)

13 BREAKEVEN

C Ltd has presented you with its break-even chart:

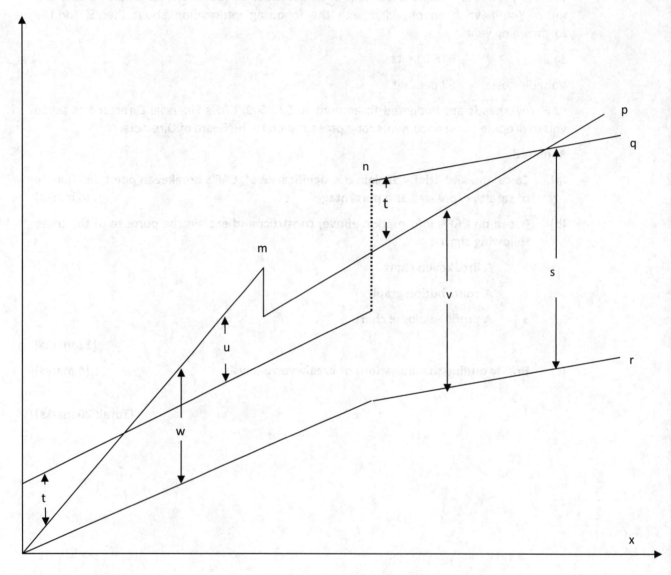

Required:

(a) Identify the components of the breakeven chart labelled *p ,q ,r, s, t, u, v w, x* and *y*.
(10 marks)

(b) Suggest what events are represented at the values of *x* that are labelled *m* and *n* on the chart.
(5 marks)

(c) Briefly comment on the usefulness of breakeven analysis to senior management of a small company.
(5 marks)

(Total: 20 marks)

14   EC LTD

EC ltd produces and sells the following two products throughout the year in a constant mix:

	Product X	*Product Y*
Variable cost per $ of sales	$0.45	$0.60
Fixed costs	$1,212,000 per period	

The management of EC has stated that total sales revenue will reach a maximum of $4,000,000, and is generated by the two products in the following proportions:

	Product X	*Product Y*
Variable cost per $ of sales	70%	30%

Required:

(a)   **Calculate the breakeven sales revenue required per period, based on the sales mix assumed above.**   **(5 marks)**

(b)   **Prepare a profit-volume chart of the above situation for the maximum sales revenue. Show on the same chart the effect of a change in the sales mix to product X 50%, product Y 50%, and clearly indicate on the chart the breakeven point for each situation.**   **(12 marks)**

(c)   **Of the fixed costs, $455,000 are attributable to Product X. Calculate the sales revenue required on Product X in order to recover the attributable fixed costs and provide a net contribution of $700,000 towards general fixed costs and profit.**
                                                      (4 marks)

                                                      (Total: 20 marks)

DECISION MAKING TECHNIQUES

15   B CHEMICALS

B Chemicals refines crude oil into petrol. The refining process uses two types of crude oil – heavy and light. A mixture of these oils is blended into either Super or Regular petrol.

In the refining process one gallon (g) of Super is made from 0.7g of heavy crude and 0.5g of light crude. One gallon of Regular is made from 0.5g of heavy crude and 0.7g of light crude oil. (There is a refining loss of 0.2g in each case.)

At present, 5,000g of heavy crude and 6,000g of light crude oil are available for refining each day. Market conditions suggest that at least two-thirds of the petrol refined should be Super. The company makes contribution of $0.25 per gallon of Super and $0.10 per gallon of Regular.

Required:

(a)   State the objective function and three constraints, one for heavy crude, one for light crude and one for market conditions.   **(6 marks)**

(b)   Graph the constraints and shade the feasible region.   **(8 marks)**

(c)   Deduce the optimal policy and the contribution generated, and comment briefly on your answer.   **(6 marks)**

(Total: 20 marks)

 Online question assistance

16   CUT AND STITCH (JUNE 10 EXAM)

Cut and Stitch (CS) make two types of suits using skilled tailors (labour) and a delicate and unique fabric (material). Both the tailors and the fabric are in short supply and so the accountant at CS has correctly produced a linear programming model to help decide the optimal production mix.

The model is as follows:

Variables:

Let W = the number of work suits produced

Let L = the number of lounge suits produced

Constraints

Tailors' time: $7W + 5L \le 3,500$ (hours) – this is line T on the diagram

Fabric: $2W + 2L \le 1,200$ (metres) – this is line F on the diagram

Production of work suits: $W \le 400$ – this is line P on the diagram

Objective is to maximise contribution subject to:

$C = 48W + 40L$

On the diagram provided the accountant has correctly identified OABCD as the feasible region and point B as the optimal point.

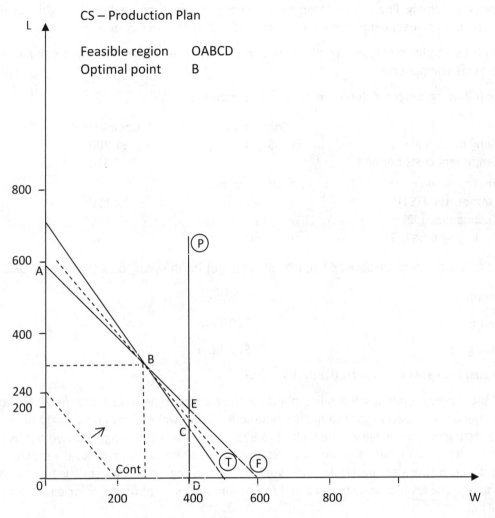

CS – Production Plan

Feasible region   OABCD
Optimal point   B

Required:

(a)   **Find by appropriate calculation the optimal production mix and related maximum contribution that could be earned by CS.**   **(4 marks)**

(b)   **Calculate the shadow prices of the fabric per metre and the tailor time per hour.**
                                                                    (6 marks)

The tailors have offered to work an extra 500 hours provided that they are paid three times their normal rate of $1.50 per hour at $4.50 per hour.

Required:

(c)   **Briefly discuss whether CS should accept the offer of overtime at three times the normal rate.**   **(6 marks)**

(d)   **Calculate the new optimum production plan if maximum demand for W falls to 200 units.**   **(4 marks)**

(Total: 20 marks)

17   DP PLC

DP plc assembles computers from bought-in components, using a computer-controlled robotic assembly line. The assembled computers are then tested by highly qualified computer engineers before they are packaged for despatch to customers.

DP plc currently assembles two different types of computer from different combinations of the same components.

The following budgeted details relate to the computers:

	Computer X	Computer Y
Selling price/unit	$800	$1,200
Component costs per unit	$150	$310
Minutes per unit	Minutes per unit	
Assembly time (S1)	80	130
Testing time (S2)	120	180
Packaging time (S3)	60	30

The following costs are derived from DP plc's budget for the year to 31 December 20X1:

Assembly	$180/hour
Testing	$60/hour
Packaging	$20/hour

No cost increases are expected until July 20X2.

DP plc is now preparing its detailed plans for the six-month period to 30 June 20X2. During this period, it expects that the assembly time available will be limited to 1,000 hours and the testing time available will be limited to 875 hours. The packaging is carried out by part-time workers, and the company believes that there are a number of local residents who would be pleased to undertake this work if the existing packaging staff were unable to complete the level of activity needed. The maximum levels of demand for each computer will be:

300 units of X (S4); and

800 units of Y (S5).

Required:

(a)   Calculate the contribution per unit for each type of computer.   **(2 marks)**

(b)   Determine the mix of computers that will maximise DP plc's profits for the six months ending 30 June 20X2, using a graphical linear programming solution, and calculate the contribution that will be earned.   **(8 marks)**

(c) DP plc now realises that there may be a limit on the number of packaging hours available. A computer package for linear programming has been used and the following solution determined:

Variables

		268.75	
		112.50	
Constraint		*Slack*	*Shadow price*
S1		23,875.00	0
S2		0	1.46
S3		0	4.75
S4		31.25	0
		687.50	0
Contribution		$107,437.50	

Required:

Write brief notes to the management team that interpret the solution produced by the computer package and make appropriate recommendations.

Note: **Do not formulate, or explain the basis of, the computer model.**   **(5 marks)**

(d) At the management meeting that discussed the report you produced in part (c) above, the senior computer engineer responsible for the testing of the computers was surprised at the times per unit being used in your calculations.

'It seems to me', she said 'that you have used the testing times per unit that were set as the targets when those models were first assembled. We seem to test them much more quickly now.'

Required:

Explain how the learning effect referred to by the senior computer engineer will affect the calculation of the optimum product mix. Use a 90% learning curve to illustrate your answer but do not determine a revised product mix.

Note: **The formula for a 90% learning curve is** $y = a^{-0.1520}$ **(5 marks)**

(Total: 20 marks)

18   BITS AND PIECES (JUNE 09 EXAM)

 Timed question with Online tutor debrief

Bits and Pieces (B&P) operates a retail store selling spares and accessories for the car market. The store has previously only opened for six days per week for the 50 working weeks in the year, but B&P is now considering also opening on Sundays.

The sales of the business on Monday through to Saturday averages at $10,000 per day with average gross profit of 70% earned.

B&P expects that the gross profit % earned on a Sunday will be 20 percentage points lower than the average earned on the other days in the week. This is because they plan to offer substantial discounts and promotions on a Sunday to attract customers. Given the price reduction, Sunday sales revenues are expected to be 60% more than the average daily sales revenues for the other days. These Sunday sales estimates are for new customers only, with no allowance being made for those customers that may transfer from other days.

B&P buys all its goods from one supplier. This supplier gives a 5% discount on all purchases if annual spend exceeds $1,000,000.

It has been agreed to pay time and a half to sales assistants that work on Sundays. The normal hourly rate is $20 per hour. In total five sales assistants will be needed for the six hours that the store will be open on a Sunday. They will also be able to take a half-day off (four hours) during the week. Staffing levels will be allowed to reduce slightly during the week to avoid extra costs being incurred.

The staff will have to be supervised by a manager, currently employed by the company and paid an annual salary of $80,000. If he works on a Sunday he will take the equivalent time off during the week when the assistant manager is available to cover for him at no extra cost to B&P. He will also be paid a bonus of 1% of the extra sales generated on the Sunday project.

The store will have to be lit at a cost of $30 per hour and heated at a cost of $45 per hour. The heating will come on two hours before the store opens in the 25 'winter' weeks to make sure it is warm enough for customers to come in at opening time. The store is not heated in the other weeks.

The rent of the store amounts to $420,000 annum.

Required:

(a) Calculate whether the Sunday opening incremental revenue exceeds the incremental costs over a year (ignore inventory movements) and on this basis reach a conclusion as to whether Sunday opening is financially justifiable. **(12 marks)**

(b) Discuss whether the manager's pay deal (time off and bonus) is likely to motivate him. **(4 marks)**

(c) Briefly discuss whether offering substantial price discounts and promotions on Sunday is a good suggestion. **(4 marks)**

(Total: 20 marks)

 Calculate your allowed time, allocate the time to the separate parts......................

19 STAY CLEAN (DEC 09 EXAM)

Stay Clean manufactures and sells a small range of kitchen equipment. Specifically the product range contains a dishwasher (DW), a washing machine (WM) and a tumble dryer (TD). The TD is of a rather old design and has for some time generated negative contribution. It is widely expected that in one year's time the market for this design of TD will cease, as people switch to a washing machine that can also dry clothes after the washing cycle has completed.

Stay Clean is trying to decide whether or not to cease the production of TD now *or* in 12 months' time when the new combined washing machine/drier will be ready. To help with this decision the following information has been provided:

(1)   The normal selling prices, annual sales volumes and total variable costs for the three products are as follows:

	DW	WM	TD
Selling price per unit	$200	$350	$80
Material cost per unit	$70	$100	$50
Labour cost per unit	$50	$80	$40
Contribution per unit	$80	$170	–$10
Annual sales	5,000 units	6,000 units	1,200 units

(2)   It is thought that some of the customers that buy a TD also buy a DW and a WM. It is estimated that 5% of the sales of WM and DW will be lost if the TD ceases to be produced.

(3)   All the direct labour force currently working on the TD will be made redundant immediately if TD is ceased now. This would cost $6,000 in redundancy payments. If Stay Clean waited for 12 months the existing labour force would be retained and retrained at a cost of $3,500 to enable them to produce the new washing/drying product. Recruitment and training costs of labour in 12 months' time would be $1,200 in the event that redundancy takes place now.

(4)   Stay Clean operates a just in time (JIT) policy and so all material cost would be saved on the TD for 12 months if TD production ceased now. Equally, the material costs relating to the lost sales on the WM and the DW would also be saved. However, the material supplier has a volume based discount scheme in place as follows:

Total annual expenditure ($)	Discount
0–600,000	0%
600,001–800,000	1%
800,001–900,000	2%
900,001–960,000	3%
960,001 and above	5%

Stay Clean uses this supplier for all its materials for all the products it manufactures. The figures given above in the cost per unit table for material cost per unit are net of any discount Stay Clean already qualifies for.

(5)   The space in the factory currently used for the TD will be sublet for 12 months on a short-term lease contract if production of TD stops now. The income from that contract will be $12,000.

(6)   The supervisor (currently classed as an overhead) supervises the production of all three products spending approximately 20% of his time on the TD production. He would continue to be fully employed if the TD ceases to be produced now.

Required:

(a) Calculate whether or not it is worthwhile ceasing to produce the TD now rather than waiting 12 months (ignore any adjustment to allow for the time value of money). **(13 marks)**

(b) Explain two pricing strategies that could be used to improve the financial position of the business in the next 12 months assuming that the TD continues to be made in that period. **(4 marks)**

(c) Briefly describe three issues that Stay Clean should consider if it decides to outsource the manufacture of one of its future products. **(3 marks)**

(Total: 20 marks)

20 CHOICE OF CONTRACTS

A company in the civil engineering industry with headquarters located 22 miles from London undertakes contracts anywhere in the United Kingdom.

The company has had its tender for a job in north-east England accepted at $288,000 and work is due to begin in March 20X3. However, the company has also been asked to undertake a contract on the south coast of England. The price offered for this contract is $352,000. Both of the contracts cannot be taken simultaneously because of constraints on staff site management personnel and on plant available. An escape clause enables the company to withdraw from the contract in the north-east, provided notice is given before the end of November and an agreed penalty of $28,000 is paid.

The following estimates have been submitted by the company's quantity surveyor:

Cost estimates

	North-east $	South-coast $
Materials:		
In inventory at original cost, Material X	21,600	
In inventory at original cost, Material Y		24,800
Firm orders placed at original cost, Material X	30,400	
Not yet ordered – current cost, Material X	60,000	
Not yet ordered – current cost, Material Z		71,200
Labour – hired locally	86,000	110,000
Site management	34,000	34,000
Staff accommodation and travel for site management	6,800	5,600
Plant on site – depreciation	9,600	12,800
Interest on capital, 8%	5,120	6,400
Total local contract costs	253,520	264,800
Headquarters costs allocated at rate of 5% on total contract costs	12,676	3,240
	266,196	278,040

	North-east	South-coast
	$	$
Contract price	288,000	352,000
Estimated profit	21,804	73,960

(1) X, Y and Z are three building materials. Material X is not in common use and would not realise much money if re-sold; however, it could be used on other contracts but only as a substitute for another material currently quoted at 10% less than the original cost of X. The price of Y, a material in common use, has doubled since it was purchased; its net realisable value if re-sold would be its new price less 15% to cover disposal costs. Alternatively it could be kept for use on other contracts in the following financial year.

(2) With the construction industry not yet recovered from the recent recession, the company is confident that manual labour, both skilled and unskilled, could be hired locally on a sub-contracting basis to meet the needs of each of the contracts.

(3) The plant which would be needed for the south coast contract has been owned for some years and $12,800 is the year's depreciation on a straight-line basis. If the north-east contract is undertaken, less plant will be required but the surplus plant will be hired out for the period of the contract at a rental of $6,000.

(4) It is the company's policy to charge all contracts with notional interest at 8% on estimated working capital involved in contracts. Progress payments would be receivable from the contractee.

(5) Salaries and general costs of operating the small headquarters amount to about $108,000 each year. There are usually ten contracts being supervised at the same time.

(6) Each of the two contracts is expected to last from March 20X3 to February 20X4 which, coincidentally, is the company's financial year.

(7) Site management is treated as a fixed cost.

Required:

As the management accountant to the company present comparative statements to show the net benefit to the company of undertaking the more advantageous of the two contracts.

Explain the reasoning behind the inclusion in (or omission from) your comparative financial statements, of each item given in the cost estimates and the notes relating thereto. **(20 marks)**

21 HS EQUATION

HS manufactures components for use in computers. The business operates in a highly competitive market where there are a large number of manufacturers of similar components. HS is considering its pricing strategy for the next 12 weeks for one of its components. The Managing Director seeks your advice to determine the selling price that will maximise the profit to be made during this period.

You have been given the following data:

Market demand

The current selling price of the component is $1,350 and at this price the average weekly demand over the last four weeks has been 8,000 components. An analysis of the market shows that, for every $50 increase in selling price, the demand reduces by 1,000 components per week. Equally, for every $50 reduction in selling price, the demand increases by 1,000 components per week.

Costs

The direct material cost of each component is $270. This price is part of a fixed price contract with the material suppliers and the contract does not expire for another year.

Production labour and conversion costs, together with other overhead costs and the corresponding output volumes, have been collected for the last four weeks and they are as follows:

Week	Output volume (units)	$000
1	9,400	7,000
2	7,600	5,688
3	8,500	6,334
4	7,300	5,446

No significant changes in cost behaviour are expected over the next 12 weeks.

Required:

(a) Calculate the optimum (profit-maximising) selling price of the component for the period. **(14 marks)**

(b) Identify and explain three reasons why it may be inappropriate for HS to use this theoretical pricing model in practice. **(6 marks)**

(Total: 20 marks)

22 MKL

Product 'M' is currently being tested by MKL and is to be launched in ten weeks' time. The 'M' is an innovative product which the company believes will change the entire market. The company has decided to use a market skimming approach to pricing this product during its introduction stage.

MKL continually reviews its product range and enhances its existing products by developing new models to satisfy the demands of its customers. The company intends to always have products at each stage of the product life cycle to ensure the company's continued presence in the market.

MKL is currently reviewing its two existing flagship products, Product K and Product L. You have been given the following information:

- Product K was introduced to the market some time ago and is now about to enter the maturity stage of its life cycle. The maturity stage is expected to last for ten weeks. Each unit has a variable cost of $38 and takes 1 standard hour to produce. The Managing Director is unsure which of four possible prices the company should charge during the next ten weeks. The following table shows the results of some market research into the level of weekly demand at alternative prices:

Selling price per unit	$100	$85	$80	$75
Weekly demand (units)	600	800	1,200	1,400

- Product L was introduced to the market two months ago using a penetration pricing policy and is now about to enter its growth stage. This stage is expected to last for 20 weeks. Each unit has a variable cost of $45 and takes 1.25 standard hours to produce. Market research has indicated that there is a linear relationship between its selling price and the number of units demanded, of the form $P = a - bx$. At a selling price of $100 per unit demand is expected to be 1,000 units per week. For every $10 increase in selling price the weekly demand will reduce by 200 units and for every $10 decrease in selling price the weekly demand will increase by 200 units.

The company currently has a production facility which has a capacity of 2,000 standard hours per week. This facility is being expanded but the extra capacity will not be available for ten weeks.

Required:

(a) Calculate which of the four selling prices should be charged for product K, in order to maximise its contribution during its maturity stage; **(5 marks)**

(b) Following on from your answer above in (a), calculate the selling price of product L during its growth stage. **(8 marks)**

(c) Compare and contrast penetration and skimming pricing strategies during the introduction stage, using product M to illustrate your answer. **(7 marks)**

(Total: 20 marks)

23 HAMMER (JUNE 10 EXAM)

Hammer is a large garden equipment supplier with retail stores throughout Toolland. Many of the products it sells are bought in from outside suppliers but some are currently manufactured by Hammer's own manufacturing division 'Nail'.

The prices (a transfer price) that Nail charges to the retail stores are set by head office and have been the subject of some discussion. The current policy is for Nail to calculate the total variable cost of production and delivery and add 30% for profit. Nail argues that all costs should be taken into consideration, offering to reduce the mark-up on costs to 10% in this case. The retail stores are unhappy with the current pricing policy arguing that it results in prices that are often higher than comparable products available on the market.

Nail has provided the following information to enable a price comparison to be made of the two possible pricing policies for one of its products.

Garden shears

Steel: the shears have 0.4kg of high quality steel in the final product. The manufacturing process loses 5% of all steel put in. Steel costs $4,000 per tonne (1 tonne = 1,000kg)

Other materials: Other materials are bought in and have a list price of $3 per kg although Hammer secures a 10% volume discount on all purchases. The shears require 0.1kg of these materials.

The labour time to produce shears is 0.25 hours per unit and labour costs $10 per hour.

Variable overheads are absorbed at the rate of 150% of labour rates and fixed overheads are 80% of the variable overheads.

Delivery is made by an outsourced distributor that charges Nail $0.50 per garden shear for delivery.

Required:

(a) Calculate the price that Nail would charge for the garden shears under the existing policy of variable cost plus 30%. **(6 marks)**

(b) Calculate the increase or decrease in price if the pricing policy switched to total cost plus 10%. **(4 marks)**

(c) Discuss whether or not including fixed costs in a transfer price is a sensible policy. **(4 marks)**

(d) Discuss whether the retail stores should be allowed to buy in from outside suppliers if the prices are cheaper than those charged by Nail. **(6 marks)**

(Total: 20 marks)

24 SNIFF CO (DEC 07 EXAM)

Sniff Limited manufactures and sells its standard perfume by blending a secret formula of aromatic oils with diluted alcohol. The oils are produced by another company following a lengthy process and are very expensive. The standard perfume is highly branded and successfully sold at a price of $39.98 per 100 millilitres (ml).

Sniff Limited is considering processing some of the perfume further by adding a hormone to appeal to members of the opposite sex. The hormone to be added will be different for the male and female perfumes. Adding hormones to perfumes is not universally accepted as a good idea as some people have health concerns. On the other hand, market research carried out suggests that a premium could be charged for perfume that can 'promise' the attraction of a suitor. The market research has cost $3,000.

Data has been prepared for the costs and revenues expected for the following month (a test month) assuming that a part of the company's output will be further processed by adding the hormones.

The output selected for further processing is 1,000 litres, about a tenth of the company's normal monthly output. Of this, 99% is made up of diluted alcohol which costs $20 per litre. The rest is a blend of aromatic oils costing $18,000 per litre. The labour required to produce 1,000 litres of the basic perfume before any further processing is 2,000 hours at a cost of $15 per hour.

Of the output selected for further processing, 200 litres (20%) will be for male customers and 2 litres of hormone costing $7,750 per litre will then be added. The remaining 800 litres (80%) will be for female customers and 8 litres of hormone will be added, costing $12,000 per litre. In both cases the adding of the hormone adds to the overall volume of the product as there is no resulting processing loss.

Sniff Limited has sufficient existing machinery to carry out the test processing.

The new processes will be supervised by one of the more experienced supervisors currently employed by Sniff Limited. His current annual salary is $35,000 and it is expected that he will spend 10% of his time working on the hormone adding process during the test month. This will be split evenly between the male and female versions of the product.

Extra labour will be required to further process the perfume, with an extra 500 hours for the male version and 700 extra hours for the female version of the hormone-added product. Labour is currently fully employed, making the standard product. New labour with the required skills will not be available at short notice.

Sniff Limited allocates fixed overhead at the rate of $25 per labour hour to all products for the purposes of reporting profits.

The sales prices that could be achieved as a one-off monthly promotion are:

- Male version: $75.00 per 100 ml

- Female version: $59.50 per 100 ml

Required:

(a)   **Outline the financial and other factors that Sniff Limited should consider when making a further processing decision.**

   Note: no calculations are required.   **(5 marks)**

(b)   **Evaluate whether Sniff Limited should experiment with the hormone adding process using the data provided. Provide a separate assessment and conclusion for the male and the female versions of the product.**   **(15 marks)**

                                                                        (Total: 20 marks)

Note: The original question as written by the examiner had the following additional requirements:

(c)   **Calculate the selling price per 100 ml for the female version of the product that would ensure further processing would break even in the test month.**   **(2 marks)**

(d)   **Sniff Limited is considering outsourcing the production of the standard perfume. Outline the main factors it should consider before making such a decision.**   **(4 marks)**

---

25 FURNIVAL

Furnival has a distillation plant that produces three joint products, P, Q and R, in the proportions 10:5:5. After the split-off point the products can be sold for industrial use or they can be taken to the mixing plant for blending and refining. The latter procedure is normally followed.

For a typical week, in which all the output is processed in the mixing plant, the following income statement can be prepared:

	Product P	Product Q	Product R
Sales volume (gallons)	1,000	500	500
Price per gallon ($)	12.50	20	10
Sales revenue ($)	12,500	10,000	5,000
Joint process cost ($)			
(apportioned using output volume)	5,000	2,500	2,500
Mixing plant cost ($):			
Process costs	3,000	3,000	3,000
Other separable costs	2,000	500	500
Total costs ($)	10,000	6,000	6,000
Profit/(loss) ($)	2,500	4,000	(1,000)

The joint process costs are 25% fixed and 75% variable, whereas the mixing plant costs are 10% fixed and 90% variable and all the 'other separable costs' are variable.

If the products had been sold at the split-off point the selling price per gallon would have been:

	Product P	Product Q	Product R
	$5.00	$6.00	$1.50

There are only 45 hours available per week in the mixing plant. Typically 30 hours are taken up with the processing of Product P, Q and R (10 hours for each product line) and 15 hours are used for other work that generates (on average) a profit of $200 per hour after being charged with a proportionate share of the plant's costs (including fixed costs). The manager of the mixing plant considers that he could sell all the plant's processing time externally at a price that would provide this rate of profit.

It has been suggested:

(i)   that, since Product R regularly makes a loss, it should be sold off at the split-off point;

(ii)   that it might be possible advantageously to change the mix of products achieved in the distillation plant. It is possible to change the output proportions to 7:8:5 at a cost of $1 for each additional gallon of Q produced by the distillation plant.

Required:

Compare the costs and benefits for each of the above proposals. Recommend, for each proposal, whether it should or should not be implemented. **(20 marks)**

26 ELECTRONIC CONTROL SYSTEM

Companies RP, RR, RS and RT are members of a group. RP wishes to buy an electronic control system for its factory and, in accordance with group policy, must obtain quotations from companies inside and outside of the group.

From outside of the group the following quotations are received:

(a) Company A quoted $33,200.

(b) Company B quoted $35,000 but would buy a special unit from RS for $13,000. To make this unit, however, RS would need to buy parts from Ilk at a price of $7,500.

The inside quotation was from RS whose price was $48,000. This would require RS buying parts from RR at a price of $8,000 and units from RT at a price of $30,000. However, RT would need to buy parts from RR at a price of $11,000.

Additional data is available as follows:

- RR is extremely busy with work outside the group and has quoted current market prices for all its products

- RS costs for the RP contract, including purchases from RR and RT, total $42,000. For the Company B contract it expects a profit of 25% on the cost of its own work

- RT prices provide for a 20% profit margin on total costs

- The variable costs of the group companies in respect of the work under consideration are:

   RR: 20% of selling price

   RS: 70% of own cost (excluding purchases from other group companies)

   RT: 65% of own cost (excluding purchases from other group companies).

Required:

From a group point of view recommend, with appropriate calculations, whether the contract should be placed with RS or Company A or Company B. **(20 marks)**

27 RECYC

Recyc plc is a company which reprocesses factory waste in order to extract good quality aluminium. Information concerning its operations is as follows:

(1) Recyc plc places an advance order each year for chemical X for use in the aluminium extraction process. It will enter into an advance contract for the coming year for chemical X at one of three levels – high, medium or low, which correspond to the requirements of a high, medium or low level of waste available for reprocessing.

(2) The level of waste available will not be known when the advance order for chemical X is entered into. A set of probabilities have been estimated by management as to the likelihood of the quantity of waste being at a high, medium or low level.

(3) Where the advance order entered into for chemical X is lower than that required for the level of waste for processing actually received, a discount from the original demand price is allowed by the supplier for the total quantity of chemical X actually required.

(4)   Where the advance order entered into for chemical X is in excess of that required to satisfy the actual level of waste for reprocessing, a penalty payment in excess of the original demand price is payable for the total quantity of chemical X actually required.

A summary of the information relating to the above points is as follows:

Level of reprocessing	Waste available 000 kg	Probability	Advance order $	Conversion discount $	Conversion premium $
			Chemical X costs per kg		
High	50,000	0.30	1.00		
Medium	38,000	0.50	1.20		
Low	30,000	0.20	1.40		
Chemical X: order conversion:					
Low to medium				0.10	
Medium to high				0.10	
Low to high				0.15	
Medium to low					0.25
High to medium					0.25
High to low					0.60

Aluminium is sold at $0.65 per kg. Variable costs (excluding chemical X costs) are 70% of sales revenue. Aluminium extracted from the waste is 15% of the waste input. Chemical X is added to the reprocessing at the rate of 1 kg per 100 kg of waste.

Required:

(a)   **Prepare a summary which shows the budgeted contribution earned by Recyc plc for the coming year for each of nine possible outcomes.**   **(14 marks)**

(b)   **State the contribution for the coming year which corresponds to the use of (i) maximax, and (ii) maximin decision criteria, and comment on the risk preference of management which is indicated by each.**   **(6 marks)**

(Total: 20 marks)

28   TICKET AGENT *Walk in the footsteps of a top tutor*

A ticket agent has an arrangement with a concert hall that holds concerts on 60 nights a year whereby he receives discounts as follows per concert:

For purchase of: *He receives a discount of:*

200 tickets   20%

300 tickets   25%

400 tickets   30%

500 tickets or more   40%

Purchases must be in full hundreds. The average price per ticket is $30.

He must decide in advance each year the number of tickets he will purchase. If he has any tickets unsold by the afternoon of the concert he must return them to the box office. If the box office sells any of these he receives 60% of their price.

His sales records over a few years show that for a concert with extremely popular artistes he can be confident of selling 500 tickets, for one with lesser known artistes 350 tickets, and for one with relatively unknown artistes 200 tickets.

His records show that 10% of the tickets he returns are sold by the box office. (**Note:** these are in addition to any sales made by the ticket agent).

His administration costs incurred in selling tickets are the same per concert irrespective of the popularity of the artistes.

Sales records show that the frequency of concerts will be:

With popular artistes	45%
With lesser known artistes	30%
With unknown artistes	25%
	100%

Required:

(a)   Calculate:

- the expected demand for tickets per concert
- the level of his purchases of tickets per concert that will give him the largest profit over a long period of time and the profit per concert that this level of purchases of tickets will yield. **(11 marks)**

(b)   Calculate the number of tickets the agent should buy, based on the following criteria:

- Maximin
- Maximax
- Minimax regret.   **(5 marks)**

(c)   Advise the ticket agent   **(4 marks)**

(Total: 20 marks)

29   SHIFTERS HAULAGE (DEC 08 EXAM)

Shifters Haulage (SH) is considering changing some of the vans it uses to transport crates for customers. The new vans come in three sizes; small, medium and large. SH is unsure about which type to buy. The capacity is 100 crates for the small van, 150 for the medium van and 200 for the large van.

Demand for crates varies and can be either 120 or 190 crates per period, with the probability of the higher demand figure being 0.6.

The sale price per crate is $10 and the variable cost $4 per crate for all van sizes subject to the fact that if the capacity of the van is greater than the demand for crates in a period then the variable cost will be lower by 10% to allow for the fact that the vans will be partly empty when transporting crates.

SH is concerned that if the demand for crates exceeds the capacity of the vans then customers will have to be turned away. SH estimates that in this case goodwill of $100 would be charged against profits per period to allow for lost future sales regardless of the number of customers that are turned away.

Depreciation charged would be $200 per period for the small, $300 for the medium and $400 for the large van.

SH has in the past been very aggressive in its decision-making, pressing ahead with rapid growth strategies. However, its managers have recently grown more cautious as the business has become more competitive.

Required:

(a)   Explain the principles behind the maximax, maximin and expected value criteria that are sometimes used to make decisions in uncertain situations.   **(5 marks)**

(b)   Prepare a profits table showing the SIX possible profit figures per period.   **(9 marks)**

(c)   Using your profit table from (b) above discuss which type of van SH should buy taking into consideration the possible risk attitudes of the managers.   **(6 marks)**

(Total: 20 marks)

Note: The original question, as written by the examiner, also had the following requirement for six marks:

Describe THREE methods other than those mentioned in (a) above, which businesses can use to analyse and assess the risk that exists in its decision-making.

---

30   THEATRE

A theatre has a seating capacity of 500 people and is considering engaging MS and her orchestra for a concert for one night only. The fee that would be charged by MS would be $10,000. If the theatre engages MS, then this sum is payable regardless of the size of the theatre audience.

Based on past experience of events of this type, the price of the theatre ticket would be $25 per person. The size of the audience for this event is uncertain, but based on past experience it is expected to be as follows:

	Probability
300 people	50%
400 people	30%
500 people	20%

In addition to the sale of the theatre tickets, it can be expected that members of the audience will also purchase confectionery both prior to the performance and during the interval. The contribution that this would yield to the theatre is unclear, but has been estimated as follows:

Contribution from confectionery sales	*Probability*
Contribution of $3 per person	30%
Contribution of $5 per person	50%
Contribution of $10 per person	20%

Required:

(a) Using expected values as the basis of your decision, advise the theatre management whether it is financially worthwhile to engage MS for the concert.

(5 marks)

(b) Prepare a two-way data table to show the profit values that could occur from deciding to engage MS for the concert. (5 marks)

(c) Explain, using the probabilities provided and your answer to (b) above, how the two-way data table can be used by the theatre management to evaluate the financial risks of the concert, including the probability of making a profit. (9 marks)

(d) Calculate the maximum price that the theatre management should agree to pay for perfect information relating to the size of the audience and the level of contribution from confectionery sales. (6 marks)

(Total: 25 marks)

31 RY DECISION TREE

RY Ltd, a transatlantic airline company, has recently launched a low-cost airline company providing flights within Europe. The market is highly competitive and two other low-cost airlines, B Ltd and G Ltd, together hold 98% of the market.

RY Ltd commissioned some market research to help with the pricing decision for one route, London to Paris, which it is thinking of offering. The research identified three possible market states and the likely number of passengers that would be attracted at three price levels on this route.

Ticket Price		£80	£90	£100
Market	*Probability*	*Passenger seats*	*Passenger seats*	*Passenger seats*
Pessimistic	0.2	80	60	30
Most likely	0.6	100	90	80
Optimistic	0.2	150	150	120

Airport charges are incurred for each customer and these are expected to be either £5 or £6 per customer depending on the negotiations with the airports involved. The probabilities for the airport charges are 0.6 for an airport charge of £5 per passenger and 0.4 for an airport charge of £6 per customer.

The fixed costs of a flight from London to Paris are £4,422.

Required:

(a) Draw a decision tree to illustrate the pricing decision faced by RY Ltd. (8 marks)

(b) Using the decision tree or otherwise, establish the optimum price that RY Ltd should charge in order to maximise profit. (6 marks)

(c) If RY Ltd knew that there would be a pessimistic market, which price should it charge in order to maximise profit? (6 marks)

(Total: 20 marks)

BUDGETING

32   NORTHLAND (JUNE 09 EXAM)

 Timed question with Online tutor debrief

Northland's major towns and cities are maintained by local government organisations (LGO), which are funded by central government. The LGOs submit a budget each year which forms the basis of the funds received.

You are provided with the following information as part of the 2010 budget preparation.

Overheads

Overhead costs are budgeted on an incremental basis, taking the previous year's actual expenditure and adding a set % to allow for inflation. Adjustments are also made for known changes. The details for these are:

Overhead cost category	2009 cost ($)	Known changes	Inflation adjustment between 2009 and 2010
Property cost	120,000	None	+5%
Central wages	150,000	Note 1 below	+3%
Stationery	25,000	Note 2 below	0%

Note 1: One new staff member will be added to the overhead team; this will cost $12,000 in 2010

Note 2: A move towards the paperless office is expected to reduce stationery costs by 40% on the 2009 spend Road repairs

In 2010 it is expected that 2,000 metres of road will need repairing but a contingency of an extra 10% has been agreed.

In 2009 the average cost of a road repair was $15,000 per metre repaired, but this excluded any cost effects of extreme weather conditions. The following probability estimates have been made in respect of 2010:

Weather type predicted	Probability	Increase in repair cost
Good	0.7	0
Poor	0.1	+10%
Bad	0.2	+25%

Inflation on road repairing costs is expected to be 5% between 2009 and 2010.

New roads

New roads are budgeted on a zero base basis and will have to compete for funds along with other capital projects such as hospitals and schools.

Required:

(a)	Calculate the overheads budget for 2010.	(3 marks)
(b)	Calculate the budgets for road repairs for 2010.	(6 marks)
(c)	Explain the problems associated with using expected values in budgeting by an LGO and explain why a contingency for road repairs might be needed.	(8 marks)
(d)	Explain the process involved for zero based budgeting.	(3 marks)

(Total: 20 marks)

 Calculate your allowed time, allocate the time to the separate parts.....................

33 EFFECTIVE BUDGETING

Statement 1: The availability of computers and sophisticated financial software has made budgeting a routine, almost automatic, process.

Statement 2: Effective budgeting is much more than just number-crunching.

Required:

(a)	Explain what is meant by 'effective budgeting' in Statement 2 and what features contribute to effective budgeting;	(3 marks)
(b)	Reconcile the apparent contradiction between *Statements 1* and *2*.	(3 marks)
(c)	Critically discuss the relative merits of periodic budgeting and continuous budgeting.	(8 marks)
(d)	Discuss the consequences of budget bias (budgetary slack) for cost control.	(6 marks)

(Total: 20 marks)

34 NN

NN Ltd manufactures and markets a range of electronic office equipment. The company currently has a turnover of $40 million per annum. The company has a functional structure and currently operates an incremental budgeting system. The company has a budget committee that is comprised entirely of members of the senior management team. No other personnel are involved in the budget-setting process.

Each member of the senior management team has enjoyed an annual bonus of between 10% and 20% of their annual salary for each of the past five years. The annual bonuses are calculated by comparing the actual costs attributed to a particular function with budgeted costs for that function during the twelve month period ended 31 December in each year.

A new Finance Director, who previously held a senior management position in a 'not for profit' health organisation, has recently been appointed. Whilst employed by the health service organisation, the new Finance Director had been the manager responsible for the implementation of a zero-based budgeting system which proved highly successful.

Required:

(a) Identify and discuss the factors to be considered when implementing a system of zero-based budgeting within NN Ltd. Include, as part of your discussion, a definition of the existing incremental budgeting system and a zero-based budgeting system. **(5 marks)**

(b) Identify and discuss the behavioural problems that the management of NN Ltd might encounter in implementing a system of zero-based budgeting, recommending how best to address such problems in order that they are overcome. **(10 marks)**

(c) Explain how the implementation of a zero-based budgeting system in NN Ltd may differ from the implementation of such a system in a 'not for profit' health organisation. **(5 marks)**

(Total: 20 marks)

35 BUDGETING SYSTEMS (JUNE 06 EXAM)

Required:

(a) Explain the weaknesses of an incremental budgeting system. **(5 marks)**

(b) Describe the main features of an activity based budgeting system and comment on the advantages claimed for its use. **(10 marks)**

(c) Discuss the ways in which participation in the budget setting process can be used to motivate managers to endeavour to meet the objectives of the company. **(5 marks)**

(Total: 20 marks)

36 BIG CHEESE CHAIRS (DEC 09 EXAM)

Big Cheese Chairs (BCC) manufactures and sells executive leather chairs. They are considering a new design of massaging chair to launch into the competitive market in which they operate.

They have carried out an investigation in the market and using a target costing system have targeted a competitive selling price of $120 for the chair. BCC wants a margin on selling price of 20% (ignoring any overheads).

The frame and massage mechanism will be bought in for $51 per chair and BCC will upholster it in leather and assemble it ready for despatch.

Leather costs $10 per metre and two metres are needed for a complete chair although 20% of all leather is wasted in the upholstery process.

The upholstery and assembly process will be subject to a learning effect as the workers get used to the new design. BCC estimates that the first chair will take two hours to prepare but this will be subject to a learning rate (LR) of 95%. The learning improvement will stop once 128 chairs have been made and the time for the 128th chair will be the time for all subsequent chairs. The cost of labour is $15 per hour.

The learning formula is shown on the formula sheet and at the 95% learning rate the value of b is −0.074000581.

Required:

(a) Calculate the average cost for the first 128 chairs made and identify any cost gap that may be present at that stage. **(8 marks)**

(b) Assuming that a cost gap for the chair exists suggest four ways in which it could be closed. **(6 marks)**

The production manager denies any claims that a cost gap exists and has stated that the cost of the 128th chair will be low enough to yield the required margin.

(c) Calculate the cost of the 128th chair made and state whether the target cost is being achieved on the 128th chair. **(6 marks)**

(Total: 20 marks)

37 HENRY COMPANY (DEC 08 EXAM)

Henry Company (HC) provides skilled labour to the building trade. They have recently been asked by a builder to bid for a kitchen fitting contract for a new development of 600 identical apartments. HC has not worked for this builder before. Cost information for the new contract is as follows:

Labour for the contract is available. HC expects that the first kitchen will take 24 man-hours to fit but thereafter the time taken will be subject to a 95% learning rate. After 200 kitchens are fitted the learning rate will stop and the time taken for the 200th kitchen will be the time taken for all the remaining kitchens. Labour costs $15 per hour.

Overheads are absorbed on a labour hour basis. HC has collected overhead information for the last four months and this is shown below:

	Hours worked	Overhead cost $
Month 1	9,300	115,000
Month 2	9,200	113,600
Month 3	9,400	116,000
Month 4	9,600	116,800

HC normally works around 120,000 labour hours in a year.

HC uses the high low method to analyse overheads.

The learning curve equation is $y = ax^b$, where $b = \log r/\log 2 = -0.074$

Required:

(a) Describe FIVE factors, other than the cost of labour and overheads mentioned above, that HC should take into consideration in calculating its bid. **(5 marks)**

(b) Calculate the total cost including all overheads for HC that it can use as a basis of the bid for the new apartment contract. **(13 marks)**

(c) If the second kitchen alone is expected to take 21.6 man-hours to fit demonstrate how the learning rate of 95% has been calculated. **(2 marks)**

(Total: 20 marks)

38   SCIENTO

Sciento Products Ltd manufactures complex electronic measuring instruments for which highly skilled labour is required. Conventional standard costing has been used for some time but problems have been experienced in setting realistic standards for labour costs.

Analysis of production times has shown that there is a learning curve effect on the labour time required to manufacture each unit and it has been decided to allow for this in establishing standard times and in the subsequent variance analysis. Records have been kept of the production times for the Electronometer, an extract of which follows:

Cumulative production (units)	Cumulative time (hours)	Average time per unit (hours)
1	200	200
2	360	180
4	648	162
8	1,166	145.8

The labour time analyses have shown that the learning curve follows the general form:

$$y = ax^b$$

where: y = average labour hours per unit

a = number of labour hours for first unit

x = cumulative number of units

b = the learning index

During period 11 the following data were recorded:

Cumulative production at start of period	526 units
Production in period	86 units
Wages paid	$71,823 for 6,861 actual hours
Materials actual cost	$20,850
Actual overheads for period	$152,600

Budgeted and standard cost data for Electronometers:

Budgeted production	86 units
Budgeted overheads	$150,903
Standard labour cost	$10 per hour
Standard material cost per unit	$250

Required:

(a)   Calculate a total standard cost for Electronometers.   (7 marks)

(b)   Calculate and analyse where possible the materials, labour and overhead cost. variances;   (10 marks)

(c)   Discuss the usefulness of allowing for the learning effect in establishing labour standards.   (3 marks)

(Total: 20 marks)

39   THE WESTERN (DEC 09 EXAM)

The Western is a local government organisation responsible for waste collection from domestic households. The new management accountant of The Western has decided to introduce some new forecasting techniques to improve the accuracy of the budgeting. The next budget to be produced is for the year ended 31 December 2010.

Waste is collected by the tonne (T). The number of tonnes collected each year has been rising and by using time series analysis the new management accountant has produced the following relationship between the tonnes collected (T) and the time period in question Q (where Q is a quarter number. So Q = 1 represents quarter 1 in 2009 and Q = 2 represents quarter 2 in 2009 and so on)

T = 2,000 + 25Q

Each quarter is subject to some seasonal variation with more waste being collected in the middle quarters of each year. The adjustments required to the underlying trend prediction are:

Quarter	Tonnes
1	−200
2	+250
3	+150
4	−100

Once T is predicted the new management accountant hopes to use the values to predict the variable operating costs and fixed operating costs that The Western will be subjected to in 2010. To this end he has provided the following operating cost data for 2009.

Volume of waste Tonnes	Total operating cost in 2009 (fixed + variable) $000s
2,100	950
2,500	1,010
2,400	1,010
2,300	990

Inflation on the operating cost is expected to be 5% between 2009 and 2010.

The regression formula is shown on the formula sheet.

Required:

(a)   **Calculate the tonnes of waste to be expected in the calendar year 2010.**   **(4 marks)**

(b)   **Calculate the variable operating cost and fixed operating cost to be expected in 2010 using regression analysis on the 2009 data and allowing for inflation as appropriate.**   **(10 marks)**

Many local government organisations operate incremental budgeting as one of their main budgeting techniques. They take a previous period's actual spend, adjust for any known changes to operations and then add a % for expected inflation in order to set the next period's budget.

(c)   **Describe two advantages and two disadvantages of a local government organisation funded by taxpayer's money using incremental budgeting as its main budgeting technique.**   **(6 marks)**

(Total: 20 marks)

40   PMF

PMF is a long-established public transport operator that provides a commuter transit link between an airport and the centre of a large city.

The following data has been taken from the sales records of PMF for the last two years:

Quarter	Number of passengers carried	
	Year 1	Year 2
1	15,620	34,100
2	15,640	29,920
3	16,950	29,550
4	34,840	56,680

The trend equation for the number of passengers carried has been found to be

$$x = 10,000 + 4,200q$$

Where	x	=	number of passengers carried per quarter
and	q	=	time period	(year 1 quarter 1: q = 1)

                                              (year 1 quarter 2: q = 2)

                                              (year 2 quarter 1: q = 5)

The seasonal adjustments have been expressed using the multiplicative model. The quarter 3 figure is 75%.

Based on data collected over the last two years, PMF has found that its quarterly costs have the following relationships with the number of passengers carried:

Cost item	Relationship
Premises costs	$y = 260,000$
Premises staff	$y = 65,000 + 0.5x$
Power	$y = 13,000 + 4x$
Transit staff	$y = 32,000 + 3x$
Other	$y = 9,100 + x$

Where	y	=	the cost per quarter ($),
and	x	=	number of passengers per quarter.

Required:

(a)   Using the trend equation for the number of passengers carried and the multiplicative time series model, determine the expected number of passengers to be carried in the third quarter of year 3.   (3 marks)

(b)   Explain why you think that the equation for the transit staff cost is in the form $y = 32,000 + 3x$.   (3 marks)

(c)   Using your answer to part (a) and the cost relationships equations, calculate for each cost item and in total, the costs expected to be incurred in the third quarter of year 3.   (5 marks)

(d)   Explain briefly why there may be differences between the actual data for the third quarter of year 3 and the values you have predicted.   (5 marks)

(e)   Spreadsheets are often used by accountants to assist in the preparation of budgets.

Describe how a spreadsheet may be used to prepare a sales budget AND explain ONE advantage of using spreadsheets to assist in this task.

(Your answer should refer to input, use of formulae, and output reports.) (4 marks)

(Total: 20 marks)

41   BUDGETING (JUNE 07 EXAM)

Required:

(a)   Outline the key stages in the planning process that links long-term objectives and budgetary control.   (6 marks)

(b)   Explain the meaning of the terms 'fixed budget', 'rolling budget' and 'zero-based budget', and discuss the circumstances under which each budget might be used.
                                                                                         (9 marks)

(c)   Discuss whether time series analysis may be preferred to linear regression as a way of forecasting sales volume.   (5 marks)

(Total: 20 marks)

STANDARD COSTING AND VARIANCE ANALYSIS

42   STANDARD COSTING

Required:

(a)   Outline the uses of standard costing and discuss the reasons why standards have to be reviewed.   **(13 marks)**

(b)   Standard costs are a detailed financial expression of organisational objectives. Outline THREE non-financial objectives that organisations might have? In your answer, identify any stakeholder group that may have a non-financial interest.

(7 marks)

(Total: 20 marks)

43   PERSEUS CO – REVISION OF BASIC VARIANCES

The Perseus Co a medium sized company, produces a single product in its one overseas factory. For control purposes, a standard costing system was recently introduced.

The standards set for the month of May were as follows:

Production and sales	16,000 units
Selling price (per unit)	$140

Materials:

Material 007	6 kilos per unit at $12.25 per kilo
Material XL90	3 kilos per unit at $3.20 per kilo
Labour	4.5 hours per unit at $8.40 per hour
Overheads (all fixed)	$86,400 per month.

(They are not absorbed into the product costs)

The actual data for the month of May is as follows:

Produced 15,400 units which were sold at $138.25 each

Materials: Used 98,560 kilos of material 007 at a total cost of $1,256,640 and used 42,350 kilos of material XL90 at a total cost of $132,979.

Labour: Paid an actual rate of $8.65 per hour to the labour force. The total amount paid out, amounted to $612,766.

Overheads (all fixed): $96,840

Required:

(a)   Prepare a standard costing profit statement, and a profit statement based on actual figures for the month of May.   **(6 marks)**

(b)   Prepare a statement of the variances which reconciles the actual with the standard profit or loss figure. (Mix and yield variances are not required.)   **(9 marks)**

(c)   Explain briefly the possible reasons for inter-relationships between material variances and labour variances.   **(3 marks)**

(d)   State TWO possible causes of an adverse labour rate variance.   **(2 marks)**

(Total: 20 marks)

44 CRUMBLY CAKES (JUNE 09 EXAM)

 Timed question with Online tutor debrief

Crumbly Cakes make cakes, which are sold directly to the public. The new production manager (a celebrity chef) has argued that the business should use only organic ingredients in its cake production. Organic ingredients are more expensive but should produce a product with an improved flavour and give health benefits for the customers. It was hoped that this would stimulate demand and enable an immediate price increase for the cakes.

Crumbly Cakes operates a responsibility based standard costing system which allocates variances to specific individuals. The individual managers are paid a bonus only when net favourable variances are allocated to them.

The new organic cake production approach was adopted at the start of March 2009, following a decision by the new production manager. No change was made at that time to the standard costs card. The variance reports for February and March are shown below (Fav = Favourable and Adv = Adverse)

Manager responsible	Allocated variances	February Variance $	March Variance $
Production manager			
	Material price (total for all ingredients)	25 Fav	2,100 Adv
	Material mix	0	600 Adv
	Material yield	20 Fav	400 Fav
Sales manager			
	Sales price	40 Adv	7,000 Fav
	Sales contribution volume	35 Adv	3,000 Fav

The production manager is upset that he seems to have lost all hope of a bonus under the new system. The sales manager thinks the new organic cakes are excellent and is very pleased with the progress made.

Crumbly Cakes operate a JIT stock system and holds virtually no inventory.

Required:

(a)   Assess the performance of the production manager and the sales manager and indicate whether the current bonus scheme is fair to those concerned.   (7 marks)

In April 2009 the following standard data applied (not adjusted for the organic ingredients):*Ingredients (per cake)*	Kg	$
Flour	0.10	0.12 per kg
Eggs	0.10	0.70 per kg
Butter	0.10	1.70 per kg
Sugar	0.10	0.50 per kg
Total input	0.40	
Normal loss (10%)	(0.04)	
Standard weight of a cake	0.36	
Standard sales price of a cake		0.85
Standard contribution per cake after all variable costs		0.35

The budget for production and sales in April was 50,000 cakes. Actual production and sales was 60,000 cakes in the month, during which the following occurred:

Ingredients used	Kg	$
Flour	5,700	$741
Eggs	6,600	$5,610
Butter	6,600	$11,880
Sugar	4,578	$2,747
Total input	23,478	$20,978
Actual loss	(1,878)	
Actual output of cake mixture	21,600	

Actual sales price of a cake = $0.99

All cakes produced must weigh 0·36 kg as this is what is advertised.

Required:

(b)   Calculate the material price, mix and yield variances and the sales price and sales contribution volume variances for April. You are not required to make any comment on the performance of the managers.   **(13 marks)**

(Total: 20 marks)

 Calculate your allowed time, allocate the time to the separate parts......................

45   MATERIAL VARIANCES

A company makes a product using two materials, X and Y, in the production process. A system of standard costing and variance analysis is in operation. The standard material requirement per tonne of mixed output is 60% material X at $30 per tonne and 40% material Y at $45 per tonne, with a standard yield of 90%.

The following information has been gathered for the three months January to March:

	January	February	March
Output achieved (tonnes)	810	765	900
Actual material input:			
X (tonnes)	540	480	700
Y (tonnes)	360	360	360
Actual material cost (X plus Y) ($)	32,400	31,560	38,600

The actual price per tonne of material Y throughout the January to March period was $45.

Required:

(a)   Prepare material variance summaries for each of January, February and March which include yield and mix variances in total plus usage and price variances for each material and in total.   **(14 marks)**

(b)   Prepare comments for management on each variance including variance trend.

(6 marks)

(Total: 20 marks)

46   CARAT

Carat plc, a premium food manufacturer, is reviewing operations for a three-month period of 20X3. The company operates a standard marginal costing system and manufactures one product, ZP, for which the following standard revenue and cost data per unit of product is available:

Selling price	$12.00
Direct material A	2.5 kg at $1.70 per kg
Direct material B	1.5 kg at $1.20 per kg
Direct labour	0.45 hrs at $6.00 per hour

Fixed production overheads for the three-month period were expected to be $62,500.

Actual data for the three-month period was as follows:

Sales and production	48,000 units of ZP were produced and sold for $580,800.
Direct material A	121,951 kg were used at a cost of $200,000.
Direct material B	67,200 kg were used at a cost of $84,000.
Direct labour	Employees worked for 18,900 hours, but 19,200 hours were paid at a cost of $117,120.
Fixed production overheads	$64,000

Budgeted sales for the three-month period were 50,000 units of Product ZP.

Required:

(a)   Calculate the following variances:

   (i)   sales volume contribution and sales price variances

   (ii)   materials price, mix and yield variances

   (iii)   labour rate, labour efficiency and idle time variances.   **(8 marks)**

(b)   Suggest possible explanations for the following variances:

   (i)   material price, mix and yield variances

   (ii)   labour rate, labour efficiency and idle time variances.   **(5 marks)**

(c)   Critically discuss the types of standard used in standard costing and their effect on employee motivation.   **(7 marks)**

(Total: 20 marks)

 Online question assistance

47 CHAFF CO (JUNE 08 EXAM)

Chaff Co processes and sells brown rice. It buys unprocessed rice seeds and then, using a relatively simple process, removes the outer husk of the rice to produce the brown rice. This means that there is substantial loss of weight in the process. The market for the purchase of seeds and the sales of brown rice has been, and is expected to be, stable. Chaff Co uses a variance analysis system to monitor its performance.

There has been some concern about the interpretation of the variances that have been calculated in month 1.

1   The purchasing manager is adamant, despite criticism from the production director, that he has purchased wisely and saved the company thousands of dollars in purchase costs by buying the required quantity of cheaper seeds from a new supplier.

2   The production director is upset at being criticised for increasing the wage rates for month 1; he feels the decision was the right one, considering all the implications of the increase. Morale was poor and he felt he had to do something about it.

3   The maintenance manager feels that saving $8,000 on fixed overhead has helped the profitability of the business. He argues that the machines' annual maintenance can wait for another month without a problem as the machines have been running well.

The variances for month 1 are as follows:

	$	
Material price	48,000	(Fav)
Material usage	52,000	(Adv)
Labour rate	15,000	(Adv)
Labour efficiency	18,000	(Fav)
Labour idle time	12,000	(Fav)
Variable overhead expenditure	18,000	(Adv)
	$	
Variable overhead efficiency	30,000	(Fav)
Fixed overhead expenditure	8,000	(Fav)
Sales price	85,000	(Adv)
Sales volume	21,000	(Adv)

Fav = Favourable, Adv = Adverse

Chaff Co uses labour hours to absorb the variable overhead.

Required:

(a)   Comment on the performance of the purchasing manager, the production director and the maintenance manager using the variances and other information above and reach a conclusion as to whether or not they have each performed well.

(9 marks)

In month 2 the following data applies:

Standard costs for 1 tonne of brown rice

- 1.4 tonnes of rice seeds are needed at a cost of $60 per tonne

- It takes 2 labour hours of work to produce 1 tonne of brown rice and labour is normally paid $18 per hour. Idle time is expected to be 10% of hours paid; this is not reflected in the rate of $18 above.

- 2 hours of variable overhead at a cost of $30 per hour

- The standard selling price is $240 per tonne

- The standard contribution per tonne is $56 per tone

Budget information for month 2 is

- Fixed costs were budgeted at $210,000 for the month

- Budgeted production and sales were 8,400 tonnes

The **actual results** for month 2 were as follows:

Actual production and sales were 8,000 tonnes

- 12,000 tonnes of rice seeds were bought and used, costing $660,000

- 15,800 labour hours were paid for, costing $303,360

- 15,000 labour hours were worked

- Variable production overhead cost $480,000

- Fixed costs were $200,000

- Sales revenue achieved was $1,800,000

Required:

(b) Calculate the variances for month 2 in as much detail as the information allows. You are not required to comment on the performance of the business or its managers for their performance in month 2. **(11 marks)**

(Total: 20 marks)

Note: The original question also included the requirement to reconcile the budget profit to the actual profit using marginal costing principles.

Walk in the footsteps of a top tutor

For tips on how to approach the question, work through the boxed notes in order.

Once each requirement has been completed review the answer in detail. Use this approach to reading and answering the question when tackling other questions.

Chaff Co processes and sells brown rice. It buys unprocessed rice seeds and then, using a relatively simple process, removes the outer husk of the rice to produce the brown rice. This means that there is substantial loss of weight in the process. The market for the purchase of seeds and the sales of brown rice has been, and is expected to be, stable. Chaff Co uses a variance analysis system to monitor its performance.

There has been some concern about the interpretation of the variances that have been calculated in month 1.

(2) No calculations required. The examiner is keen that accountants are able to interpret the numbers that they calculate and understand what they mean in the context of performance.

(3) Resulted in favourable material price variance. But consider material quality. Poorer quality material may have resulted in adverse material usage, sales price and sales volume variances.

1   The purchasing manager is adamant, despite criticism from the production director, that he has purchased wisely and saved the company thousands of dollars in purchase costs by buying the required quantity of cheaper seeds from a new supplier.

2   The production director is upset at being criticised for increasing the wage rates for month 1; he feels the decision was the right one, considering all the implications of the increase. Morale was poor and he felt he had to do something about it.

3   The maintenance manager feels that saving $8,000 on fixed overhead has helped the profitability of the business. He argues that the machines' annual maintenance can wait for another month without a problem as the machines have been running well.

(4) Resulted in adverse labour rate variance.

(6) Resulted in a favourable fixed overhead variance but may be linked to adverse variable overhead expenditure variance.

(5) Improved morale linked to favourable labour efficiency, variable overhead efficiency and labour idle time variances.

The variances for month 1 are as follows:

	$	
Material price	48,000	(Fav)
Material usage	52,000	(Adv)
Labour rate	15,000	(Adv)
Labour efficiency	18,000	(Fav)
Labour idle time	12,000	(Fav)
Variable overhead expenditure	18,000	(Adv)
Variable overhead efficiency	30,000	(Fav)
Fixed overhead expenditure	8,000	(Fav)
Sales price	85,000	(Adv)
Sales volume	21,000	(Adv)

(7) Check that each variance has been explained.

Fav = Favourable, Adv = Adverse

Chaff Co uses labour hours to absorb the variable overhead.

(1) Start by reading the requirement and allocating time (1.8 mins per mark). Now read through the question. Annotate or make notes whilst reading.

Required:

(a) **Comment on the performance of the purchasing manager, the production director and the maintenance manager using the variances and other information above and reach a conclusion as to whether or not they have each performed well.** **(9 marks)**

(8) Now answer the requirement
– Plan the answer first. Aim for nine separate points.
– There are 9 marks available. This is achievable if the requirement is broken down.
– Consider each manager in turn. 2 to 3 marks will be available for commenting on the performance of each manager.
– I mark will be available for a conclusion on each manager's performance.
– Points must be relevant and succinct in order to maximise marks and ensure that the requirement is answered in the allocated time.

(10) It's now the following month.

In month 2 the following data applies:

Standard costs for 1 tonne of brown rice

(11) Standard info.

– 1.4 tonnes of rice seeds are needed at a cost of $60 per tonne

– It takes 2 labour hours of work to produce 1 tonne of brown rice and labour is normally paid $18 per hour. Idle time is expected to be 10% of hours paid; this is not reflected in the rate of $18 above.

– 2 hours of variable overhead at a cost of $30 per hour

– The standard selling price is $240 per tonne

– The standard contribution per tonne is $56 per tonne

Budget information for month 2 is

– Fixed costs were budgeted at $210,000 for the month

– Budgeted production and sales were 8,400 tonnes

The **actual results** for month 2 were as follows:

Actual production and sales were 8,000 tonnes

(12) Actual info.

– 12,000 tonnes of rice seeds were bought and used, costing $660,000

– 15,800 labour hours were paid for, costing $303,360

– 15,000 labour hours were worked

– Variable production overhead cost $480,000

– Fixed costs were $200,000

– Sales revenue achieved was $1,800,000

<table>
<tr><td>(9) Start by reading the requirement and allocating the time (1.8 mins per mark).</td></tr>
</table>

Required:

(b) Calculate the variances for month 2 in as much detail as the information allows. You are not required to comment on the performance of the business or its managers for their performance in month 2.　　**(11 marks)**

(Total: 20 marks)

> (13) Now answer the requirement:
> Plan the answer first. A review of the information shows that the following variances can be calculated:
> (1) Sales price (2) Sales volume (3) Material price (4) Material usage (5) Labour rate (6) Labour productive efficiency (7) Labour excess idle time (8) Variable overhead expenditure (9) Variable overhead efficiency (10) Fixed overhead expenditure
> These are all the basic variances. Practice before the exam to ensure these calculations can be completed quickly and accurately.

48　WC

WC is a company that installs kitchens and bathrooms for customers who are renovating their houses. The installations are either pre-designed 'off-the-shelf' packages or highly customised designs for specific jobs.

The company operates with three divisions: Kitchens, Bathrooms and Central Services. The Kitchens and Bathrooms divisions are profit centres but the Central Services division is a cost centre.　The costs of the Central Services division, which are thought to be predominantly fixed, include those incurred by the design, administration and finance departments. The Central Services costs are charged to the other divisions based on the budgeted Central Services costs and the budgeted number of jobs to be undertaken by the other two divisions.

The budgeting and reporting system of WC is not very sophisticated and does not provide much detail for the Directors of the company.

The budgeted details for last year were:

	Kitchens	Bathrooms
Number of jobs	4,000	2,000
	$	$
Average price per job	10,000	7,000
Average direct costs per job	5,500	3,000
Central Services recharge per job	2,500	2,500
Average profit per job	2,000	1,500

The actual results were as follows:

	Kitchens	Bathrooms
Number of jobs	2,600	2,500
	$	$
Average price per job	13,000	6,100
Average direct costs per job	8,000	2,700
Central Services recharge per job	2,500	2,500
Average profit per job	2,500	900

The actual costs for the Central Services division were $17.5 million.

Required:

(a) **Calculate the budgeted and actual profits for each of the profit centres and for the whole company for the year.** **(4 marks)**

(b) **Calculate the sales price variances and the sales mix profit and sales quantity profit variances.** **(6 marks)**

(c) **Prepare a statement that reconciles the budgeted and actual profits and shows appropriate variances in as much detail as possible.** **(10 marks)**

(Total: 20 marks)

49 STICKY WICKET (JUNE 10 EXAM)

Sticky Wicket (SW) manufactures cricket bats using high quality wood and skilled labour using mainly traditional manual techniques. The manufacturing department is a cost centre within the business and operates a standard costing system based on marginal costs.

At the beginning of April 2010 the production director attempted to reduce the cost of the bats by sourcing wood from a new supplier and de-skilling the process a little by using lower grade staff on parts of the production process. The standards were not adjusted to reflect these changes.

The variance report for April 2010 is shown below (extract).

	Adverse	Favourable
Variances	$	$
Material price		5,100
Material usage	7,500	
Labour rate		43,600
Labour efficiency	48,800	
Labour idle time	5,400	

The production director pointed out in his April 2010 board report that the new grade of labour required significant training in April and this meant that productive time was lower than usual. He accepted that the workers were a little slow at the moment but expected that an improvement would be seen in May 2010. He also mentioned that the new wood being used was proving difficult to cut cleanly resulting in increased waste levels.

Sales for April 2010 were down 10% on budget and returns of faulty bats were up 20% on the previous month. The sales director resigned after the board meeting stating that SW had always produced quality products but the new strategy was bound to upset customers and damage the brand of the business.

Required

(a) **Assess the performance of the production director using all the information above taking into account both the decision to use a new supplier and the decision to de-skill the process.** **(7 marks)**

In May 2010 the budgeted sales were 19,000 bats and the standard cost card is as follows:

	Std cost	Std cost
	$	$
Materials (2kg at $5/kg)	10	
Labour (3hrs at $12/hr)	36	
Marginal cost		46
Selling price		68
Contribution		22

In May 2010 the following results were achieved:

40,000kg of wood were bought at a cost of $196,000, this produced 19,200 cricket bats. No inventory of raw materials is held. The labour was paid for 62,000 hours and the total cost was $694,000. Labour worked for 61,500 hours.

The sales price was reduced to protect the sales levels. However, only 18,000 cricket bats were sold at an average price of $65.

Required:

(b) **Calculate the materials, labour and sales variances for May 2010 in as much detail as the information allows. You are not required to comment on the performance of the business.** **(13 marks)**

(Total: 20 marks)

50 SPIKE CO (DEC 07 EXAM)

Spike Limited manufactures and sells good quality leather bound diaries. Each year it budgets for its profits, including detailed budgets for sales, materials and labour. If appropriate, the departmental managers are allowed to revise their budgets for planning errors.

In recent months, the managing director has become concerned about the frequency of budget revisions. At a recent board meeting he said 'There seems little point budgeting any more. Every time we have a problem the budgets are revised to leave me looking at a favourable operational variance report and at the same time a lot less profit than promised.'

Two specific situations have recently arisen, for which budget revisions were sought:

Materials

A local material supplier was forced into liquidation. Spike Limited's buyer managed to find another supplier, 150 miles away at short notice. This second supplier charged more for the material and a supplementary delivery charge on top. The buyer agreed to both the price and the delivery charge without negotiation. 'I had no choice', the buyer said, 'the production manager was pushing me very hard to find any solution possible!' Two months later, another, more competitive, local supplier was found.

A budget revision is being sought for the two months where higher prices had to be paid.

Labour

During the early part of the year, problems had been experienced with the quality of work being produced by the support staff in the labour force. The departmental manager had complained in his board report that his team were 'unreliable, inflexible and just not up to the job'.

It was therefore decided, after discussion of the board report, that something had to be done. The company changed its policy so as to recruit only top graduates from good quality universities. This has had the effect of pushing up the costs involved but increasing productivity in relation to that element of the labour force.

The support staff departmental manager has requested a budget revision to cover the extra costs involved following the change of policy.

Required:

(a) **Discuss each request for a budget revision, putting what you see as both sides of the argument and reach a conclusion as to whether a budget revision should be allowed.** **(8 marks)**

The market for leather bound diaries has been shrinking as the electronic versions become more widely available and easier to use. Spike Limited has produced the following data relating to leather bound diary sales for the year to date:

Budget

Sales volume	180,000 units
Sales price	$17.00 per unit
Standard contribution	$7.00 per unit

The total market for diaries in this period was estimated in the budget to be 1.8m units. In fact, the actual total market shrank to 1.6m units for the period under review.

Actual results for the same period

Sales volume	176,000 units
Sales price	$16.40 per unit

Required:

(b) **Calculate the total sales price and total sales volume variance.** **(4 marks)**

(c) **Analyse the total sales volume variance into components for market size and market share.** **(4 marks)**

(d) **Comment on the sales performance of the business.** **(4 marks)**

(Total: 20 marks)

Note: The original question also included the following requirement for 5 marks:

Describe the circumstances when a budget revision should be allowed and when it should be refused.

---

51   SECURE NET (DEC 09 EXAM)

Secure Net (SN) manufacture security cards that restrict access to government owned buildings around the world.

The standard cost for the plastic that goes into making a card is $4 per kg and each card uses 40g of plastic after an allowance for waste. In November 100,000 cards were produced and sold by SN and this was well above the budgeted sales of 60,000 cards.

The actual cost of the plastic was $5.25 per kg and the production manager (who is responsible for all buying and production issues) was asked to explain the increase. He said 'World oil price increases pushed up plastic prices by 20% compared to our budget and I also decided to use a different supplier who promised better quality and increased reliability for a slightly higher price. I know we have overspent but not all the increase in plastic prices is my fault'

The actual usage of plastic per card was 35g per card and again the production manager had an explanation. He said 'The world-wide standard size for security cards increased by 5% due to a change in the card reader technology, however, our new supplier provided much better quality of plastic and this helped to cut down on the waste.'

SN operates a just in time (JIT) system and hence carries very little inventory.

Required:

(a)   Calculate the total material price and total material usage variances ignoring any possible planning error in the figures.   **(4 marks)**

(b)   Analyse the above total variances into component parts for planning and operational variances in as much detail as the information allows.   **(8 marks)**

(c)   Assess the performance of the production manager.   **(8 marks)**

                                                                                          (Total: 20 marks)

52   PH

PH operates a modern factory that converts chemicals into fertiliser. Because the demand for its product is seasonal, the company expects that there will be an average level of idle time equivalent to 20% of hours paid. This is incorporated into the company's standard costs, and the standard labour rate of $6.00 per hour paid is then adjusted accordingly. Any difference between the expected and actual amount of idle time is reported as the 'idle time variance' and is valued at the adjusted wage rate.

Data for each of the four months January to April 20X2 is as follows:

	January	February	March	April
Actual hours paid	10,000	14,000	17,000	30,000
Actual productive hours	7,200	10,304	12,784	23,040
Standard hours produced	6,984	9,789	11,889	20,966
Idle time variance	$6,000 (A)	$6,720 (A)	$6,120 (A)	?
Efficiency variance	$1,620 (A)	$3,863 (A)	$6,713 (A)	?

Required:

(a)   Calculate the idle time variance and the efficiency variance for April.   **(4 marks)**

(b)   Using the data provided and your answer to (a) above as appropriate, prepare a percentage variance chart that shows the trend of these variances. (Use graph paper and show both variances on the same chart.) Comment on the usefulness of presenting the information in this format.   **(12 marks)**

(c)   Comment briefly on the possible inter-relationships between the idle time variance and the efficiency variance.   **(4 marks)**

(Total: 20 marks)

53   MARSHALL

Marshall operates a business that sells advanced photocopying machines and offers on-site servicing. There is a separate department that provides servicing. The standard cost for one service is shown below along with the operating statements for the Service Department for the six months to 30 September. Each service is very similar and involves the replacement of two sets of materials and parts.

Marshall's budgets for 5,000 services per month.

Standard cost for one service

	$
Materials – 2 sets @ $20 per set	40
Labour – 3 hours @ $11 per hour	33
Variable overheads – 3 hours @ $5 per hour	15
Fixed overheads – 3 hours @ $8 per hour	24
	112

Operating Statements for six months ending 30 September

Months	1	2	3	4	5	6	Total
Number of services per month	5,000	5,200	5,400	4,800	4,700	4,500	29,600
	$	$	$	$	$	$	$
Flexible budget costs	560,000	582,400	604,800	537,600	526,400	504,000	3,315,200
Less variances:							
Materials							
Price	5,150 F	3,090 F	1,100 F	(2,040) A	(5,700) A	(2,700) A	(1,100) A
Usage	(6,000) A	2,000 F	(4,000) A	(12,000) A	(2,000) A	0	(22,000) A
Labour							
Rate	26,100 F	25,725 F	27,331 F	18,600 F	17,400 F	15,515 F	130,671 F
Efficiency	5,500 F	9,900 F	12,100 F	(12,100) A	(4,400) A	(11,000) A	0
Variable overheads:							
Expenditure	(3,500) A	(3,500) A	(2,500) A	(4,500) A	500 F	2,500 F	(11,000) A
Efficiency	2,500 F	4,500 F	5,500 F	(5,500) A	(2,000) A	(5,000) A	0
Fixed overheads:							
Expenditure	(3,000) A	(5,000) A	(5,000) A	(15,000) A	5,000 F	5,000 F	(18,000) A
Volume	0	4,800 F	9,600 F	(4,800) A	(7,200) A	(12,000) A	(9,600) A
Actual costs	533,250	540,885	560,669	574,940	524,800	511,685	3,246,229

Required:

(a) Prepare a summary financial statement showing the overall performance of the Service Department for the six months to 30 September 200X. **(6 marks)**

(b) Write a report to the Operations Director of Marshall commenting on the performance of the Service Department for the six months to 30 September 200X.

Suggest possible causes for the features you have included in your report and state the further information that would be helpful in assessing the performance of the department. **(14 marks)**

(Total: 20 marks)

PERFORMANCE MEASUREMENT AND CONTROL

54 JUMP PERFORMANCE APPRAISAL (JUNE 10 EXAM)

Jump has a network of sports clubs which is managed by local managers reporting to the main board. The local managers have a lot of autonomy and are able to vary employment contracts with staff and offer discounts for membership fees and personal training sessions. They also control their own maintenance budget but do not have control over large amounts of capital expenditure.

A local manager's performance and bonus is assessed relative to three targets. For every one of these three targets that is reached in an individual quarter, $400 is added to the manager's bonus, which is paid at the end of the year. The maximum bonus per year is therefore based on 12 targets (three targets in each of the four quarters of the year). Accordingly the maximum bonus that could be earned is 12 × $400 = $4,800, which represents 40% of the basic salary of a local manager. Jump has a 31 March year end.

The performance data for one of the sports clubs for the last four quarters is as follows :

	Qtr to 30 June 2009	Qtr to 30 Sept 2009	Qtr to 31 Dec 2009	Qtr to 31 March 2010
Number of members	3,000	3,200	3,300	3,400
Member visits	20,000	24,000	26,000	24,000
Personal training sessions booked	310	325	310	339
Staff days	450	480	470	480
Staff lateness days	20	28	28	20
Days in quarter	90	90	90	90

Agreed targets are:

1   Staff must be on time over 95% of the time (no penalty is made when staff are absent from work)

2   On average 60% of members must use the clubs' facilities regularly by visiting at least 12 times per quarter 3. On average 10% of members must book a personal training session each quarter

Required:

(a)   **Calculate the amount of bonus that the manager should expect to be paid for the latest financial year.**   **(6 marks)**

(b)   **Discuss to what extent the targets set are controllable by the local manager (you are required to make a case for both sides of the argument).**   **(9 marks)**

(c)   **Describe two methods as to how a manager with access to the accounting and other records could unethically manipulate the situation so as to gain a greater bonus.**   **(5 marks)**

(Total: 20 marks)

55   PACE COMPANY (DEC 08 EXAM)

Pace Company (PC) runs a large number of wholesale stores and is increasing the number of these stores all the time. It measures the performance of each store on the basis of a target return on investment (ROI) of 15%. Store managers get a bonus of 10% of their salary if their store's annual ROI exceeds the target each year. Once a store is built there is very little further capital expenditure until a full four years have passed.

PC has a store (store W) in the west of the country. Store W has historic financial data as follows over the past four years:

	2005	2006	2007	2008
Sales ($000)	200	200	180	170
Gross profit ($000)	80	70	63	51
Net profit ($000)	13	14	10	8
Net assets at start of year ($000)	100	80	60	40

The market in which PC operates has been growing steadily. Typically, PC's stores generate a 40% gross profit margin.

Required:

(a)   **Discuss the past financial performance of store W using ROI and any other measure you feel appropriate and, using your findings, discuss whether the ROI correctly reflects Store W's actual performance.**   **(7 marks)**

(b)   **Explain how a manager in store W might have been able to manipulate the results so as to gain bonuses more frequently.**   **(4 marks)**

PC has another store (store S) about to open in the south of the country. It has asked you for help in calculating the gross profit, net profit and ROI it can expect over each of the next four years. The following information is provided:

Sales volume in the first year will be 18,000 units. Sales volume will grow at the rate of 10% for years two and three but no further growth is expected in year 4. Sales price will start at $12 per unit for the first two years but then reduce by 5% per annum for each of the next two years.

Gross profit will start at 40% but will reduce as the sales price reduces. All purchase prices on goods for resale will remain constant for the four years.

Overheads, including depreciation, will be $70,000 for the first two years rising to $80,000 in years three and four.

Store S requires an investment of $100,000 at the start of its first year of trading.

PC depreciates non-current assets at the rate of 25% of cost. No residual value is expected on these assets.

Required:

(c)   **Calculate (in columnar form) the revenue, gross profit, net profit and ROI of store S over each of its first four years.**   **(9 marks)**

                                                                 (Total: 20 marks)

---

*Note:*The original question, as written by the examiner, also included the following requirement for 4 marks:

Calculate the minimum sales volume required in year 4 (assuming all other variables remain unchanged) to earn the manager of S a bonus in that year.

---

56   PROPOSALS FOR DIVISION X

Division X is in a stable market. The first draft of its plan for the next three years is regarded as unacceptable to group management because it shows a slow decline in profit and return on investment:

	Year 1	Year 2	Year 3
	$m	$m	$m
Profit before interest and tax (PBIT)	3.0	2.7	2.4
Asset base (at beginning of year)	24.0	25.0	26.0

Proposals which may improve the situation in the next three years are being discussed; ONLY ONE can be accepted because of cash limitations. Projects are evaluated with a 10% required return on investment. These proposed projects are shown below.

(i)   **Special-purpose machine**

Capital expenditure in years 1 and 2, followed by operating cash flow in year 3:

Year 1	Year 2	Year 3	NPV
$m	$m	$m	$m
−0.5	−0.5	2.0	0.634

(ii)   **R&D project**

Revenue expenditure in years 1 and 2, followed by operating cash flow in year 3:

Year 1	Year 2	Year 3	NPV
$m	$m	$m	$m
−1.0	−1.0	4.0	1.269

(iii)   **Advertising**

This can be done in each year if required. Each annual campaign costs $1m, but produces additional contributions of $0.4m in the year of the campaign and $1.1m in the subsequent year. A decision has been made to run annual campaigns in years 1 and 2 only. The combined cash flows are:

Year 1	Year 2	Year 3	NPV
$m	$m	$m	$m
−0.6	+0.5	+1.1	0.694

Managers are currently evaluated on return on investment (ROI), and are paid bonuses when this reaches or exceeds 10%. At 10% ROI the manager of division X will receive 25% of his salary of $50,000 pa. For each 1 % increase in ROI above 10%, and *pro rata*, he will receive an additional 2.5% of basic salary with an upper bonus limit of 50% of salary for that year.

Thus, for the first draft of the plan, the bonus based on the ROI has been correctly calculated as:

	Year 1	Year 2	Year 3
Bonus	$15,625	$13,500	$ Zero

Calculations ignore tax and depreciation. The asset base represents the assets employed in the division at the beginning of each year, and excludes cash balances which are transferred to the group, and is used for the calculation of residual income (RI) and ROI.

Required:

(a) Calculate the ROI, and the manager's bonus each year for the three alternative proposals. Comment on the effects of the bonus system on the manager's choice of project. **(13 marks)**

(b) A proposal is under consideration to change the bonus scheme to 2% of residual income (RI) with a limit of 50% of salary. A 10% rate of interest would be used in the calculation of RI.

For the plan including the special-purpose machine, the bonus, based on the RI, has been correctly calculated as:

	Year 1	Year 2	Year 3
Bonus	$12,000	$3,000	$25,000

Required:

Calculate the RI and bonuses each year, both for the first draft of the plan and for the R&D and Advertising alternatives. Comment briefly on whether the proposed revised bonus system would influence the manager's choice of project in a different way from that based on the ROI. **(7 marks)**

(Total: 20 marks)

57 TIP (DEC 09 EXAM)

Thatcher International Park (TIP) is a theme park and has for many years been a successful business, which has traded profitably. About three years ago the directors decided to capitalise on their success and reduced the expenditure made on new thrill rides, reduced routine maintenance where possible (deciding instead to repair equipment when it broke down) and made a commitment to regularly increase admission prices. Once an admission price is paid customers can use any of the facilities and rides for free.

These steps increased profits considerably, enabling good dividends to be paid to the owners and bonuses to the directors. The last two years of financial results are shown below.

	2008	2009
	$	$
Sales	5,250,000	5,320,000
Less expenses:		
Wages	2,500,000	2,200,000
Maintenance – routine	80,000	70,000
Repairs	260,000	320,000
Directors salaries	150,000	160,000
Directors bonuses	15,000	18,000
Other costs (including depreciation)	1,200,000	1,180,000
Net profit	1,045,000	1,372,000
Book value of assets at start of year	13,000,000	12,000,000
Dividend paid	500,000	650,000
Number of visitors	150,000	140,000

TIP operates in a country where the average rate of inflation is around 1% per annum.

Required:

(a) Assess the financial performance of TIP using the information given above.

(14 marks)

During the early part of 2008 TIP employed a newly qualified management accountant. He quickly becameconcerned about the potential performance of TIP and to investigate his concerns he started to gather data to measure some non-financial measures of success. The data he has gathered is shown below:

Table 1

	2008	2009
Hours lost due to breakdown of rides (see note 1)	9,000 hours	32,000 hours
Average waiting time per ride	20 minutes	30 minutes

Note 1: TIP has 50 rides of different types. It is open 360 days of the year for 10 hours each day

(b) Assess the quality of the service that TIP provides to its customers using Table 1 and any other relevant data and indicate the risks it is likely to face if it continues with its current policies.

(6 marks)

(Total: 20 marks)

58 Y AND Z

Y and Z are two divisions of a large company that operate in similar markets. The divisions are treated as investment centres and every month they each prepare an operating statement to be submitted to the parent company. Operating statements for these two divisions for October are shown below:

Operating statements for October

	Y	Z
	$000	$000
Sales revenue	900	555
Less variable costs	345	312
Contribution	555	243
Less controllable fixed costs (includes depreciation on divisional assets)	98	42
Controllable income	460	201
Less apportioned central costs	338	180
Net income before tax	122	21
Total divisional net assets	$9.76m	$1.26m

The company currently has a target return on capital of 12% per annum. However, the company believes its cost of capital is likely to rise and is considering increasing the target return on capital. At present the performance of each division and the divisional management are assessed primarily on the basis of Return on Investment (ROI).

Required:

(a)   Calculate the annualised Return on Investment (ROI) for divisions Y and Z, and discuss the relative performance of the two divisions using the ROI data and other information given above.   **(9 marks)**

(b)   Calculate the annualised Residual Income (RI) for divisions Y and Z, and explain the implications of this information for the evaluation of the divisions' performance.

(6 marks)

(c)   Briefly discuss the strengths and weaknesses of ROI and RI as methods of assessing the performance of divisions.   Explain two further methods of assessment of divisional performance that could be used in addition to ROI or RI.   **(5 marks)**

(Total: 20 marks)

59   FP

FP sells and repairs photocopiers. The company has operated for many years with two departments, the Sales Department and the Service Department, but the departments had no autonomy. The company is now thinking of restructuring so that the two departments will become profit centres.

The Sales Department

This department sells new photocopiers. The department sells 2,000 copiers per year. Included in the selling price is $60 for a one-year guarantee. All customers pay this fee. This means that, during the first year of ownership, if the photocopier needs to be repaired then the repair costs are not charged to the customer. On average 500 photocopiers per year need to be repaired under the guarantee. The repair work is carried out by the Service Department who, under the proposed changes, would charge the Sales Department for doing the repairs. It is estimated that on average the repairs will take 3 hours each and that the charge by the Service Department will be $136,500 for the 500 repairs.

The Service Department

This department has two sources of work – the work needed to satisfy the guarantees for the Sales Department and repair work for external customers. Customers are charged at full cost plus 40%. The details of the budget for the next year for the Service Department revealed standard costs of:

Parts	*At cost*
Labour	$15 per hour
Variable overheads	$10 per labour hour
Fixed overheads	$22 per labour hour

The calculation of these standards is based on the estimated maximum market demand and includes the expected 500 repairs for the Sales Department. The average cost of the parts needed for a repair is $54. This means that the charge to the Sales Department for the repair work, including the 40% mark-up, will be $136,500.

Proposed change

It has now been suggested that FP should be structured so that the two departments become profit centres and that the managers of the Departments are given autonomy. The individual salaries of the managers would be linked to the profits of their respective departments.

Budgets have been produced for each department on the assumption that the Service Department will repair 500 photocopiers for the Sales Department and that the transfer price for this work will be calculated in the same way as the price charged to external customers.

However the manager of the Sales Department has now stated that he intends to have the repairs done by another company, RS, because it has offered to carry out the work for a fixed fee of $180 per repair and this is less than the price that the Service Department would charge.

Required:

(a) Calculate the individual profits of the Sales Department and the Service Department, and of FP as a whole from the guarantee scheme if:

(i) the repairs are carried out by the Service Department and are charged at full cost plus 40%;

(ii) the repairs are carried out by the Service Department and are charged at marginal cost;

(iii) the repairs are carried out by RS. **(10 marks)**

(b) (i) Explain, with reasons, why a 'full cost plus' transfer pricing model may *not* be appropriate for FP. **(3 marks)**

(ii) Comment on THREE other issues that the managers of FP should consider if they decide to allow RS to carry out the repairs. **(3 marks)**

(c) Briefly explain TWO advantages and TWO disadvantages of structuring the departments as profit centres. **(4 marks)**

(Total: 20 marks)

60 CTD

CTD has two divisions – FD and TM. FD is an iron foundry division which produces mouldings that have a limited external market and are also transferred to TM division. TM division uses the mouldings to produce a piece of agricultural equipment called the 'TX' which is sold externally. Each TX requires one moulding. Both divisions produce only one type of product.

The performance of each Divisional Manager is evaluated individually on the basis of the residual income (RI) of his or her division. The company's average annual 12% cost of capital is used to calculate the finance charges. If their own target residual income is achieved, each Divisional Manager is awarded a bonus equal to 5% of his or her residual income. All bonuses are paid out of Head Office profits.

The following budgeted information is available for the forthcoming year:

	TM division TX per unit	FD division Moulding per unit
External selling price ($)	500	80
Variable production cost ($)	*366	40
Fixed production overheads ($)	60	20
Gross profit ($)	74	20
Variable selling and distribution cost ($)	25	**4
Fixed administration overhead ($)	25	4
Net profit ($)	24	12
Normal capacity (units)	15,000	20,000
Maximum production capacity (units)	15,000	25,000
Sales to external customers (units)	15,000	5,000
Capital employed	$1,500,000	$750,000
Target RI	$105,000	$85,000

* The variable production cost of TX includes the cost of an FD moulding.

** External sales only of the mouldings incur a variable selling and distribution cost of $4 per unit.

FD division currently transfers 15,000 mouldings to TM division at a transfer price equal to the total production cost plus 10%.

Fixed costs are absorbed on the basis of normal capacity.

Required:

(a) Calculate the bonus each Divisional Manager would receive under the current transfer pricing policy and discuss any implications that the current performance evaluation system may have for each division and for the company as a whole.

(14 marks)

(b) Both Divisional Managers want to achieve their respective residual income targets. Based on the budgeted figures, calculate:

(i) the maximum transfer price per unit that the Divisional Manager of TM division would pay;

(ii) the minimum transfer price per unit that the Divisional Manager of FD division would accept.

(6 marks)

(Total: 20 marks)

61 DIVISION A

Division A, which is a part of the ACF Group, manufactures only one type of product, a Bit, which it sells to external customers and also to division C, another member of the group. ACF Group's policy is that divisions have the freedom to set transfer prices and choose their suppliers.

The ACF Group uses residual income (RI) to assess divisional performance and each year it sets each division a target RI. The group's cost of capital is 12% a year.

Division A

Budgeted information for the coming year is:

Maximum capacity	150,000 Bits
External sales	110,000 Bits
External selling price	$35 per Bit
Variable cost	$22 per Bit
Fixed costs	$1,080,000
Capital employed	$3,200,000
Target residual income	$180,000

Division C

Division C has found two other companies willing to supply Bits:

X could supply at $28 per Bit, but only for annual orders in excess of 50,000 Bits. Z could supply at $33 per Bit for any quantity ordered.

Required:

(a) Division C provisionally requests a quotation for 60,000 Bits from division A for the coming year.

    (i) Calculate the transfer price per Bit that division A should quote in order to meet its residual income target. **(6 marks)**

    (ii) Calculate the two prices division A would have to quote to division C, if it became group policy to quote transfer prices based on opportunity costs. **(4 marks)**

(b) Evaluate and discuss the impact of the group's current and proposed policies on the profits of divisions A and C, and on group profit. Illustrate your answer with calculations. **(10 marks)**

(Total: 20 marks)

62 BRIDGEWATER CO (JUNE 08 EXAM)

Bridgewater Co provides training courses for many of the mainstream software packages on the market.

The business has many divisions within Waterland, the one country in which it operates. The senior managers of Bridgewater Co have very clear objectives for the divisions and these are communicated to divisional managers on appointment and subsequently in quarterly and annual reviews. These are:

1   Each quarter, sales should grow and annual sales should exceed budget

2   Trainer (lecture staff) costs should not exceed $180 per teaching day

3   Room hire costs should not exceed $90 per teaching day

4   Each division should meet its budget for profit per quarter and annually

It is known that managers will be promoted based on their ability to meet these targets. A member of the senior management is to retire after quarter 2 of the current financial year, which has just begun. The divisional managers anticipate that one of them may be promoted at the beginning of quarter 3 if their performance is good enough.

The manager of the Northwest division is concerned that his chances of promotion could be damaged by the expected performance of his division. He is a firm believer in quality and he thinks that if a business gets this right, growth and success will eventually follow.

The current quarterly forecasts, along with the original budgeted profit for the Northwest division, are as follows:

	Q1	Q2	Q3	Q4	Total
	$000	$000	$000	$000	$000
Sales	40.0	36.0	50.0	60.0	186.0
less:					
Trainers	8.0	7.2	10.0	12.0	37.2
Room hire	4.0	3.6	5.0	6.0	18.6
Staff training	1.0	1.0	1.0	1.0	4.0
Other costs	3.0	1.7	6.0	7.0	17.7
Forecast net profit	24.0	22.5	28.0	34.0	108.5
Original budgeted profit	25.0	26.0	27.0	28.0	106.0
Annual sales budget					180.0
Teaching days	40	36	50	60	

Required:

(a)   **Assess the financial performance of the Northwest division against its targets and reach a conclusion as to the promotion prospects of the divisional manager**

(8 marks)

The manager of the Northwest division has been considering a few steps to improve the performance of his division.

Voucher scheme

As a sales promotion, vouchers will be sold for $125 each, a substantial discount on normal prices. These vouchers will entitle the holder to attend four training sessions on software of their choice. They can attend when they want to but are advised that one training session per quarter is sensible. The manager is confident that if the promotion took place immediately, he could sell 80 vouchers and that customers would follow the advice given to attend one session per quarter. All voucher holders would attend planned existing courses and all will be new customers.

Software upgrade

A new important software programme has recently been launched for which there could be a market for training courses. Demonstration programs can be bought for $1,800 in quarter 1. Staff training would be needed, costing $500 in each of quarters 1 and 2 but in quarters 3 and 4 extra courses could be offered selling this training. Assuming similar class sizes and the usual sales prices, extra sales revenue amounting to 20% of normal sales are expected (measured before the voucher promotion above). The manager is keen to run these courses at the same tutorial and room standards as he normally provides. Software expenditure is written off in the income statement as incurred.

Delaying payments to trainers

The manager is considering delaying payment to the trainers. He thinks that, since his commitment to quality could cause him to miss out on a well deserved promotion, the trainers owe him a favour. He intends to delay payment on 50% of all invoices received from the trainers in the first two quarters, paying them one month later than is usual.

Required:

(b)   Revise the forecasts to take account of all three of the proposed changes. **(6 marks)**

(c)   Comment on each of the proposed steps and reach a conclusion as to whether, if all the proposals were taken together, the manager will improve his chances of promotion.   **(6 marks)**

(Total: 20marks)

> *Note:* The original question also included the following requirement for 4 marks:
>
> **Suggest two improvements to the performance measurement system used by Bridgewater Co that would encourage a longer term view being taken by its managers.**

63   OLIVER'S SALON (JUNE 09 EXAM)

 Timed question with Online tutor debrief

Oliver is the owner and manager of Oliver's Salon which is a quality hairdresser that experiences high levels of competition. The salon traditionally provided a range of hair services to female clients only, including cuts, colouring and straightening

A year ago, at the start of his 2009 financial year, Oliver decided to expand his operations to include the hairdressing needs of male clients. Male hairdressing prices are lower, the work simpler (mainly hair cuts only) and so the time taken per male client is much less.

The prices for the female clients were not increased during the whole of 2008 and 2009 and the mix of services provided for female clients in the two years was the same.

The latest financial results are as follows:

	2008		2009	
	$	$	$	$
Sales		200,000		238,500
Less cost of sales:				
Hairdressing staff costs	65,000		91,000	
Hair products – female	29,000		27,000	
Hair products – male			8,000	
		94,000		126,000
Gross profit		106,000		112,500
Rent	10,000		10,000	
Administration salaries	9,000		9,500	
Electricity	7,000		8,000	
Advertising	2,000		5,000	
Total expenses		28,000		32,500
Profit		78,000		80,000

Oliver is disappointed with his financial results. He thinks the salon is much busier than a year ago and was expecting more profit. He has noted the following extra information:

1   Some female clients complained about the change in atmosphere following the introduction of male services, which created tension in the salon.

2   Two new staff were recruited at the start of 2009. The first was a junior hairdresser to support the specialist hairdressers for the female clients. She was appointed on a salary of $9,000 per annum. The second new staff member was a specialist hairdresser for the male clients. There were no increases in pay for existing staff at the start of 2009 after a big rise at the start of 2008 which was designed to cover two years' worth of increases.

Oliver introduced some non-financial measures of success two years ago.

	2008	2009
Number of complaints	12	46
Number of male client visits	0	3,425
Number of female client visits	8,000	6,800
Number of specialist hairdressers for female clients	4	5
Number of specialist hairdressers for male clients	0	1

Required:

(a)   Calculate the average price for hair services per male and female client for each of the years 2008 and 2009.   **(3 marks)**

(b)   Assess the financial performance of the Salon using the data above.   **(11 marks)**

(c)   Analyse and comment on the non-financial performance of Oliver's business, under the headings of quality and resource utilisation.   **(6 marks)**

(Total: 20 marks)

 Calculate your allowed time, allocate the time to the separate parts.....................

---

64   TIES ONLY (DEC 07 EXAM)

Ties Only Limited is a new business, selling high quality imported men's ties via the internet. The managers, who also own the company, are young and inexperienced but they are prepared to take risks. They are confident that importing quality ties and selling via a website will be successful and that the business will grow quickly. This is despite the well recognised fact that selling clothing is a very competitive business.

They were prepared for a loss-making start and decided to pay themselves modest salaries (included in administration expenses in table 1 below) and pay no dividends for the foreseeable future.

The owners are so convinced that growth will quickly follow that they have invested enough money in website server development to ensure that the server can handle the very high levels of predicted growth. All website development costs were written off as incurred in the internal management accounts that are shown below in table 1.

Significant expenditure on marketing was incurred in the first two quarters to launch both the website and new products. It is not expected that marketing expenditure will continue to be as high in the future.

Customers can buy a variety of styles, patterns and colours of ties at different prices.

The business's trading results for the first two quarters of trade are shown in the table below:

		Quarter 1		Quarter 2
	$	$	$	$
Sales		420,000		680,000
Less: Cost of sales		(201,600)		(340,680)
Gross profit		218,400		339,320
Less: Expenses				
Website development	120,000		90,000	
Administration	100,500		150,640	
Distribution	20,763		33,320	
Launch marketing	60,000		40,800	
Other variable expenses	50,000		80,000	
Total expenses		(351,263)		(394,760)
Loss for quarter		(132,863)		(55,440)

Required:

(a) **Assess the financial performance of the business during its first two quarters using only the data in table 1 above.** **(8 marks)**

(b) **Briefly consider whether the losses made by the business in the first two quarters are a true reflection of the current and likely future performance of the business.** **(4 marks)**

The owners are well aware of the importance of non-financial indicators of success and therefore have identified a small number of measures to focus on. These are measured monthly and then combined to produce a quarterly management report.

The data for the first two quarters management reports is shown below:

Table 2	Quarter 1	Quarter 2
Website hits*	690,789	863,492
Number of ties sold	27,631	38,857
On time delivery	95%	89%
Sales returns	12%	18%
System downtime	2%	4%

* A website hit is automatically counted each time a visitor to the website opens the home page of Ties Only Limited.

The industry average conversion rate for website hits to number of ties sold is 3.2%. The industry average sales return rate for internet-based clothing sales is 13%.

Required:

(c)   Comment on each of the non-financial data in table 2 above taking into account, where appropriate, the industry averages provided, providing your assessment of the performance of the business.   (8 marks)

(Total: 20 marks)

Note: The original question as written by the examiner gave 12 marks to part (a) and 11 marks to part (b). The suggested answers are thus more extensive than now required.

 Online question assistance

65   NON-FINANCIAL MEASURES

Many firms still focus on profitability as their main measure of performance, despite increasing evidence that non-financial measures are often more important.

Required:

(a)   Explain the arguments for using the profit measure as the all-encompassing measure of the performance of a business.   (5 marks)

(b)   Explain the limitations of this profit-measurement approach and of undue dependence on the profit measure.   (5 marks)

(c)   Explain the problems of using a broad range of non-financial measures for the short- and long-term control of a business.   (5 marks)

(d)   An insurance company is considering introducing a balanced scorecard. State the four perspectives of the balanced scorecard and recommend, with explanations, ONE performance measure for each perspective.   (5 marks)

(Total: 20 marks)

66   PUBLIC SECTOR ORGANISATION

A public sector organisation is extending its budgetary control and responsibility accounting system to all departments. One such department concerned with public health and welfare is called 'Homecare'. The department consists of staff who visit elderly 'clients' in their homes to support them with their basic medical and welfare needs.

A monthly cost control report is to be sent to the department manager, a copy of which is also passed to a Director who controls a number of departments. In the system, which is still being refined, the budget was set by the Director and the manager had not been consulted over the budget or the use of the monthly control report.

Shown below is the first month's cost control report for the Homecare department:

Cost Control Report – Homecare Department
Month ending May 20X0

	Budget	Actual	(Overspend)/ underspend
Visits	10,000	12,000	(2,000)
	$	$	$
Department expenses:			
Supervisory salary	2,000	2,125	(125)
Wages (Permanent staff)	2,700	2,400	300
Wages (Casual staff)	1,500	2,500	(1,000)
	Budget	Actual	(Overspend)/ underspend
	$	$	$
Office equipment depreciation	500	750	(250)
Repairs to equipment	200	20	180
Travel expenses	1,500	1,800	(300)
Consumables	4,000	6,000	(2,000)
Administration and telephone	1,000	1,200	(200)
Allocated administrative costs	2,000	3,000	(1,000)
	15,400	19,795	(4,395)

In addition to the manager and permanent members of staff, appropriately qualified casual staff are appointed on a week to week basis to cope with fluctuations in demand. Staff use their own transport, and travel expenses are reimbursed. There is a central administration overhead charge over all departments. Consumables consist of materials which are used by staff to care for clients. Administration and telephone are costs of keeping in touch with the staff who often operate from their own homes.

As a result of the report, the Director sent a memo to the manager of the Homecare department pointing out that the department must spend within its funding allocation and that any spending more than 5% above budget on any item would not be tolerated. The Director requested an immediate explanation for the serious overspend.

You work as the assistant to the Directorate Management Accountant. On seeing the way the budget system was developing, he made a note of points he would wish to discuss and develop further, but was called away before these could be completed.

Required:

Develop and explain the issues concerning the budgetary control and responsibility accounting system which are likely to be raised by the management accountant. You should refer to the way the budget was prepared, the implications of a 20% increase in the number of visits, the extent of controllability of costs, the implications of the funding allocation, social aspects and any other points you think appropriate. You may include numerical illustrations and comment on specific costs, but you are not required to reproduce the cost control report. **(20 marks)**

67 WOODSIDE CHARITY (JUNE 07 EXAM)

Woodside is a local charity dedicated to helping homeless people in a large city. The charity owns and manages a shelter that provides free overnight accommodation for up to 30 people, offers free meals each and every night of the year to homeless people who are unable to buy food, and runs a free advice centre to help homeless people find suitable housing and gain financial aid. Woodside depends entirely on public donations to finance its activities and had a fundraising target for the last year of $700,000. The budget for the last year was based on the following forecast activity levels and expected costs.

Free meals provision:	18,250 meals at $5 per meal
Overnight shelter:	10,000 bed-nights at $30 per night
Advice centre:	3,000 sessions at $20 per session
Campaigning and advertising:	$150,000

The budgeted surplus (budgeted fundraising target less budgeted costs) was expected to be used to meet any unexpected costs. Included in the above figures are fixed costs of $5 per night for providing shelter and $5 per advice session representing fixed costs expected to be incurred by administration and maintaining the shelter. The number of free meals provided and the number of beds occupied each night depends on both the weather and the season of the year. The Woodside charity has three full-time staff and a large number of voluntary helpers.

The actual costs for the last year were as follows:

Free meals provision:	20,000 meals at a variable cost of $104,000
Overnight shelter:	8,760 bed-nights at a variable cost of $223,380
Advice centre:	3,500 sessions at a variable cost of $61,600
Campaigning and advertising:	$165,000

The actual costs of the overnight shelter and the advice centre exclude the fixed costs of administration and maintenance, which were $83,000.

The actual amount of funds raised in the last year was $620,000.

Required:

(a) **Prepare an operating statement, reconciling budgeted surplus and actual shortfall and discuss the charity's performance over the last year.** **(13 marks)**

(b) **Discuss problems that may arise in the financial management and control of a not-for-profit organisation such as the Woodside charity.** **(7 marks)**

(Total: 20 marks)

Section 2

ANSWERS TO PRACTICE QUESTIONS

SPECIALIST COST AND MANAGEMENT ACCOUNTING TECHNIQUES

1 ABC

Key answer tips

This is standard bookwork on ABC – ensure you learn such aspects as you may have to apply such points to a specific organisation in the real exam.

(a) Activity Based Costing (ABC) has been implemented across a range of organisations to enhance management information systems. The introduction of ABC changed the focus of cost accumulation from processes to activities. In this way, decision-relevant costs could be identified since management could, in principle, alter the activities undertaken. Traditional methods of product costing were often volume related (e.g. hours of labour used) but this did not develop with the growth in activities that had no relation to volume, or in multi-product businesses where there are complex production processes.

There are general conditions under which ABC is most likely to operate and these relate to the following factors:

(i) Where there is a requirement to apportion costs (e.g. in a multi-product business).

(ii) Where there are significant overheads to apportion.

(iii) Where the availability of sophisticated information retrieval systems allows management to track product costs as they pass through a production system.

Multi-product businesses

The main issue is that there have to be at least two products in the business otherwise there are no costs to apportion between products. For a single product company, all the costs of the business are identifiable with the product.

However, ABC might still be useful in single product businesses when management decisions are required to determine the level of production. In such cases, optimum levels of output can be defined once costs can be split between fixed and variable elements. ABC will help identify variable costs as those that vary with the level of activities that incur costs. In principle, fixed costs are then those costs that do not vary with activity, and hence it becomes possible to undertake profitability analysis in relation to activity levels.

Other advantages of ABC in a multi-product business relate to the accurate valuation of inventory and facilitating the effective management of inventory levels with multiple products. There is also reduced cross-subsidisation of products: with costs accurately identified with products, it becomes easier for management to distinguish which products are profitable from those that are not.

The significance of overheads and the ABC method of charging costs

Since ABC is a cost apportionment system then it is principally beneficial when there is a high proportion of overhead costs to apportion to products. If a business incurs only direct costs, there is no issue for ABC to resolve.

ABC is based on the premise that activities lead to costs being incurred and that costs should therefore be apportioned on the basis of the activities that different products consume. In this way, management can better understand the behaviour of overheads as they relate to decisions.

ABC apportions costs by first identifying the activities that generate costs. Cost drivers are then chosen that reflect the events that create costs when the activities are undertaken. The costs associated with each activity are then collected into cost pools where there are common cost drivers. Finally, costs are allocated to products on the basis of the activities they use. In summary, if product overheads can be seen in terms of activities, and activities have costs associated with them, then the use of activities by a product can be costed.

Retrieval systems

A basic requirement for any cost allocation system is information availability. This is particularly so for ABC systems which rely heavily on activity information. Moreover, production systems are far more complex than in the days when traditional absorption costing was most effective. For example, manufacturing processes rely far more on quality control monitoring, inspection and set-up processes than they ever did and are not necessarily related to the volume of activity. With many products, and variants on products, the monitoring of costs itself becomes a large and complex process. With complexity inevitably follows greater support services, of which a major category would be computer support services.

In addition, ABC requires the monitoring of activities that have not involved monitoring previously. This raises issues of information capture and it is in new technology that answers to this are most likely to be found.

(b)   One of the key problems in assessing manager performance is in ensuring that costs on which managers' performance is judged are controllable and hence traceable to manager decisions. Manager performance will be unfairly assessed if non-controllable costs are incorrectly taken into account, and the manager is made accountable for them. ABC is often claimed to rest on a more accurate information base than absorption costing, and hence the impact of management decisions is potentially more easily seen under ABC than it is under traditional volume-related absorption methods. Thus, it becomes possible to more closely align management decisions with their consequences and improve performance appraisal.

For example, in allocating and apportioning overheads, the re-apportionment of service department costs is reduced or eliminated under ABC. This is because ABC establishes separate cost pools for support activities and the costs of these activities are assigned to products directly on the basis of the appropriate driver. The accuracy of ABC in this context rests on the accurate identification of cost pools and cost drivers.

Also, ABC absorbs costs into products in a wider variety of ways than traditional absorption methods, which rely mostly on labour and/or machine hours. In extending the range of absorption bases, ABC is able to more closely track costs to the causes of the costs which then links to management decisions.

The foregoing does not rule out accurate costing using traditional absorption methods, especially when a business has most of its costs varying with production volume. However, when overheads do not vary with output, other means of determining absorption rates are preferable, such as those based on cost drivers. Thus, the scope for arbitrariness in manager performance appraisal is reduced.

2 BRICK BY BRICK (JUN 10 EXAM)

(a) Costs and quoted prices for the GC and the EX using labour hours to absorb overheads:

		GC $	EX $
Materials		3,500	8,000
Labour	300 hrs × $15/hr	4,500	
	500hrs × $15/hr		7,500
Overheads	300 hrs × $10/hr (W1)	3,000	
	500hrs × $10/hr		5,000
Total cost		11,000	20,500
Quoted price		16,500	30,750

(W1) Overhead absorption rate is calculated as $400,000/40,000hrs = $10/hr

(b) Costs and quoted prices for the GC and the EX using ABC to absorb overheads:

		GC $	EX $
Materials		3,500	8,000
Labour	300 hrs × $15/hr	4,500	
	500 hrs × $15/hr		7,500
Overheads			
− Supervisor	(W2)/(W3)	180	1,080
− Planers	(W2)/(W3)	280	1,400
− Property	(W2)/(W3)	1,800	3,000
Total cost		10,260	20,980
Quoted price		15,390	31,470

(W2)

	Costs	Number of drivers	Cost per driver
Supervisor	90,000	500	180
Planners	70,000	250	280
Property	240,000	40,000	6

(W3)

	Supervisor	Planner	Property
Cost per driver (W2)	$180	$280	$6
GC	180 × 1 = 180	280 × 1 = 280	6 × 300 = 1,800
EX	180 × 6 = 1,080	280 × 5 = 1,400	6 × 500 = 3,000

(c) The pricing policy is a matter for BBB to decide. They could elect to maintain the current 50% mark-up on cost and if they did the price of the GC would fall by around 7% in line with the costs. This should make them more competitive in the market.

They could also reduce the prices by a little less than 7% (say 5%) in order to increase internal margins a little.

It is possible that the issue lies elsewhere. If the quality of the work or the reputation and reliability of the builder is questionable then reducing prices is unlikely to improve sales. It is conceivable that BBB has a good reputation for EX but not for GC, but more likely that a poor reputation would affect all products. Equally poor service levels or lack of flexibility in meeting customer needs may be causing the poor sales performance. These too will not be 'corrected' by merely reducing prices.

It is also possible that the way salesmen discuss or sell their products for the GC is not adequate so that in some way customers are being put off placing the work with BBB.

BBB is in competition and it perhaps needs to reflect this in its pricing more (by 'going rate pricing') and not seek to merely add a mark-up to its costs.

BBB could try to penetrate the market by pricing some jobs cheaply to gain a foothold. Once this has been done the completed EX or GC could be used to market the business to new customers.

The price of the EX would also need consideration. There is no indication of problems in the selling of the EX and so BBB could consider pushing up their prices by around 2% in line with the cost increase. On the figures in my answer the price goes up for a typical extension to $31,470 from $30,750 a rise of $720. This does not seem that significant and so might not lose a significant number of sales.

The reliability and reputation of a builder is probably more important than the price that they charge for a job and so it is possible that the success rate on job quotes may not be that price sensitive.

(d) Marginal costs are those costs that are incurred as a consequence of the job being undertaken. In this case they would include only the materials and the labour. If overheads are included then this is known as total absorption costing.

Overheads are for many businesses fixed by nature and hence do not vary as the number of jobs changes. In a traditional sense any attempt to allocate costs to products (by way of labour hours for example) would be arbitrary with little true meaning being added to the end result. The overhead absorption rate (OAR) is merely an average of these costs (over labour hours) and is essentially meaningless. This switch (to marginal costing) would also avoid the problem of the uncertainty of budget volume. Budget volume is needed in order to calculate the fixed cost absorption rate.

The marginal cost (MC) is more understandable by managers and indeed customers and a switch away from total absorption cost (TAC) could have benefits in this way. Clearly if overheads are going to be excluded for the cost allocations then they would still have to be covered by way of a bigger margin added to the costs. In the end all costs have to be paid for and covered by the sales in order to show a profit.

A more modern viewpoint is that activity causes costs to exist. For example, it is the existence of the need for site visits that gives rise to the need for a supervisor and therefore, for his costs. If the activities that drive costs are identified, more costs can then be directly traced to products, hence eradicating the need for arbitrary apportionment of many overhead costs. This has the benefit of all costs being covered, rather than the potential shortfall that can arise if marginal cost plus pricing is used.

In the long run businesses have to cover all costs including fixed overheads in order to make a profit, whichever pricing strategy is adopted.

3   JOLA PUBLISHING CO (JUNE 08 EXAM)

Key answer tips

Candidates will be expected to understand why overhead allocation differs between activity based costing and traditional absorption costing. The examiner is unlikely to test only the numbers.

(a)   The first thing to point out is that the overhead allocations to the two products have not changed by that much. For example the CB has absorbed only $0.05 more overhead. The reason for such a small change is that the overheads are dominated by property costs (75% of total overhead) and the 'driver' for these remains machine hours once the switch to ABC is made. Thus no difference will result from the switch to ABC in this regard.

The major effect on the cost will be for quality control. It is a major overhead (23% of total) and there is a big difference between the relative number of machine hours for each product and the number of inspections made (the ABC driver). The CB takes less time to produce than the TJ, due to the shortness of the book. It will therefore carry a smaller amount of overhead in this regard. However, given the high degree of government regulation, the CB is subject to 'frequent' inspections whereas the TJ is inspected only rarely. This will mean that under ABC the CB will carry a high proportion of the quality control cost and hence change the relative cost allocations.

The production set up costs are only a small proportion of total cost and would be, therefore, unlikely to cause much of a difference in the cost allocations between the two products. However this hides the very big difference in treatment. The CB is produced in four long production runs, whereas the TJ is produced monthly in 12 production runs. The relative proportions of overhead allocated under the two overhead treatments will be very different. In this case the TJ would carry much more overhead under ABC than under a machine hours basis for overhead absorption.

Tutorial note

Many candidates demonstrated an understanding of this area but failed to get enough depth to score a good mark. There are thirteen minutes available, which should be sufficient time to plan and write up a succinct and relevant answer. Rather than just discussing overheads in general, a good approach would be to review each of the three overhead costs in turn. It should be possible to get two marks for the discussion of each overhead. A general introduction and overall conclusion would gain another two marks.

(b)   Cost per unit calculation using machine hours for overhead absorption

	CB ($)		TJ ($)
Paper (400g at $2/kg)	0.80	(100g at $1/kg)	0.10
Printing (50ml at $30/ltr)	1.50	(150ml at $30/ltr)	4.50
Machine cost (6 mins at $12/hr)	1.20	(10 mins at $12/hr)	2.00
Overheads (6 mins at $24/hr) (W1)	2.40	(10 mins at $24/hr)	4.00
Total cost	5.90		10.60
Sales price	9.30		14.00
Margin	3.40		3.40

(W1) Workings for overheads:

Total overhead $2,880,000

Total machine hours $(1,000,000 \times 6 \text{ mins}) + (120,000 \times 10 \text{ mins})$ = 7,200,000 mins

= 120,000 hours

Cost per hour   = $2,880,000 ÷120,000

= $24 per hour

	CB ($)		TJ ($)
Paper (400g at $2/kg)	0.80	(100g at $1/kg)	0.10
Printing (50ml at $30/ltr)	1.50	(150ml at $30/ltr)	4.50
Machine cost (6 mins at $12/hr)	1.20	(10 mins at $12/hr)	2.00
Overheads (W2)	2.41	(W2)	3.88
Total cost	5.91		10.48
Sales price	9.30		14.00
Margin	3.39		3.52

(c)   Cost per unit calculations under ABC

(W2) Working for ABC overheads   alternative approach

	Total	CB	TJ	No of	Cost/	CB	TJ
	$	$	$	drivers	driver	$	$
Property costs	2,160,000	1,800,000	360,000	120,000	18/hr	1.80	3.00
Quality control	668,000	601,200	66,800	200	3340/ inspection	0.6012	0.56
Production set up	52,000	13,000	39,000	16	3250/ run	0.013	0.325
Total	2,880,000	2,414,200	465,800	Cost per unit		2.41	3.88
Production level		1,000,000	120,000				
Cost per unit		2.41	3.88				

The above overheads have been split on the basis of the following activity levels:

	Driver	CB	TJ
Property costs	Machine hours	100,000	20,000
Quality control	Inspections	180	20
Production set up	Set ups	4	12

A cost per driver approach is also acceptable.

Tutorial note

Ensure your answer is well laid out in a logical manner so you get follow- through marks, even if you make a silly error earlier on.

Note: The original question asked for implementation problems. The suggested solution is as follows:

There are many problems with ABC, which, despite its academic superiority, cause issues on its introduction.

- Lack of understanding: ABC is not fully understood by many managers and therefore is not fully accepted as a means of cost control.

- Difficulty in identifying cost drivers: In a practical context, there are frequently difficulties in identifying the appropriate drivers. For example, property costs are often significant and yet a single driver is difficult to find.

- Lack of appropriate accounting records: ABC needs a new set of accounting records, this is often not immediately available and therefore resistance to change is common. The setting up of new cost pools is needed which is time consuming.

ACCA marking scheme		Marks
(a)	Comment on rent and rates	2
	Comment on quality control	2
	Comment on production set up cost	2
	Comment on overall effect	2
	Maximum	7
(b)	Paper cost CB	½
	Paper cost TJ	½
	Printing ink cost CB	½
	Printing ink cost TJ	½
	Machine cost CB	½
	Machine cost TJ	½
	Overhead OAR	1
	Overhead cost CB	½
	Overhead cost TJ	½
	Margins	1
	Maximum	5
(c)	Split of rent and rates	1½
	Split of quality control	1½
	Split of production set up cost	1½
	Overhead cost per unit CB	1½
	Overhead cost per unit TJ	1½
	Direct cost as above	1
	Maximum	8
	Total	**20**

Examiner's comments (extract)

An activity based costing question. As is common with my questions I facilitated a commentary on some calculations already done (in part a) and then followed that up with a requirement to some calculations themselves parts (b) and (c).

In part (a) some candidates misread the requirement and gave text book explanations of the process involved in ABC. This gained very few marks. The old adage of 'answer the question' would have served well here. Vague references to 'activities' without referring to the specific activities in the question gained only a few marks. I wanted candidates to explain why these products costs had changed following the introduction of ABC.

Parts (b) and (c) were extremely well done by many.

Part (d) (i.e. the additional requirement) also produced some good answers. The requirement asked for implementation problems not merely "issues" and so marks were lost through poor focus.

4   ABKABER PLC

Key answer tips

Part (a) is a routine calculation of profit using ABC and traditional methods

Part (b) asks for a discussion of ABC for Abkaber. It is vital that you relate as many of your points as possible to the specific circumstances given.

(a)   (i)   **Absorption costing using labour hour absorption rate**

Total overhead cost	=	$2,400,000 + $6,000,000 + $3,600,000
	=	$12,000,000
Total labour hours	=	200,000 + 220,000 + 80,000
	=	500,000
Overhead absorption rate/labour hour	=	$12,000,000/500,000 = $24

	Sunshine	Roadster	Fireball
Units of production and sale	2,000	1,600	400
Direct labour hours	200,000	220,000	80,000
	$	$	$
Direct labour ($5/hour)	1,000,000	1,100,000	400,000
Materials (at $400/600/900)	800,000	960,000	360,000
Overheads ($24/direct labour hour)	4,800,000	5,280,000	1,920,000
Total costs	6,600,000	7,340,000	2,680,000

	Sunshine	Roadster	Fireball
	$	$	$
Cost per unit	3,300	4,587.5	6,700
Selling price	4,000	6,000.0	8,000
Profit/(loss) per unit	700	1,412.5	1,300
Total profit/(loss) per product	1,400,000	2,260,000	520,000

Total profit = $4,180,000

(ii) **Activity Based Costing**

Number of deliveries to retailers	100 + 80 + 70	=	250
Charge rate for deliveries	$2,400,000/250	=	$9,600
Number of set-ups	35 + 40 + 25	=	100
Charge rate for set-ups	$6,000,000/100	=	$60,000
Number of purchase orders	400 + 300 + 100	=	800
Charge rate for purchase orders	$3,600,000/800	=	$4,500

	Sunshine	Roadster	Fireball
Units of production and sale	2,000	1,600	400
	$	$	$
Direct labour (as above)	1,000,000	1,100,000	400,000
Materials (as above)	800,000	960,000	360,000
Overheads:			
Deliveries at $9,600 (100:80:70)	960,000	768,000	672,000
Set-ups at $60,000 (35:40:25)	2,100,000	2,400,000	1,500,000
Purchase orders at $4,500	1,800,000	1,350,000	450,000
(400:300:100)			
Total costs	6,660,000	6,578,000	3,382,000
	$	$	$
Cost per unit	3,330	4,111.25	8,455
Selling price	4,000	6,000.00	8,000
Profit/(loss) per unit	670	1,888.75	(455)
Total profit/(loss) per product	$1,340,000	$3,022,000	$(182,000)

Total profit = $4,180,000

(b) **The Finance Director**

Using the labour hours method of allocation, the Fireball makes an overall profit of $520,000 but using ABC it makes a loss of $182,000. There is a significant difference in the levels of cost allocated, and so in profitability, between the two methods.

The major reason for the difference appears to be that while labour hours are not all that significant for Fireball production, the low volumes of Fireball sales cause a relatively high amount of set-ups, deliveries and purchase processes, and this is recognised by ABC.

If the Fireball model is to continue, a review of the assembly and distribution systems may be needed in order to reduce costs.

The Marketing Director

The marketing director suggests that ABC may have a number of problems and its conclusions should not be believed unquestioningly. These problems include:

- For decisions such as the pricing of the new motorbike rental contract, what is really needed is the incremental cost to determine a break-even position. While ABC may be closer to this concept than a labour hours allocation basis, its accuracy depends upon identifying appropriate cost drivers.

- There may be interdependencies between both costs and revenues that ABC is unlikely to capture. Where costs are truly common to more than one product then this may be difficult to capture by any given single activity.

- As with labour hours allocations it is the future that matters. Any relationship between costs and activities based upon historic experience and observation may be unreliable as a guide to the future.

The Managing Director

- ABC normally assumes that the cost per activity is constant as the number of times the activity is repeated increases. In practice there may be a learning curve, such that costs per activity are non-linear. As a result, the marginal cost of increasing the number of activities is not the same as the average.

- Also in this case, fixed costs are included which would also mean that the marginal cost does not equal the average cost.

- The MD is correct in stating that some costs do not vary with either labour hours or any cost driver, and thus do not fall easily under ABC as a method of cost attribution as there is no cause and effect relationship. Depreciation on the factory building might be one example.

The Chairman

From a narrow perspective of reporting profit, it is true that the two methods give the same overall profit of $4,180,000, as is illustrated in answer (a). There are, however, a number of qualifications to this statement:

- If the company carried inventory then the method of cost allocation would, in the short term at least, affect inventory values and thus would influence profit.

- If the ABC information can be relied on as a method of identifying overhead costs that vary with activity, a decision might be taken to cease Fireball production, as it generates a negative profit of $182,000. This 'loss' was not apparent using traditional absorption costing and a direct labour hour absorption rate. Although we do not know the extent to which overheads would be reduced by ceasing production of fireball, ABC suggests that there is a possibility that closure would improve profitability, by up to $182,000 each year.

5   LIFECYCLE COSTING

(a)   It is generally accepted that most products will have quite a distinct product life cycle, as illustrated below:

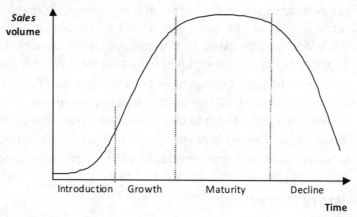

At the **introductory stage** the product is launched. It success depends upon awareness and trial of the product by consumers; this stage is likely to be accompanied by extensive marketing and promotion. A high level of set-up costs will already have been incurred by this stage, including research and development, product design and building of production facilities.

If the product is accepted, it will move into the **growth stage,** where sales volume increases dramatically; unit costs fall as fixed costs are recovered over greater volumes. Marketing and promotion will continue through this stage.

As market saturation is approached, with sales growth slowing, the product is entering its **maturity stage.** Initially profits will continue to increase, as initial set-up and fixed costs are recovered and marketing and distribution economies achieved. However, price competition and product differentiation will start to erode profitability as firms compete for the limited new customers remaining.

Eventually, in the **decline stage,** the product will move towards obsolescence as it is replaced by new and better alternatives. The product will be abandoned when profits fall to an unacceptable level, or when further capital commitment is required. Meanwhile, a replacement product will need to have been developed, incurring new levels of R&D and other product set-up costs.

In an advanced manufacturing environment, where products have low labour content, and are designed to make use of standard components and minimise wastage, rectification and warranty costs, the direct unit cost is relatively low. A very high proportion of the total costs over the product's life cycle will be in the form of initial development, design and production set-up costs, and ongoing fixed costs that are committed to at this stage.

In addition, in a globally competitive market, product life cycles are decreasing, making initial costs even more disproportionate in the early stages. The time scale between launch of one product and commencement of development of its successor can be very short, as can be seen in the modern car and computer industries. The recognition of product life cycles, with corresponding strategic planning of new development, marketing and finance, is of great importance for modern businesses.

(b)   The commitment of a high proportion of a product's life cycle costs at the very early stages of the cycle has led to the need for accounting systems that compare the revenues from a product with all the costs incurred over the entire product life cycle.

Life cycle costing (LCC) is such a system, tracking and accumulating the actual costs and revenues attributable to each product from inception to abandonment. In this way, the final profitability of a given product is determined at the end of its life, whilst accumulated costs at any stage can be compared with life-cycle budgeted costs, product by product, for the purposes of planning and control.

Comparing this approach with the more traditional management accounting practices:

- Most accounting reporting systems are based upon periodic accounts, reporting product profitability in isolated calendar-based amounts, rather than focusing on the revenues and costs accumulated over the life cycle to date

- Recognition of the commitment needed over the entire life cycle of a product will generally lead to more effective resource allocation than the traditional annual budgeting system

- R&D, design, production set-up, marketing and customer service costs are traditionally reported on an aggregated basis for all products and recorded as a period expense. Life cycle costing traces these costs to individual products over their entire life cycles, to aid comparison with product revenues generated in later periods

- Relationships between early decisions re product design and production methods and ultimate costs can therefore be identified and used for subsequent planning.

(c) Activity Based Management (ABM) systems focus on the underlying causes of costs, the activities of the business. These would include design, production scheduling, set up, marketing and servicing. Costs are collected and reported by activity, through the use of cost drivers in Activity Based Costing (ABC).

The benefits arising from adoption of ABM include:

- better understanding of costs and their causes, leading to more effective cost management

- use of this information at the planning stage can lead to better use of resources

- highlights opportunities to reduce or eliminate non value-adding activities – e.g. by the introduction of quality control systems that will reduce product rectification work and handling of customer complaints etc

- the product value-analysis process that will often be part of ABM leads to improved product design, increased use of standard components, more efficient use of material and labour, which will all add to cost reductions

- identification of cost driver rates gives a measure of the cost efficiency of activities, which may be used in performance appraisal and comparison between similar activities in different areas of the business.

Note: Any TWO relevant benefits are acceptable

6   MANPAC

Key answer tips

A good question which examines life cycle costing, target costing, marketing-based approaches to pricing and the product life cycle.

A well prepared candidate should score strongly here. Remember to relate your answer to MANPAC – an innovative computer game.

SY Company is the first to launch this type of product.

(a)   **Life cycle costing**

According to Bromwich and Bhimani, life cycle costing is the accumulation of costs for activities that occur over the entire life cycle of a product, from inception to abandonment.

If this were to apply to MANPAC then, from the moment the creators of the game thought about writing an interactive 3D game, any time and costs spent on the project should have been charged to the product. One would expect computer games products to incur very significant design and development costs. All design costs should be specifically charged to the MANPAC.

In order to maximise benefits over the life cycle of the MANPAC, life cycle costing advocates the following:

- Minimise time to the market: the MANPAC is the first of its kind to be launched. In order to gain dominance in the market it would be important to launch the product as far ahead of the competition as possible. It is easier to be a market leader if there is little or no competition.

- Maximise the length of the life cycle: this may be done by staggering the launch in different markets, segmenting the product in the future, selling accessories to the product, for example the MANPAC may be upgraded by superior software half way through its life.

- Design costs out of the product: 80 to 90% of a product's cost are committed at the design stage. In order to maximise benefit over the whole life cycle the product must be designed in a cost conscious manner with a view to the longer term impact on a product's costs.

Target costing

Currently SY Company uses cost-plus pricing. This is a push or bottom-up system starting with a forecast cost per unit, onto which a mark-up is added in order to calculate the selling price. Target costing is a pull system.

Target costing consists of several steps:

(i)   Start by understanding the market place. What sort of computer game might customers desire? And, importantly, how much are customers prepared to pay for the product?

(ii) Once this target price has been determined, the required long-term profit margin must be established.

(iii) In order to reach the target cost, simply deduct the profit margin from the target price.

(iv) It is only once the target cost has been agreed that the design team can begin their work. The MANPAC must be designed within a pre-determined cost ceiling.

(v) When designing the product it will be important to consider areas such as:

- Minimise the number of components

- Use common parts where possible. What existing products use components that can also be used on MANPAC?

- Consider extra features and accessories that may be included

- How will the product be packaged?

It is essential that during manufacturing the target cost is achieved at all times. Staff must accept the cost and then do everything within their power to ensure the cost is achieved. Staff must accept responsibility for achieving the cost.

(b) When launching a brand new innovative product that is the first on the market, there are generally two strategies that may be employed:

Penetration pricing

This is where the product is launched at a very low price in order to gain rapid acceptance of the product.

Penetration pricing may be used for several reasons:

- To encourage customers to try a new and different product
- To discourage competition (profit margins are very low)
- If demand is very elastic, a low price generates a very high demand
- If there are significant economies of scale to be gained from high volume.

Market skimming

Here the product is launched at a very high price.

This policy may be successful in the following circumstances:

- If the new product is very different and ground-breaking, some customers are willing to pay a high price at the beginning of the product's life cycle

- If demand is totally unknown upon launch. If the skimming price is too high it can always be lowered

- If demand is very inelastic

- If the product has a relatively short life cycle. The manufacturers have very little time to recover the development costs and to generate a profit on the product.

It seems likely that the MANPAC should have launched at a market skimming (very high) price. There are several reasons for this:

- Development costs are huge
- Product life cycle is relatively short – two or three years perhaps

- Sales volumes are unlikely to be massive
- Hence, each unit sold is likely to be required to generate a reasonable profit in order to recover the design costs from a few units in a short space of time
- The product is innovative – it is a 3D interactive game – and some customers will be prepared to pay an extremely high price in the early stages in order to be one-up on their peers. If people are prepared to pay a high price, then perhaps SY Company should charge one.

(c) The product life cycle of the MANPAC is likely to be broken down into four stages.

1 **Introduction**

The product is introduced to the market. The product has been designed, developed and packaged. Several million pounds will have already have been spent on MANPAC up to this point.

Advertising and marketing: when the product is first launched on the market, demand is likely to be small. Lack of familiarity with the new product and its sources of availability will militate against large initial sales, and it will usually be necessary to spend heavily on advertising to bring the product to the attention of potential customers.

Pricing: as discussed previously MANPAC should perhaps have launched at a very high price.

A combination of relatively high unit costs, relatively low sales volume, and the potential problem of rejection by the market conspire to make this the riskiest stage in the life cycle.

2 **Growth**

Assuming the product successfully negotiates the perils of the introduction stage, it will enter the growth phase, where demand for the product increases steadily and average costs fall with the economies of scale that accompany the greater production volume. This stage should offer the greatest potential for profit to the producer, despite the fact that competitors will be prompted to enter the growing market.

Pricing decisions: as competition begins to increase in order to maintain market share, it is likely that the retail price of MANPAC will have to fall.

Advertising and marketing: SY Company should spend heavily on advertising and will try to increase brand awareness in the market place.

Cost reduction and control: as volumes increase and unit costs begin to fall, managers should avoid assuming that the product is cost efficient. The target cost (if used) should continually be reduced during this stage and staff should continue to develop new cost efficient production methods.

3 **Maturity**

By this stage the MANPAC will have reached the mass market and the increase in demand will begin to slow down. The sales curve will flatten out and eventually start to decline. Profitability will generally be at a lower level than in the growth phase.

Pricing: as competition is at its keenest in this stage, it is likely that the price of the game will be at its lowest.

Marketing and advertising: in order to maintain market share, managers must continue to spend on advertising. The emphasis may well be on increasing brand loyalty and developing a sense of prestige/quality associated with the MANPAC game.

Product development: in order to generate higher profits, SY Company may try to extend this phase in the product's life cycle. The product may be modified or improved, as a means of sustaining its demand. Managers may try to reach new market segments.

Cost reduction and control: the unit cost should be at its lowest during this phase. It remains important for the manufacturing process to remain lean and well managed. A value analysis exercise may be undertaken on an ad-hoc basis.

4   **Decline**

The fall in sales accelerates when the market reaches saturation point. It is likely that new technology will mean that superior interactive games are being launched. Although it is still possible to make profits for a short period during this stage, it is only a matter of time before the rapidly dwindling sales volumes herald the onset of losses for all producers who remain in the market. The product has effectively reached the end of its life cycle and more profitable opportunities must be sought elsewhere.

The final decision that must be reached is when to withdraw the product from the market.

Note: Only ONE issue is required for each stage.

7   WARGRIN (DEC 08 EXAM)

(a)   Lifecycle costing is a concept which traces all costs to a product over its complete lifecycle, from design through to cessation. It recognises that for many products there are significant costs to be incurred in the early stages of its lifecycle. This is probably very true for Wargrin Limited. The design and development of software is a long and complicated process and it is likely that the costs involved would be very significant.

The profitability of a product can then be assessed taking all costs in to consideration.

It is also likely that adopting lifecycle costing would improve decision-making and cost control. The early development costs would have to be seen in the context of the expected trading results therefore preventing a serious over spend at this stage or under pricing at the launch point.

Key answer tips

Easy marks were available for an explanation of this core costing technique. Common errors included candidates confusing lifecycle costing with the product life cycle and/ or a lack of discussion of lifecycle costing within the context of the scenario.

(b) **Budgeted results for game**

	Year 1 ($)	Year 2 ($)	Year 3 ($)	Total ($)
Sales	240,000	480,000	120,000	840,000
Variable cost (W1)	40,000	80,000	20,000	140,000
Fixed cost (W1)	80,000	120,000	80,000	280,000
Marketing cost	60,000	40,000		100,000
Profit	60,000	240,000	20,000	320,000

On the face of it the game will generate profits in each of its three years of life. Games only have a short lifecycle as the game players are likely to become bored of the game and move on to something new.

The pattern of sales follows a classic product lifecycle with poor levels of sales towards the end of the life of the game.

The stealth product has generated $320,000 of profit over its three year life measured on a traditional basis. This represents 40% of turnover – ahead of its target. Indeed it shows a positive net profit in each of its years on existence.

The contribution level is steady at around 83% indicating reasonable control and reliability of the production processes. This figure is better than the stated target.

Considering traditional performance management concepts, Wargrin Limited is likely to be relatively happy with the game's performance.

However, the initial design and development costs were incurred and were significant at $300,000 and are ignored in the annual profit calculations. Taking these into consideration the game only just broke even making a small $20,000 profit. Whether this is enough is debatable, it represents only 2.4% of sales for example. In order to properly assess the performance of a product the whole lifecycle needs to be considered.

Workings

(W1) Split of variable and fixed cost for Stealth

	Volume	Cost $
High	14,000 units	150,000
Low	10,000 units	130,000
Difference	4,000 units	20,000

Variable cost per unit = $20,000/4,000 unit = $5 per unit

Total cost = fixed cost + variable cost

$150,000 = fixed cost + (14,000 × $5)

$150,000 = fixed cost +$70,000

Fixed cost = $80,000 (and $120,000 if volume exceeds 15,000 units in a year.)

Key answer tips

Candidates must be comfortable with the high low method. The examiner is keen to test techniques such as this within the context of a longer calculation question. Good candidates ignored the design and development costs (a sunk cost).

Candidates needed to leave enough time to interpret the calculations and to discuss the expected performance of the game. Almost half of the marks were available for the written points.

(c) Incremental budgeting is a process whereby this year's budget is set by reference to last year's actual results after an adjustment for inflation and other incremental factors. It is commonly used because:

- It is quick to do and a relatively simple process.
- The information is readily available, so very limited quantitative analysis is needed.
- It is appropriate in some circumstances. For example in a stable business the amount of stationery spent in one year is unlikely to be significantly different in the next year, so taking the actual spend in year one and adding a little for inflation should be a reasonable target for the spend in the next year.

There are problems involved with incremental budgeting:

- It builds on wasteful spending. If the actual figures for this year include overspends caused by some form of error then the budget for the next year would potentially include this overspend again.
- It encourages organisations to spend up to the maximum allowed in the knowledge that if they don't do this then they will not have as much to spend in the following year's budget.
- Assessing the amount of the increment can be difficult.
- It is not appropriate in a rapidly changing business.
- Can ignore the true (activity based) drivers of a cost leading to poor budgeting.

Key answer tips

Easy marks were available here. Candidates must be aware of all of the different approaches to budgeting together with their pros and cons.

Note: The original question also required a dsicussion of the setting of a meaningful standard. The suggested solution is shown below:

Design and development costs: Setting a standard cost for this classification of cost would be very difficult. Presumably each game would be different and present the program writers with different challenges and hence take a varying amount of time.

Variable production cost: A game will be produced on a CD or DVD in a fairly standard format. Each CD/DVD will be identical and as a result setting a standard cost would be possible. Allowance might need to be made for waste or faulty CDs produced. Some machine time will be likely and again this should be the same for all items and therefore setting a standard would be valid.

Fixed production cost: The standard fixed production cost of a game will be the product of the time taken to produce the game and the standard fixed overhead absorption rate for the business. This brings into question whether this is 'meaningful'. Allocating fixed costs to products in a standard way may not provide meaningful data. It can sometimes imply a variability (cost per unit) that is not the case and can therefore confuse non-accountants, causing poor decisions. The time per unit will be fairly standard.

Marketing costs: Games may have different target audiences and therefore require different marketing strategies. As such setting a standard may be difficult to do. It may be possible to set standards for each marketing media chosen. For example the rates for a page advert in a magazine could be set as a standard.

		ACCA marking scheme	
			Marks
(a)		Performance assessment over whole life cycle	1.0
		Improved decision making/ cost control	1.0
		Relate to Wargrin	2.0
			———
			4.0
(b)		Sales	1.0
		Variable cost	1.0
		Fixed cost	2.0
		Marketing cost	1.0
		Comments on profit performance (against standard targets)	2.0
		Consideration of all lifecycle costs	2.0
			———
			9.0
(c)		Why incremental budgeting common – 1 mark per idea (max 3)	3.0
		Problems of incremental budgets – 1 mark per idea (max 4)	4.0
			———
			7.0
			———
Total			20
			———

Examiner's comments (extract)

Question 4 was partly based on lifecycle costing, which is not a topic that has been examined that often in other papers or indeed syllabi. This probably means a lack of good questions in the materials. As a result I did try and keep this question straightforward.

In part (a) a very large number of candidates confused life cycle costing with the product lifecycle. I was treated to large numbers of PLC diagrams and long winded explanations of the different stages of it. Most of which scored no marks at all. I did give credit if the PLC discussion stumbled into mentions of the costs.

The calculations in part (b) were quite well done by most. This was expected as it was far from difficult. The high low overhead calculation should have been a gift as this topic is fully examined at F2. A depressing number of candidates could not handle the stepped fixed cost aspect however. Part (b) also asked for an assessment of performance and I provided targets for net profit % and contribution %. The number of candidates that simply ignored these targets in the assessment of performance was staggering. Far too many simply provided a description of the figures (sales have gone up in the second year by x%, but then fall again in year 3). This is not an assessment of performance! Too many missed the point completely that the game's performance looked good until the initial development costs were included. This is the whole point behind lifecycle costing.

Part (c) should have been a gift of 6 marks and certainly for around 30% of candidates it was. This should have been nearer 70% of candidates. Some did not even know what incremental budgeting was, getting it confused with some form of rolling budget. I was amazed at this, as this is pure knowledge that some simply do not have.

Part (d) (i.e. the additional requirement) seemed to baffle almost all marginal and below candidates. This question asked is the standard "meaningful"? You can set standards for everything but not all would have meaning. For example the development time for a game could not really be standardised. Games would, presumably, be very different in their complexity and hence would take significantly different amounts of time to develop. This concept was not understood by the majority. Most also ignored my suggestion in the question to consider each of the cost classifications in turn, which is poor technique.

8   EDWARD CO (DEC 07 EXAM)

Key answer tips

This was an in-depth question on target costing that was done poorly by many students. The examiner has made it very clear that he will examine these themes again!

(a)   **Target costing process**

Target costing begins by specifying a product an organisation wishes to sell. This will involve extensive customer analysis, considering which features customers value and which they do not. Ideally only those features valued by customers will be included in the product design.

The price at which the product can be sold at is then considered. This will take in to account the competitor products and the market conditions expected at the time that the product will be launched. Hence a heavy emphasis is placed on external analysis before any consideration is made of the internal cost of the product.

From the above price a desired margin is deducted. This can be a gross or a net margin. This leaves the cost target. An organisation will need to meet this target if their desired margin is to be met.

Costs for the product are then calculated and compared to the cost target mentioned above.

If it appears that this cost cannot be achieved then the difference (shortfall) is called a cost gap. This gap would have to be closed, by some form of cost reduction, if the desired margin is to be achieved.

Tutorial note

Easy marks were available here and a well prepared candidate should have been able to score full marks. Aim for at least three well explained points. Separate each point out using headings or a new paragraph. This will make it easier for the marker to review. The following headings could have been used:

1   *Estimate selling price*

2   *Deduct required profit*

3   *Calculate target cost*

4   *Close Gap*

(b)

Tutorial note

This section was more challenging and required the application of book knowledge. Brainstorm ideas first. This should focus attention on thinking of enough separate points and should help to give your answer a natural structure. This is the hard part done. It should then be fairly straightforward to write up the answer in the time remaining.

Benefits of adopting target costing

- The organisation will have an early external focus to its product development. Businesses have to compete with others (competitors) and an early consideration of this will tend to make them more successful. Traditional approaches (by calculating the cost and then adding a margin to get a selling price) are often far too internally driven.

- Only those features that are of value to customers will be included in the product design. Target costing at an early stage considers carefully the product that is intended. Features that are unlikely to be valued by the customer will be excluded. This is often insufficiently considered in cost plus methodologies.

- Cost control will begin much earlier in the process. If it is clear at the design stage that a cost gap exists then more can be done to close it by the design team. Traditionally, cost control takes place at the 'cost incurring' stage, which is often far too late to make a significant impact on a product that is too expensive to make.

- Costs per unit are often lower under a target costing environment. This enhances profitability. Target costing has been shown to reduce product cost by between 20% and 40% depending on product and market conditions. In traditional cost plus systems an organisation may not be fully aware of the constraints in the external environment until after the production has started. Cost reduction at this point is much more difficult as many of the costs are 'designed in' to the product.

- It is often argued that target costing reduces the time taken to get a product to market. Under traditional methodologies there are often lengthy delays whilst a team goes 'back to the drawing board'. Target costing, because it has an early external focus, tends to help get things right first time and this reduces the time to market.

(c)   **Cost per unit and cost gap calculation**

	$ per unit
Component 1	
$(4.10 + \dfrac{\$2,400}{4,000 \, \text{units}})$	4.70
Component 2	
$(\dfrac{25}{100} \times 0.5 \times \dfrac{100}{98})$	0.128
Material – other	8.10
Assembly labour	
$(\dfrac{30}{60} \times \$12.60/\text{hr} \times \dfrac{100}{90})$	7.00
Variable production overhead (W1)	
$(\dfrac{30}{60} \times \$20/\text{hr})$	10.00
Fixed production overhead (W1)	
$(\dfrac{30}{60} \times \$12/\text{hr})$	6.00
	———
Total cost	35.928
Desired cost ($44 × 0.8)	35.20
	———
Cost gap	0.728
	———

Working 1: Production overhead cost. Using a high low method

Extra overhead cost between month 1 and 2	$80,000
Extra assembly hours	4,000
Variable cost per hour	$20/hr
Monthly fixed production overhead	
$700,000 − (23,000 × $20/hr)	$240,000
Annual fixed production overhead ($240,000 × 12)	$2,880,000

$$\text{FPO absorption rate } \frac{\$2,880,000}{240,000\,\text{hrs}} = \qquad \$12/\text{hr}$$

Tutorial note

There is plenty of time to do this calculation (23 minutes) and so there is no need to panic or rush. Set out a cost card for the radio and then work through each of the costs mentioned in the question, including each cost as a separate line in the cost card. Clearly reference any workings back to the cost card. Remember to pick up the easy marks first -the more difficult hi-low and overhead absorption calculations were only worth four of the total marks. Even if these harder areas were ignored a good pass could still be obtained. Don't forget to identify the cost gap.

Note: The original question included a requirement to discuss closing the cost gap. The suggested solution to this requirement was as follows:

Steps to reduce a cost gap include:

Review radio features

Remove features from the radio that add to cost but do not significantly add value to the product when viewed by the customer. This should reduce cost but not the achievable selling price. This can be referred to as value engineering or value analysis.

Team approach

Cost reduction works best when a team approach is adopted. Edward Limited should bring together members of the marketing, design, assembly and distribution teams to allow discussion of methods to reduce costs. Open discussion and brainstorming are useful approaches here.

Review the whole supplier chain

Each step in the supply chain should be reviewed, possibly with the aid of staff questionnaires, to identify areas of likely cost savings. Areas which are identified by staff as being likely cost saving areas can then be focussed on by the team. For example, the questionnaire might ask 'are there more than five potential suppliers for this component?' Clearly a 'yes' response to this question will mean that there is the potential for tendering or price competition.

Components

Edward Limited should look at the significant costs involved in components. New suppliers could be sought or different materials could be used. Care would be needed not to damage the perceived value of the product. Efficiency improvements should also be possible by reducing waste or idle time that might exist. Avoid, where possible, non-standard parts in the design.

Assembly workers

Productivity gains may be possible by changing working practices or by de-skilling the process. Automation is increasingly common in assembly and manufacturing and Edward Limited should investigate what is possible here to reduce the costs. The learning curve may ultimately help to close the cost gap by reducing labour costs per unit.

Clearly reducing the percentage of idle time will reduce product costs. Better management, smoother work flow and staff incentives could all help here. Focusing on continuous improvement in production processes may help.

Overheads

Productivity increases would also help here by spreading fixed overheads over a greater number of units. Equally Edward Limited should consider an activity based costing approach to its overhead allocation, this may reveal more favourable cost allocations for the digital radio or ideas for reducing costs in the business.

ACCA marking scheme			Marks
(a)	Process description		1
	Product specification		1
	Selling price		1
	Cost calculation		1
		maximum	3
(b)	1 mark per benefit:		4
(c)	Cost calculation:		
	Component 1		2
	Component 2		2
	Material other		1
	Assembly labour		2
	Variable production overhead		1
	High low calculation		2
	Fixed production OAR calculation		1
	Fixed production overhead		1
	Cost gap identified		1
			13
Total			**20**

Examiner's comments (extract)

The management accounting aspect of the syllabus is an important aspect.

Requirement (a) – most candidates gained at least half marks for describing the target costing process. However, I would have expected any well prepared candidate to pick up full marks for something that is after all simply 'knowledge' of a core topic. A substantial number of candidates had very little idea as to what target costing is, opting to guess in a large number of different ways. This suggests most candidates were not prepared for this.

Requirement (b) – the 'benefits' of target costing was less well done and this was expected. I am generally interested in why something is done as well as how it is done. This principle will be reflected again in future questions.

Requirement (c) – candidates scored good marks in Part (c); however all should revise high-low as I am disposed to use it again to provide overhead data within a question. High-low was poorly done by large numbers of candidates, which was a little disappointing given its simplicity and its existence in the F2 (and 1.2) syllabus. Allowances for waste and idle time were often incorrectly done. Any form of attempt scored something but this is an area that will be revisited and I would advise a look at the model answer and revise the correct method. Adding 10% to a cost (or time taken) is not the same as correctly adjusting by a factor of 100/90 (assuming a 10% loss for waste in this case).

Walk in the footsteps of a top tutor

The following answer was written to time to show what is achievable in the allocated time and how the answer can be structured to maximise marks.

(a)   Target costing in Edward Co should be carried out as follows:

    1   **Product Specification**

        Target costing begins by specifying the product that the organisation wishes to sell. For Edward Co, the product is the new digital radio. The radio's features should fulfil the customer's needs.

    2   **Price**

        The price of the radio should be set next. Competitor's prices and market conditions must be considered.

    3   **Margin**

        Edward Co's required margin should then be deducted from the price. This will result in a target cost.

(b)   Benefits of early adoption of target costing include:

Early External Focus

Edward Co will consider customer needs, competitors and market conditions, from the start of product development. This early external focus should increase the chance of success.

Customers' Needs

Only features which will help to fulfil the needs of the customer will be included in the product. This should save time, money and increase the chance of success.

Early Cost Control

Steps can be taken to control costs right from the beginning of the development process.

Lower Costs

Target costing has been shown to reduce product cost by 20-40% depending on the market conditions.

Note: For requirements (a) – (b) marks would be allocated for other relevant points.

(c)   Cost gap

Step 1: Calculate the target cost

Target selling price	=	$44.00
Target margin (20%) =		($8.80)
		———
Target cost	=	$35.20
		———

Tutorial note

Work through each cost in turn and include as a separate line in a cost card. Set up separate, clearly referenced workings if necessary. Do not get stuck on the difficult areas but instead take a guess and move on. The key is to complete the cost card and to get most of it correct.

Step 2: Calculate the expected cost

	$
Component 1 – Board	4.10
– Delivery costs $2,000/ 4,000	0.60
Component 2 – 0.25m × $0.50/m × 100/98	0.128
Other material	8.10
Assembly labour	7.00
$12.60 per hour × 0.5 hours × 100/90	
Production overheads (W1) – variable	10.00
– fixed	6.00
	———
Total expected cost	35.928
	———

(W1) **Production overheads**

	Overheads ($)	Labour Hours
Hi	700,000	23,000
Low	620,000	19,000
Difference	80,000	4,000

Variable overhead per labour hour = $80,000/4,000 = $20 per hour
Variable overhead per unit = 0.5 hours × $20 per hour = $10

Total overhead of $700,000 = Fixed overhead + variable overhead of
$$($20 × 3,000 \text{ hours})$$

700,000 – $460,000 = Fixed overhead of $240,000 (This is the monthly amount)

Fixed OAR = Annual fixed overhead of ($240,000 × 12)/ 240,000 assembly hours
= $12 per labour hour

Fixed overhead per unit = $12 per hour × 0.5 hours = $6

Step 3: Calculate the Cost Gap

Target cost = $35.20

Expected cost = $35.928

Cost gap = **Difference of $0.728**

9   YAM CO (JUNE 09 EXAM)

(a)   The output capacity for each process is as follows:

The total processing hours of the factory is given but can be proven as follows:

18 hours × 5 days × 50 weeks × 50 production lines = 225,000 hours.

Given this, the production capacity for pressing must be 225,000 hours/0·5 hours per metre = 450,000 metres. Using this method the production capacity for all processes is as follows:

	Product A	Product B	Product C
Pressing	450,000	450,000	562,500
Stretching	900,000	562,500	900,000
Rolling	562,500	900,000	900,000

The bottleneck is clearly the pressing process which has a lower capacity for each product. The other processes will probably be slowed to ensure smooth processing.

Tutorial note

*Clearly an alternative approach is simply to look at the original table for processing speed and pick out the slowest process. This is pressing. (full marks available for that **explained** observation). This would have been a much more straightforward approach in the exam.*

(b)   **TPAR for each product**

	Product A	Product B	Product C
Selling price	70.0	60.0	27.0
Raw materials	3.0	2.5	1.8
Throughput	67.0	57.5	25.2
Throughput per bottleneck hour*	134.0	115.0	63.0
Fixed costs per hour (W1)	90.0	90.0	90.0
TPAR	1.49	1.28	0.7
*Working**	67/0.5 = 134	57.5/0.5 = 115	25.2/0.4 = 63

(W1) **The fixed cost per bottleneck hour can be calculated as follows:**

Total fixed costs are $18,000,000 plus the labour cost. Labour costs $10 per hour for each of the 225,000 processing hours, a cost of $2,250,000.

Total fixed cost is therefore $18,000,000 + $2,250,000 = $20,250,000

Fixed cost per bottleneck hours is $20,250,000/225,000 = $90 per hour

Key answer tips

Calculate the TPAR in three stages:

–   Firstly, calculate the throughput per bottleneck hour.

–   Secondly, calculate the fixed cost per hour.

–   Finally, calculate the TPAR.

Carry forward marks would be awarded if the incorrect bottleneck process was identified in requirement (a).

(c)   (i)   Yam could improve the TPAR of product C in various ways:

Speed up the bottleneck process. By increasing the speed of the bottleneck process the rate of throughput will also increase, generating a greater rate of income for Yam if the extra production can be sold. Automation might be used or a change in the detailed processes. Investment in new machinery can also help here but the cost of that would need to be taken into account.

Increase the selling prices. It can be difficult to increase selling prices in what we are told is a competitive market. Volume of sales could be lost leaving Yam with unsold stock or idle equipment. On the other hand, given the business appears to be selling all it can produce, then a price increase may be possible.

Reduce the material prices. Reducing material prices will increase the net throughput rate. Metal is available from many sources being far from a unique product. Given the industry is mature the suppliers of the raw material could be willing to negotiate on price; this could have volume or quality based conditions attached. Yam will have to be careful to protect its quality levels. Bulk buying increases stock levels and the cost of that would need to be considered.

Reduce the level of fixed costs. The fixed costs should be listed and targets for cost reduction be selected. ABC techniques can help to identify the cost drivers and with management these could be used to reduce activity levels and hence cost. Outsourcing, de-skilling or using alternative suppliers (for stationery for example) are all possible cost reduction methods.

(ii) A TPAR of less than one indicates that the rate at which product C generates throughput (sales revenue less material cost) is less than the rate at which Yam incurs fixed cost. So on a simple level, producing a product which incurs fixed cost faster than it generates throughput does not seem to make commercial sense. Clearly the TPAR could be improved (using the methods above) before cessation is considered any further.

However, cessation decisions involve consideration of many wider issues (only three required).

- Long-term expected net cash flows from the product allowing for the timing of those cash flows (NPV) are an important factor in cessation decisions

- Customer perception could be negative in that they will see a reduction in choice

- Lost related sales: if product C is lost will Yam lose customers that bought it along with another product?

- What use could be made of the excess capacity that is created

- Throughput assumes that all costs except raw materials are fixed; this may not necessarily be the case and only avoidable fixed costs need to be taken into account for a cessation decision. If few fixed costs can be avoided then product C is making a contribution that will be lost if the product ceased.

Tutorial note

Note that 11 of the 20 marks in this question are for the written requirements. This is typical of the examiner and therefore it is imperative to practice answering these written requirements.

ACCA marking scheme				
				Marks
(a)		Identification of bottleneck		1.0
		Explanation		2.0
				———
			Maximum	3.0
(b)		Sales prices (per product)		0.5
		Raw material cost (per product)		0.5
		Throughput per bottleneck hour (per product)		0.5
		Fixed costs		1.5
		Fixed cost per hour		0.5
		TPAR (per product)		0.5
				———
			Maximum	8.0
(c)	(i)	Increase speed of bottleneck		1.0
		Increase selling prices – difficult to do		1.0
		Reduce material prices		1.0
		Reduce level of fixed costs		1.0
				———
		Maximum		4.0
	(ii)	Explain a TPAR		2.0
		Long-term cash flows		1.0
		Lost related sales		1.0
		Use of spare capacity		1.0
		Fixed costs		1.0
		Any other reasonable factor e.g. lost contribution		1.0
				———
			Maximum	5.0
				———
Total				20
				———

Examiner's Comments (extract)

As is my usual style I tried to make the discursive elements of a question independent of the numbers. The idea here is to give all candidates a chance to demonstrate performance management skills regardless of any problems they may have had with the numbers.

It was clear that many candidates had poor knowledge of throughput accounting. Few could properly identify the bottleneck process. Many used total hours per product as their guide to a wrong answer.

In the throughput calculations many included labour in the calculation of contribution, whereas its exclusion is more normal. Labour is properly treated as a fixed cost and yet many did not include it in the overheads part of the calculations.

Most candidates could give some reasonable suggestions on how to improve a TPAR, however not enough scored the four easy marks on offer.

The final part of the question was least well done, as expected. It is an easy mistake to feel that an unprofitable product should cease to be made but the world is a more complicated place. Current profitability is a factor but the future is more relevant. The impact of the withdrawal on customers and staff and the effect on competition are all relevant. No detailed knowledge of future cash flows was expected at this stage of studies.

10 FLOPRO PLC

Key answer tips

This question draws on a range of basic management accounting techniques including product costing, contribution analysis and limiting factor analysis. The well prepared candidate will have a good background knowledge of these topics in addition to an understanding of the central syllabus topic of throughput accounting. Candidates should be able to demonstrate an understanding of the theory behind TA as well as being able to carry out a practical exercise.

(a)   The net profit for each product is calculated as follows:

	Product A	Product B
	$	$
Direct material cost	2	40
Variable production overhead cost	28	4
Fixed production overhead $40 (W1) × hours	10	6
	—	—
Total cost	40	50
Selling price	60	70
	—	—
Net profit	20	20
	—	—

(W1)

Fixed production overhead is absorbed at an average rate per hour:

Total hours (120,000 × 0.25) + (45,000 × 0.15) = 36,750

Absorption rate per hour = $1,470,000/36,750 = $40

(b)   (i)   Throughput return per bottleneck hour

= (selling price – material cost)/bottleneck hours per unit

Product A = (60 – 2)/0.02 = $2,900

Product B = (70 – 40)/0.0l5 = $2,000

Flopro should sell product A up to its maximum demand and then product B using the remaining capacity

Maximum demand of product A = 120,000 × 120% = 144,000 units

Bottleneck hours required for A = 144,000 × 0.02 = 2,880 hours

Bottleneck hours available for B = 3,075 – 2,880 = 195 hours

Output of product B which is possible = 195/0.015 = 13,000 units

The maximum net profit may be calculated as:

	$
Throughput return product A 144,000 × ($60 – 2)	8,352,000
Throughput return product B 13,000 × ($70 – 40)	390,000
Total throughput return	8,742,000
Less: Overhead cost	
shown as variable in (a) ((120,000 × $28) + (45,000 × $4))	(3,540,000)
Fixed	(1,470,000)
Net profit	3,732,000

(ii) Throughput return per bottleneck hour for product B (as calculated above)

$$= (70 – 40)/0.015 = \$2,000$$

Cost per bottleneck hour = ($3,540,000 + $1,470,000)/3,075

$$= \$1,629.27$$

Throughput accounting ratio for product B = $2,000/$1,629.27 = 1.2275

(iii) Where throughput accounting principles are applied, a product is worth producing and selling so long as its throughput return per bottleneck hour is greater than the production cost per throughput hour. This may be measured by the throughput accounting ratio. Where the ratio is greater than one, return exceeds cost and the focus should be on improving the size of the ratio.

Efforts may be made to improve the position for each product and in total by focusing on areas such as:

- Improved throughput ($) per unit by increasing selling price or reducing material cost per unit. Product B has a very high material element ($40 per unit)

- Improving the throughput ($) per unit by reducing the time required on the bottleneck resource. Reducing the time for product B from 0.015 hours to 0.01 hours through change methods would improve its ratio

- Improving the overall position by reducing the cost of spare capacity. This may be achieved by operational re-design aimed at reducing or eliminating the impact of any bottlenecks.

11 ENVIRONMENTAL MANAGEMENT ACCOUNTING

(a) 1 **Waste disposal costs**

FTX is likely to incur environmental costs associated with waste: for example, landfill taxes, or the costs of disposal of raw materials and chemicals not used in drug production, FTX may also be vulnerable to fines for compliance failures such as pollution.

Control measures could be implemented to identify how much material is wasted in production by using the 'mass balance' approach, whereby the weight of materials bought is compared to the product yield. From this process, potential cost savings may be identified. The cost of packaging lends itself particularly well to this analysis: by analysing how much packaging the drug uses and what percentage of that packaging is recyclable, FTX could also reduce its costs whilst being environmentally friendly.

2 **Water consumption costs**

Like any other business, FTX will pay for water twice: first to buy it, and, secondly, to dispose of it. If FTX looks to reduce its water bill, it is important for the business to identify where water is used in the drug production process and how consumption can be decreased.

3 **Energy consumption costs**

Like any other business or household, FTX should be able to reduce its energy costs significantly by switching production to night-time for example (when electricity is cheaper). Furthermore, environmental management accounts may help to identify inefficiencies and wasteful practices and therefore opportunities for cost savings.

4 **Transport and travel costs**

Environmental Management Accounting can often help to identify savings in terms of business travel and transport of goods and materials. An obvious control measure, in this case, would be the replacement of FTX's vehicles by more fuel-efficient vans or cars.

(b) Environmental Management Accounting is a specialised part of the management accounts that focuses on things such as the cost of energy and water. EMA uses some standard accountancy techniques to identify, analyse, manage and hopefully reduce environmental costs in a way that provide mutual benefit to the company and the environment.

EMA techniques could include the following:

- **Input/outflow analysis**

  This technique records material inflows and balances this with outflows on the basis that, what comes in must go out. So, if 100kg of materials have been bought and only 80kg of materials have been produced, for example, then the 20kg difference must be accounted for in some way. It may be, for example, that 10% of it has been sold as scrap and 10% of it is waste. By accounting for outputs in this way, both in terms of physical quantities and, at the end of the process, in monetary terms too, businesses are forced to focus on environmental costs.

- **Flow cost accounting**

  This technique uses not only material flows but also the organisational structure. It makes material flows transparent by looking at the physical quantities involved, their costs and their value. It divides the material flows into three categories: material, system and delivery and disposal. The values and costs of each of these three flows are then calculated. The aim of flow cost accounting is to reduce the quantity of materials which, as well as having a positive effect on the environment, should have a positive effect on a business' total costs in the long run.

- **Activity-based costing**

  ABC allocates internal costs to cost centres and cost drivers on the basis of the activities that give rise to the costs. In an environmental accounting context, it distinguishes between environment-related costs, which can be attributed to joint cost centres, and environment-driven costs, which tend to be hidden on general overheads.

- **Lifecycle costing**

  Within the context of environmental accounting, lifecycle costing is a technique which requires the full environmental consequences, and therefore costs, arising from production of a product to be taken account across its whole lifecycle, literally 'from cradle to grave'.

12 CHOCOLATES ARE FOREVER (CAF)

(a) The Breakeven point is that number if units produced and sold at which CAF will make no profit or no loss:

$$\text{Breakeven point} = \frac{\text{Fixed costs}}{\text{Contribution per unit}}; \quad \text{Breakeven point} = \frac{\$20,000}{\$12-\$7}$$

Breakeven point = 4,000 units.

The margin of safety expresses the gap between budgeted sales and breakeven sales. It measures by how much CAF needs to fall short of budgeted sales before it starts making a loss:

$$\text{Margin of Safety} = \frac{\text{Budgeted Sales} - \text{Breakeven Sales}}{\text{Budgeted Sales}} \times 100\%$$

$$\text{Margin of Safety} = \frac{6,000 \text{ units} - 4,000 \text{ units}}{6,000 \text{ units}} \times 100\%; \quad \text{Margin of Safety} = 33.33\,\%$$

(b) A **breakeven chart** is a graphical representation of the data. It shows the breakeven point when the total cost line and the total revenue line intersect. The total cost line is a total variable cost line sitting on the fixed cost line. The Sales revenue line is also depicted and comes from the origin. (no sales, no revenue). The Margin of Safety can then be read off the chart on the horizontal axis – the difference between the budgeted output and the breakeven output.

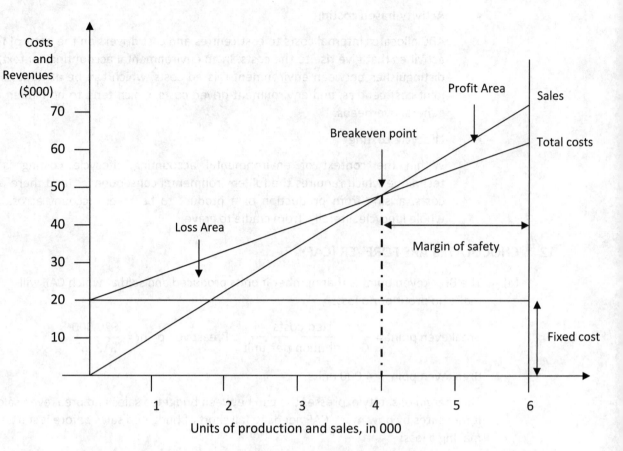

A contribution breakeven chart is based on the same principles as a basic breakeven chart, but it shows the variable cost line instead of the fixed cost line.

The same lines for total cost and sales revenue are shown so the breakeven point and profit can be read off in the same way as with a conventional chart. However, it is possible also to read the contribution for any level of activity.

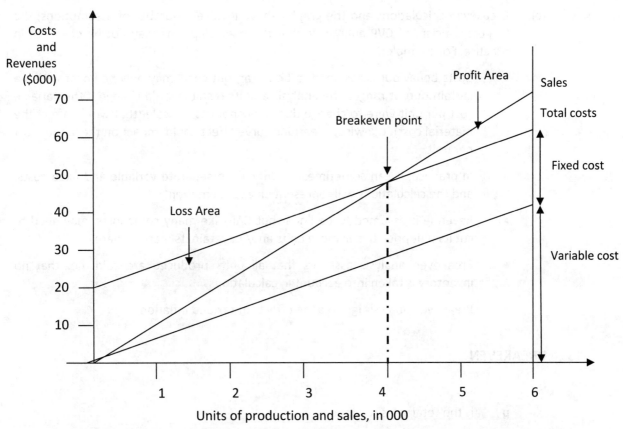

The Profit-Volume chart is an alternative chart, which is simpler, but gives a lot of the same information. By drawing a line between the fixed costs at zero output (where the amount of loss will equal the fixed costs) and the breakeven point – where the profit line crosses the x axis – the chart may be used to work out the expected profit at any level of output.

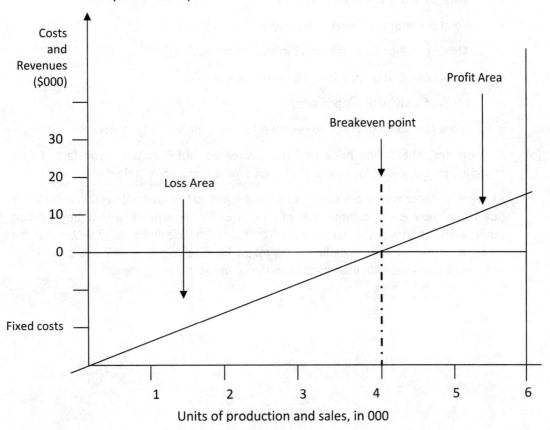

(c)   Breakeven calculations and the graphs above involve a number of assumptions; the biggest criticism of CVP analysis is that these assumptions may not be observed in practice. For example:

- Costs behaviour is assumed to be linear, but costs may only be linear within a certain output range. The analysis and its results would change if the variable cost per unit were to change due to economies of scale (that would affect the material cost). Likewise, a learning curve effect could impact on the labour cost per unit.

- In practice, it can sometimes be difficult to separate variable and fixed costs, and the calculations will represent an approximation.

- Revenue is assumed to be linear but CAF, like many companies, may need to cut its unit price to sell more units and/ or retain its market share.

- Breakeven analysis assumes that all units produced are sold, i.e. that no inventory is taken into account in calculations.

- Breakeven analysis ignores the effects of tax and inflation.

13   BREAKEVEN

(a)

p	is the total sales revenue
q	Total Cost (Fixed cost + variable cost)
r	Total variable cost
s	Fixed costs at the specific level of activity
t	Total loss at the specific level of activity
u	Total profit at that level of activity
v	Total contribution at the specific level of activity
w	Total contribution at a lower level of activity
x	Level of activity of output sales
y	monetary value of cost and revenue function for level of activity.

(b)   At event 'm', the selling price per unit decreases, but it remains constant. P is a straight line, but with a lower gradient above 'm' compared to below 'm'.

At event 'n' there is an increase in fixed costs equal to the dotted line. This is probably due to an increase in capital expenditure in order to expand output beyond this point. Also, at this point, the variable cost per unit declines as reflected by the gradient of the variable cost line. This might be due to more efficient production methods associated with increased investment in capital equipment.

(c)   Breakeven analysis is of limited use in a multi-product company, but the analysis can be a useful aid to management of a small single product company. The following are some of the main benefits:

•   Breakeven analysis forces management to consider the functional relationship between costs, revenue and activity, and gives an insight to how costs and revenues cProduct Pe with cProduct Pes in the level of activity.

•   Breakeven analysis forces management to consider the fixed costs at various levels of activity and the sellin gprice that will be required to achieve various levels of output.

ACCA Marking scheme		
		Marks
(a)	Each component 0.5 marks, x 10 components	5
(b)	Event m	1
	Event n	1
(c)	Every valid comment, maximum 3	3
Total		10

14   EC LTD

(a)   Breakeven revenue = $\dfrac{\text{Fixed costs £1,212,000}}{\text{Average contribution to Sales ratio 50.5\% (W1)}}$

Breakeven revenue = $2,400,000.

Working 1: Average Contribution to Sales Ratio (on a £100 total sales basis)

	Product X	Product Y	Total
Sales	$70	$30	$100
Contribution	$70 * 0.55 = $38.50	$30 * 0.4 = $12	$50.50

If £50.50 contribution is achieved for every £100 worth of sales,

Average contribution to Sales ratio = $\dfrac{\$50.50}{\$100}$ = 0.505 or 50.5%

(b)

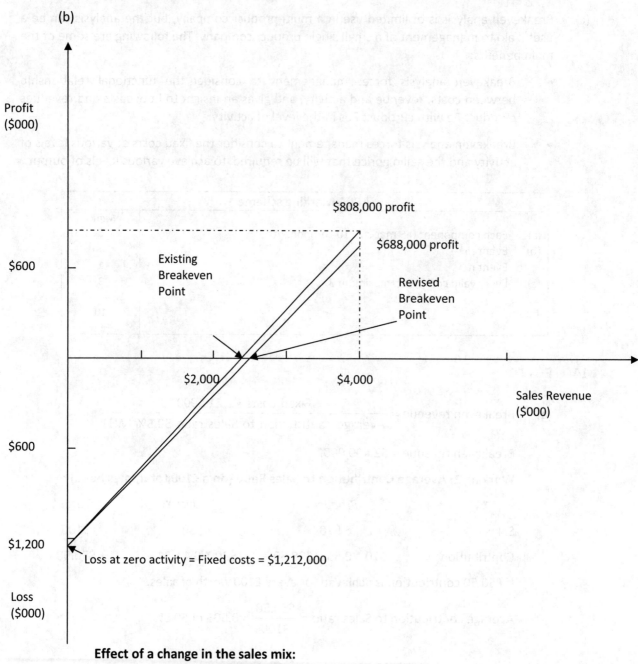

Effect of a change in the sales mix:

	Product X	Product Y	Total
Sales	$50	$50	$100
Contribution	$50 * 0.55 = $27.50	$50 * 0.4 = $20	$47.50

If £47.50 contribution is achieved for every £100 worth of sales,

Average contribution to Sales ratio = 47.50 % and

$$\text{Breakeven revenue} = \frac{\text{Fixed costs £1,212,000}}{\text{Average contribution to Sales ratio 47.5\% (W1)}}$$

Breakeven revenue = $2,551,579.

(c) $$\text{Sales revenue required} = \frac{\text{Attributable fixed costs } \$455,000 + \$700,000}{\text{X's contribution to Sales ratio 55\%}}$$

Sales revenue required = $2,100,000.

DECISION MAKING TECHNIQUES

15   B CHEMICALS

Key answer tips

With any linear programming question the key is to work through the different steps in a systematic manner.

(a)   **Formulation of LP problem**

Let x = the gallons of Super petrol produced;

   y = the gallons of Regular petrol produced each day; and

   C = the total contribution

The company needs to maximise an objective function C = $0.25x + 0.1y$

Subject to constraints:

supply of heavy crude $0.7x + 0.5y \leq 5,000$ (1)

supply of light crude $0.5x + 0.7y \leq 6,000$ (2)

market conditions $x \geq 2/3\ (x + y)$

rearranging $3x \geq 2x + 2y$

or x $\geq 2y$ (3)

also x, y ≥ 0

(b) **Graph**

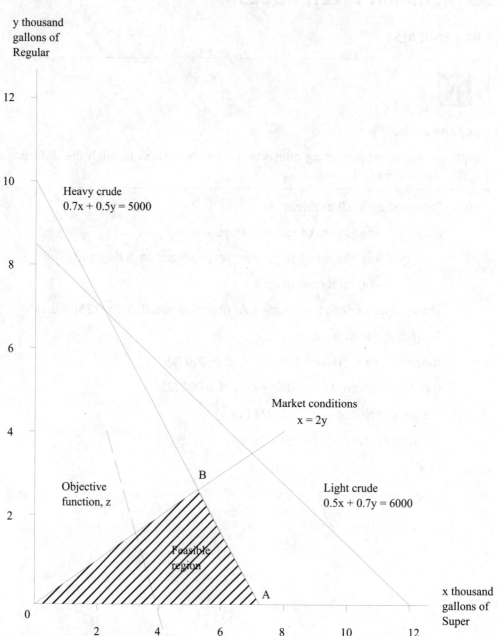

y thousand
gallons of
Regular

Heavy crude
0.7x + 0.5y = 5000

Market conditions
x = 2y

B

Objective
function, z

Light crude
0.5x + 0.7y = 6000

Feasible
region

A

x thousand
gallons of
Super

Note: the objective function is also shown.

(c) **Optimal policy and comment**

From the graph, which also shows an objective function (z = 10,000 has been drawn), it is clear that the optimal solution lies at point A. This is the point where the line 0.7x + 0.5y = 5,000 cuts the horizontal axis, where y = 0 and x = 7,142.85.

The optimal production policy involves producing no Regular petrol and 7,142.85 gallons of Super petrol. The contribution that this generates is:

7,142.85 × $0.25 = $1,785.71 per day.

Comment

- Whilst the solution to the LP problem might involve no Regular petrol, a policy that abandons refining of one product may risk longer-term demand for that product
- The conclusion drawn is only as reliable as the underlying estimates whose accuracy should be checked
- It would only require a small change in estimates to move the optimal solution from A to B.

16   CUT AND STITCH

(a)   The optimal production mix can be found by solving the two equations given for F and T.

$7W + 5L = 3,500$

$2W + 2L = 1,200$

Multiplying the second equation by 2·5 produces:

$7W + 5L = 3,500$

$5W + 5L = 3,000$

$2W = 500$

$W = 250$

Substituting W = 250 in the fabric equation produces:

$2 \times 250 + 2L = 1,200$

$2L = 700$

$L = 350$

The optimal solution is when 250 work suits are produced and 350 lounge suits are produced. **The contribution gained is $26,000**:

$C = 48W + 40L$

$C = (48 \times 250) + (40 \times 350)$

$C = 26,000$

(b)   The shadow prices can be found by adding one unit to each constraint in turn.

Shadow price of T

$7W + 5L = 3,501$

$2W + 2L = 1,200$

Again multiplying the second equation by 2.5 produces:

$7W + 5L = 3,501$

$5W + 5L = 3,000$

$2W = 501$

$= 250.5$

Substituting W = 250.5 in the fabric equation produces:

$(2 \times 250.5) + 2L = 1,200$

$2L = 1,200 - 501$

$L = 349.5$

Contribution earned at this point would be = (48×250.5) + $(40 \times 349.5) = 26,004$ which is an increase of $4.

Hence the shadow price of T is $4 per hour.

Shadow price of F

$7W + 5L = 3,500$

$2W + 2L = 1,201$

Again multiplying the second equation by 2.5 produces:

$7W + 5L = 3,500.0$

$5W + 5L = 3,002.5$

$2W = 497.5$

$W = 248.75$

Substituting W = 248.75 in the fabric equation produces:

$(2 \times 248.75) + 2L = 1,201$

$2L = 1,201 - 497.5$

$L = 351.75$

Contribution earned at this point would be = $(48 \times 248.75) + (40 \times 351.75) = 26,010$, which is an increase of $10. Hence the shadow price of F is $10 per metre.

(c)   The shadow price represents the maximum premium above the normal rate a business should be willing to pay for more of a scarce resource. It is equal to the increased contribution that can be gained from gaining that extra resource.

The shadow price of labour here is $4 per hour. The tailors have offered to work for $4.50 – a premium of $3.00 per hour. At first glance the offer seems to be acceptable.

However, many businesses pay overtime at the rate of time and a half and some negotiation should be possible to create a win/win situation. Equally some consideration should be given to the quality aspect here. If excessive extra hours are worked then tiredness can reduce the quality of the work produced.

(d)   If maximum demand for W falls to 200 units, the constraint for W will move left to 200 on the × axis of the graph. The new optimum point will then be at the intersection of:

W = 200 and

$2W + 2L = 1,200$

Solving these equations simultaneously, if:

W = 200, then $(2 \times 200) + 2L = 1,200$

Therefore L = 400.

So, the new production plan will be to make 400L and 200W

		Marks
ACCA marking scheme		
(a)	Optimal point calculation	3
	Contribution	1
		4
(b)	For each shadow price	3
		6
(c)	Rate discussion	3
	Other factors e.g. tiredness, negotiation	3
		6
(d)	Find optimum point	1
	Solve 2 equations	2
	Conclusion	1
		4
Total		20

17 DP PLC

Key answer tips This is a very straightforward linear programming question. If you are a little uncertain when it comes to drawing LP graphs you should practise calculating and drawing them as they offer easy marks in the exam.

(a)   **Computer**

	X		Y	
	$	$	$	$
Selling price		800		1,200
Components	150		310	
Assembly	240		390	
Testing	120		180	
Packaging	20		10	
		(530)		(890)
Contribution per unit		270		310

(b)   Let X = the number of computer X to be produced in next 6 months

Y = the number of computer Y to be produced in the next 6 months

Assembly time is limited to 1,000 × 60 minutes = 60,000

Testing time is limited to 875 × 60 minutes = 52,500

Assembly time (minutes) 80x + 130y = 60,000 (S1)

Testing time (minutes) 120x + 180y = 52,500 (S2)

Sales functions $0 \le x \le 300$ (S4)

$0 \le y \le 800$ (S5)

Objective function (contribution) $270x + 310y = C$

Subject to constraints

Assembly time $80X + 130Y + S1 = 60,000$

Testing time $120X + 180Y + S2 = 52,500$

Note: There is no constraint for packaging time as this is unlimited.

Demand for X $X + S4 = 300$

Demand for Y $Y + S5 = 800$

$X, Y \ge 0$.

Plotting the objective function

If $C = 100,000$

When $x = 0$

              $y = 322$

When $y = 0$

              $X = 370$

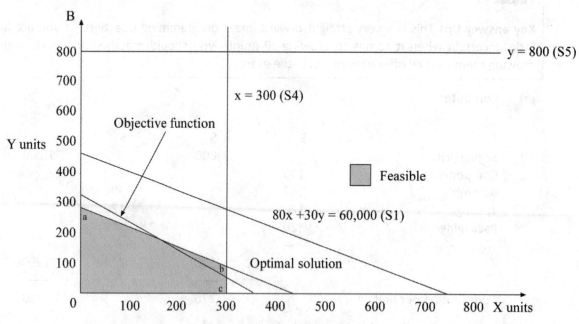

The graph above shows that the optimal solution is at b where:

X = 300 units

Y = 92 units

Product contributions:

		$
Product X	(300 × $270)	81,000
Product Y	(92 × $310)	28,520
Total contribution		109,520

(c) **REPORT**

To: Management Team, DP plc

From: Management Accountant

Date: 28 November 20X1

Subject: Budget for the six months to 30 June 20X2

Introduction

I have now had a chance to look at the implications of the projected shortage of packaging hours. As you will see, I have concluded that we may need to employ assembly workers in a new way.

Findings

The fact that there is a packaging time constraint reduces the budgeted contribution from $109,520 to $107,437.50 according to the computer package. This means that the packaging time is an effective constraint on operations.

The computer tells me that the optimal activity is to produce 268.75 units of computer X and 112.50 units of computer Y. These figures can be rounded to 269 and 112 respectively. As we know the maximum demand for X is 300 and for Y is 800, we will have unsatisfied demand of 31 units of X and 688 units of Y.

The computer shows that both testing time and packaging time will be fully utilised. If the amount available of these could be increased, then each extra testing minute would yield an increase in contribution of $1.46, and each extra packaging minute would yield an increase in contribution of $4.75. Assembly time however, is in surplus – we have 23,875 assembly minutes in surplus, or 398 hours.

Conclusion

We should try to employ assembly workers in new ways, say to test and package the products, after receiving appropriate training. This would utilise our spare resource and reduce/eliminate our capacity problems. It is not clear without further investigation, however, whether this is a practicable solution.

Signed: Management Accountant

(d) As testing time is one of the factors that limits the activity level of the company, the senior test engineer's statement is very important. In particular it seems that the learning period is now ended. The resulting reduction in the test times taken affects our solution, so the possible level of activity will change.

With a 90% learning curve, the average time taken per unit is reduced by 10% each time the cumulative output is doubled. When the steady state is reached, it is possible that testing time will no longer be a limiting factor.

Other management decisions that may be affected by the learning curve effect on labour costs include:

- Pricing decisions: decreasing labour costs per unit will allow for a more competitive price to be set;

- Work scheduling: understanding the learning curve allows correct scheduling of labour and enables deliveries to take place on time;

- Standard setting: definite standards should be set only once the steady state has been reached;

- Budgeting; our cash budgets should take into account the effect of the reduction in variable costs.

18   BITS AND PIECES (JUNE 09 EXAM)

(a)   The decision to open on Sundays is to be based on incremental revenue and incremental costs:

	Ref	$	$
Incremental revenue	(W1)		800,000
Incremental costs			
• Cost of sales	(W2)	335,000	
• Staff	(W3)	45,000	
• Lighting	(W4)	9,000	
• Heating	(W5)	9,000	
• Manager's bonus	(W6)	8,000	
• Total costs			(406,000)
Net incremental revenue			394,000

Conclusion

On the basis of the above it is clear that the incremental revenue exceeds the incremental costs and therefore it is financially justifiable.

(W1)   **Incremental revenue**

Day	Sales	Gross profit	Gross profit	Cost of Sales
	$	%	$	$
Average	10,000	70%		
Sunday (+60% of average)	16,000	50%	8,000	8,000
Annually (50 days)	800,000		400,000	400,000
Current results (300 days)	3,000,000	70.0%	2,100,000	
New results	3,800,000	65.8%	2,500,000	

(W2)   **Purchasing and discount on purchasing**

Extra purchasing from Sunday trading is $800,000 − $400,000 = $400,000

Current annual purchasing is $18,000 × 50 =$900,000

New annual purchasing is ($900,000 + $400,000) × 0.95 = $1,235,000

Incremental cost is $1,235,000 − $900,000 = $335,000 (a $65,000 discount)

(W3) **Staff costs**

Staff costs on a Sunday are 5 staff × 6 hours × $20 per hour × 1.5 = $900 per day Annual cost is $900 × 50 days = $45,000

(W4) **Lighting costs**

Lighting costs are 6 hours × $30 per hour × 50 days = $9,000

(W5) **Heating costs**

Heating cost in winter is 8 hours × $45 per hour × 25 days = $9,000

(W6) **Manager's bonus**

This is based on the incremental revenue $800,000 × 1% = $8,000 (or $160 per day)

Tutorial note

Only relevant cash flows should be taken into consideration when making this decision, i.e. the future incremental cash flows that occur as a result of Sunday opening. Prepare a summary of the relevant cash flows and reference in workings, where required.

(b)   The manager's rewards can be summarised as follows:

Time off

This appears far from generous. The other staff are being paid time and a half and yet the manager does not appear to have this option and also is only being given time off in lieu (TOIL) at normal rates. Some managers may want their time back as TOIL so as to spend time with family or social friends; others may want the cash to spend. One would have thought some flexibility would have been sensible if the manager is to be motivated properly.

Bonus

The bonus can be calculated at $8,000 per annum (W6); on a day worked basis, this is $160 per day. This is less than that being paid to normal staff; at time and a half they earn 6 hours × $20 × 1.5 = $180 per day. It is very unlikely to be enough to keep the presumably better qualified manager happy. Indeed the bonus is dependent on the level of new sales and so there is an element of risk involved for the manager. Generally speaking higher risk for lower returns is far from motivating.

The level of sales could of course be much bigger than is currently predicted. However, given the uplift on normal average daily sales is already +60%, this is unlikely to be significant.

(c)   **Discounts and promotion**

When new products or in this case opening times are launched then some form of market stimulant is often necessary. B&P has chosen to offer substantial discounts and promotions. There are various issues here:

Changing buying patterns: It is possible that customers might delay a purchase a day or two in order to buy on a Sunday. This would cost the business since the margin earned on Sunday is predicted to be 20% points lower than on other days.

Complaints: Customers that have already bought an item on another day might complain when they see the same product on sale for much less when they come back in for something else on a Sunday. Businesses need to be strong in this regard in that they have to retain control over their pricing policy. Studies have shown that only a small proportion of people will actually complain in this situation. More might not, though, be caught out twice and hence will change the timing of purchases (as above).

Quality: The price of an item can say something about its quality. Low prices tend to suggest poor quality and vice versa. B&P should be careful so as not to suggest that

		Marks
ACCA marking scheme		
(a)	Existing total sales	1.0
	New sales	1.0
	Incremental sales	1.0
	Existing purchasing	2.0
	Discount allowed for	1.0
	Incremental Sunday purchasing costs	1.0
	Staff cost	2.0
	Lighting cost	1.0
	Heating cost	1.0
	Manager's bonus	1.0
	Maximum	12
(b)	Time off at normal rate not time and a half	1.0
	Lack of flexibility	1.0
	Bonus per day worked calculation and comment	1.0
	Risk	1.0
	Maximum	4
(c)	Changing customer buying pattern	2.0
	Complaints risk	2.0
	Quality link	2.0
	Maximum	6
Total		20

Examiner's comments (extract)

This question (in the second two parts) required some common business sense. This is sadly lacking in many. The manager's pay deal offered him less money per hour than the staff (on current prediction of incremental sales) and time off on a one to one basis when the staff got time and a half. Most managers would be savvy enough to recognise a poor deal when they saw it. Equally a weekend day is for many a family day and a day off in the week is a poor substitute for that.

The offering of substantial discounts may well encourage sales (a mark earning point). However, surely it is likely that customers could switch from weekday shopping to weekend shopping to save money. Surprisingly few realised this.

Marks gained for part (a) were reasonable with incremental sales, staff costs, and lighting being done correctly by most candidates. For some reason the incremental heating cost was incorrectly calculated by many, with candidates electing to heat the stores all year as opposed to just the winter months as stated in the question.

There were two sunk costs to be excluded (rent and supervisor salary). It is always advisable for a candidate to indicate that the cost is to be excluded rather than simply not mention it at all.

Very few realised that the manager's pay deal was not overly generous both in terms of time off and the amount of cash on offer. Many candidates seemed to think that the mere existence of time off and the offer of money was enough to motivate. The amount of time off and cash was ignored. This is again naive, demonstrating a lack of understanding or experience.

19   STAY CLEAN (DEC 09 EXAM)

(a)

	Reasons	$
Paper	– Book value is irrelevant because it is a sunk cost, as there is no other use replacement would not occur so the opportunity cost or scrap sale proceeds is the relevant value.	2,500
Ink	– Since this involves a future cost if the work is undertaken the purchase price should be used. Since the remaining inventory has no foreseeable use it has no value so the entire purchase cost is used.	3,000
Skilled labour	– Since the weekend working is caused if the work is undertaken the full cost is relevant:	
	125 hours @ \$4/hr = \$500	
	125 hours @ \$5/hr = \$625	1,125
Unskilled labour	– The weekend work results in 50 hours time off in lieu, this with the 75 other hours worked totals 125 hours which is less than the 200 hours of idle time which are already being paid for, thus there is no incremental cost.	Nil

Variable overhead	– This is a future cost which will be incurred if the work is undertaken	1,400
Printing press	– The depreciation is a past cost and should be ignored, however, the use of the press has an opportunity cost. If this work is undertaken then the press is not available for hire. The opportunity cost is the contribution which would be earned from hiring: 200 hours @ ($6 – $3)	600
Production fixed costs	– As these costs are unaffected by the decision they should be ignored	Nil
Estimating costs	– These costs are past or sunk costs and should be ignored.	Nil
Minimum price		$8,625

Key answer tip

It is important to explain clearly why costs are included as relevant or excluded as not relevant.

(b) An opportunity cost is the value which represents the cost of the next best alternative or the benefit forgone by accepting one course of action in preference to others when allocating scarce resources.

If there is only one scarce resource, decisions can be made by ranking alternatives according to their contributions per unit of the scarce resource. However, in reality there will be many scarce resources, and different alternatives will use alternative combinations of those scarce resources. In these situations opportunity costs are used to identify the optimum use of those resources.

20   CHOICE OF CONTRACTS

Note		North East		South Coast	
		$	$	$	$
	Contract price		288,000		352,000
(1)	Material X: inventory	19,440			
(2)	Material X: firm orders	27,360			
(3)	Material X: not yet ordered	60,000			
(4)	Material Y			49,600	
(5)	Material Z			71,200	
(6)	Labour	86,000		110,000	
(8)	Staff accommodation and travel	6,800		5,600	
(9)	Penalty clause			28,000	
(10)	Loss of plant hire income			6,000	
			(199,600)		(270,400)
	Profit		88,400		81,600

The company should undertake the North-east contract. It is better than the South coast contract by $6,800 ($88,400 – $81,600).

Notes:

(1)   Material X can be used in place of another material which the company uses. The value of material X for this purpose is 90% × $21,600 = $19,440. If the company undertakes the North-east contract it will not be able to obtain this saving. This is an opportunity cost.

(2)   Although the material has not been received yet the company is committed to the purchase. Its treatment is the same therefore as if it was already in inventory. The value is 90% × $30,400 = $27,360.

(3)   The future cost of material X not yet ordered is relevant.

(4)   The original cost of material Y is a sunk cost and is therefore not relevant. If the material was to be sold now its value would be 24,800 × 2 × 85% = $42,160, i.e. twice the purchase price less 15%, however, if the material is kept it can be used on other contracts, thus saving the company from future purchases. The second option is the better. The relevant cost of material Y is 2 × 24,800 = $49,600. If the company uses material Y on the South-coast contract, it will eventually have to buy an extra $49,600 of Y for use on other contracts.

(5)   The future cost of material Z is an incremental cost and is relevant.

(6)   As the labour is to be sub-contracted it is a variable cost and is relevant.

(7)   Site management is a fixed cost and will be incurred whichever contract is undertaken (and indeed if neither is undertaken), and is therefore not relevant.

(8)   It is assumed that the staff accommodation and travel is specific to the contracts and will only be incurred if the contracts are undertaken.

(9)   If the South-coast contract is undertaken the company has to pay a $28,000 penalty for withdrawing from the North-east contract. This is a relevant cost with regard to the South-coast contract.

(10)   The depreciation on plant is not a cash flow. It is therefore not relevant. The opportunity cost of lost plant hire is relevant, however.

(11)   It is assumed that the notional interest has no cash flow implications.

(12)   It is assumed that the HQ costs are not specific to particular contracts.

21   HS EQUATION

(a) $p = a - bq$ where p is price and q is demand for product
When price = $1,350, demand = 8,000 units
When price = $1,400, demand = 7,000 units

So:

(1) $1,350 = a - 8,000q$

and

(2) $1,400 = a - 7,000q$

   so subtracting equation (1) from equation (2)

   $50 = 1,000b$

$b = 0.05$

and substituting in equation (2):

$1,400 = a - 0.05 \times 7,000$

$a = 1,750$

so Price = $1,750 - 0.05q$ and marginal revenue = $1,750 - 0.1q$

To find variable production cost per unit, we need to separate fixed and variable costs from the historic cost data:

Using the high-low method, dividing the difference in cost for the highest and lowest activity levels by the change in activity

Variable production cost per unit $= \$(7,000 - 5,446) \times 1,000 / (9,400 - 7,300)$

$= \$1,554 \times 1,000 / 2,100$

$= \$740$

Direct material cost   = $270
Total variable cost   = $(270 + 740)

$= \$1,010$

Price is maximised where marginal cost (= variable cost) = marginal revenue

$1,010 = 1,750 - 0.1q$

$q = 7,400$ units

and price $= 1,750 - 0.05 \times 7,400$

$= \$1,380$

optimum price is $1,380

(b) **Tutorial note:** Note that the question only asks for two reasons

There are a number of reasons why it may be inappropriate for HS to use this model in practice:

- The model depends on the market structure being one in which there is:

  – Perfect competition (which is the closest situation to HS's market)

  – Monopolistic competition

  – Monopoly or

  – Oligopoly

  Whilst the market is highly competitive, it is unlikely that there is perfect competition (in which the action of one company cannot affect the market price).

- The model assumes that costs and demand follow a linear relationship and that there are no step changes in fixed costs. Again this may hold over a small range of volumes but is unlikely to be true for all possible volumes.

- This model can only be used if the company has detailed knowledge of demand and cost curves. It is unlikely that in practice HS would be able to derive accurate cost and demand curves.

22 MKL

(a) The selling price that should be charged for Product K is the one that maximises total contribution, i.e. a price of $75 for a demand of 1,400 units:

Selling price per unit	$	100	$	85	$	80	$	75
Variable Cost	$	38	$	38	$	38	$	38
Unit contribution	$	62	$	47	$	42	$	37
Demand units		600 units		800 units		1200 units		1400 units
Total Weekly contribution	$	37,200	$	37,600	$	50,400	$	51,800

(b) 1,400 units of Product K will use up 1,400 standard hours; in order to utilise all of the spare capacity, we now need to use 600 hours for Product L, for the first 10 weeks.

$$\frac{600 \text{ hours}}{1.25 \text{ hours}} = 480 \text{ units will use all the spare capacity.}$$

To maximise profits, the optimum price P will be expressed as $P = a - bQ$.

Here, $a = \$100 + (\frac{1,000}{200} \times \$10)$

So $a = \$150$ and $b = \frac{\$10}{200}$ 0.05

$P = \$150 - 0.05Q$

$P = \$150 - 0.05 \times 480$ units

P = $126 for the first 10 weeks.

For the following 10 weeks when the extra capacity becomes available, the optimum price P will be expressed as P = a − bQ and we need to equate MC = MR to maximise profits, with

MR = a − 2bQ.

Profit maximised when	MC = MR
When	$45 = a − 2bQ
When	$45 = $150 − 0.10Q
When	Q = 1,050 units
And	P = $150 − 0.05x 1,050
	P = $97.50

(c) **Skimming**

Given that the product is innovative and unlike any current products on the market, then a skimming strategy would seem a very good fit. As the product in new and exciting, charging a high early price would help target the early adopters in the introduction stage. This would also have the advantage of allowing product M to be produced in relatively low volumes, whilst still generating good cashflows to recoup the substantial R&D and launch costs traditionally linked to this kind of products.

Finally, as the market is untested for the product, it allows the firm to start with a high intro price and adjust downwards accordingly.

Penetration Pricing

This tactic represents the alternative approach when launching a new product; it involves charging an initial low price to quickly gain market share. It offers the advantage of scaring off potential entrants to the market and may allow the firm to exploit economies of scale. However, given that our product M is differentiated and there will be little, if any, immediate competition, we think the company is right to adopt a skimming strategy for its pricing.

23 HAMMER (JUNE 10)

(a) Price under existing policy

	$
Steel (0.4/0.95 × $4.00)	1.68
Other materials ($3.00 × 0·9 × 0·1)	0.27
Labour (0.25 × $10)	2.50
Variable overhead (0.25 × $15)	3.75
Delivery	0.50
Total variable cost	8.70
Mark-up 30%	2.61
Transfer price	11.31

(b)   The only difference would be to add the fixed costs and adjust the mark-up %.

	$
Existing total variable cost	8.70
Extra fixed cost (0.25 × $15 × 0.8)	3.00
Total cost	11.70
Mark-up 10%	1.17
Transfer price	12.87

The price difference is therefore 12.87 – 11.31 = $1.56 per unit

(c)   As far as the manufacturer is concerned, including fixed costs in the transfer price will have the advantage of covering all the costs incurred. In theory this should guarantee a profit for the division (assuming the fixed overhead absorption calculations are accurate). In essence the manufacturer is reducing the risk in his division.

The accounting for fixed costs is notoriously difficult with many approaches possible. Including fixed costs in the transfer price invites manipulation of overhead treatment.

One of the main problems with this strategy is that a fixed cost of the business is being turned into a variable cost in the hands of the seller (in our case the stores). This can lead to poor decision-making for the group since, although fixed costs would normally be ignored in a decision (as unavoidable), they would be relevant to the seller because they are part of their variable buy in price.

(d)   **Degree of autonomy allowed to the stores in buying policy.**

If the stores are allowed too much freedom in buying policy Hammer could lose control of its business. Brand could be damaged if each store bought a different supplier's shears (or other products). On the other hand, flexibility is increased and profits could be made for the business by entrepreneurial store managers exploiting locally found bargains. However, the current market price for shears may only be temporary (sale or special offer) and therefore not really representative of their true market 'value'. If this is the case, then any long-term decision to allow retail stores to buy shears from external suppliers (rather than from Nail) would be wrong.

The question of comparability is also important. Products are rarely 'identical' and consequently, price differences are to be expected. The stores could buy a slightly inferior product (claiming it is comparable) in the hope of a better margin. This could seriously damage Hammer's brand.

Motivation is also a factor here, however. Individual managers like a little freedom within which to operate. If they are forced to buy what they see as an inferior product (internally) at high prices it is likely to de-motivate. Also with greater autonomy, the performance of the stores will be easier to assess as the store managers will have control over greater elements of their business.

		Marks
ACCA marking scheme		
(a)	Steel	1
	Other material	1
	Labour	1
	Variable overhead	1
	Delivery	1
	Mark-up	1
		___
	Total	6
(b)	Fixed cost	2
	Mark-up	2
		___
	Total	4
(c)	Covers all cost	1
	Risk	1
	Fixed cost accounting	1
	Converts a FC to VC	2
		___
	Total (max)	4
(d)	Market price may be temporary	1
	Brand	1
	Profitability	1
	Flexibility	1
	Control	1
	Motivation	1
	Performance assessment	1
	Comparability	1
		___
	Total (max)	6
		___
	Total	20
		___

24   SNIFF CO (DEC 07)

Key answer tips

This is an in-depth question on relevant costing and the further processing decisions.

In part (a) the financial factors may seem obvious, i.e. process further if the profit will increase as a result. However, there are five marks available and so it is not enough to simply make this comment. Consider what will drive profit, e.g. future incremental sales and costs, sales volume. Each of these factors can then be explained briefly.

The main non-financial factor involves the health concerns surrounding the use of the hormones. Ethics is a key motivation of the examiner and so make sure issues such as this are discussed.

In part (b) it is vital that you apply the principles of relevant costing accurately. i.e. you should only include future incremental cash flows:

- Future – Exclude sunk costs such as the market research

- Incremental – The supervisor's salary and fixed costs should be ignored. On the other hand opportunity costs should be included for labour

(a)   Sniff should consider the following factors when making a further processing decision:

Financial factors

- **Incremental revenue.** Sniff should only process the perfume further if the incremental revenues from the new product exceeds the incremental costs of processing the perfume.

- **Incremental costs.** A decision to further process can involve more materials and labour. Care must be taken to only include those costs that change as a result of the decision and therefore sunk costs should be ignored. Sunk costs would include, for example, fixed overheads that would already be incurred by the business before the further process decision was taken. The shortage of labour means that its 'true' cost will be higher and need to be included.

    Also, Sniff should consider both the Direct costs and the indirect costs (although they may not all be easily identifiable) such as:

    1   The additional space required

    2   Branding costs

    3   Patent costs

    4   Supervisors costs.

Other factors

- **Impact on overall sales volumes.** Sniff is selling a 'highly branded' product. Existing customers may well be happy with the existing product. If the further processing changes the existing product too much there could be an impact on sales and loyalty.

- **Impact on reputation.** As is mentioned in the question, adding hormones to a product is not universally popular. Many groups exist around the world that protest against the use of hormones in products. Sniff could be damaged by this association.

- **Potential legal cases** being brought regarding allergic reactions to hormones.

(b)

Tutorial note

There are 27 minutes to answer this requirement and therefore no need to panic. A logical, planned structure is essential. Start by calculating the contribution for 1,000 litres of standard perfume, working through each cost and sales item in turn. Once this is done, set up a separate working for the male and female versions. Calculate the extra costs and revenues of further processing. Take a guess if you are not sure of a particular area and move on. Don't forget to conclude, using the financial and non-financial factors.

Market research is a sunk cost and therefore should be ignored for the purpose of the calculation.

Production costs for 1,000 litres of the standard perfume

		$
Aromatic oils	10 ltrs × $18,000/ltr	180,000
Diluted alcohol	990 ltrs × $20/ltr	19,800
Material cost		199,800
Labour	2,000 hrs × $15/hr	30,000
Total		229,800
Cost per litre		229.80
Sales price per litre		399.80

Lost contribution per hour of labour used on new products

($399,800 − $199,800) ÷ 2,000 hrs = $100/hr

Incremental costs

	Male version		*Female version*	
		$		$
Hormone	2 ltr × $7,750/ltr	15,500	8 ltr × $12,000/ltr	96,000
Supervisor	Sunk cost	0	Sunk cost	0
Labour	500 hrs × $100/hr	50,000	700 hrs × $100/hr	70,000
Fixed cost	Sunk cost	0	Sunk cost	0
Research	Sunk cost	0	Sunk cost	0
Total		65,500		166,000

Incremental revenues

	Male version		Female version	
		$		$
Standard	200 ltr × $399.80/ltr	79,960	800 ltr × $399.80	319,840
Hormone	202 ltr × $750/ltr	151,500	808 ltr × $595/ltr	480,760
Inc. revenue		71,540		160,920
Benefit/(cost)		6,040		(5,080)

The Male version of the product is worth processing further in that the extra revenue exceeds the extra cost by $6,040.

The Female version of the product is not worth processing further in that the extra cost exceeds the extra revenue by $5,080.

In both cases the numbers appear small. Indeed, the benefit of $6,040 may not be enough to persuade management to take the risk of damaging the brand and the reputation of the business. To put this figure into context: the normal output generates a contribution of $170 per litre and on normal output of about 10,000 litres this represents a monthly contribution of around $1.7m (after allowing for labour costs).

Future production decisions are a different matter. If the product proves popular, however, Sniff might expect a significant increase in overall volumes. If Sniff could exploit this and resolve its current shortage of labour then more contribution could be created. It is worth noting that resolving its labour shortage would substantially reduce the labour cost allocated to the hormone added project. Equally, the prices charged for a one off experimental promotion might be different to the prices that can be secured in the long run.

Note: The original question had parts (c) and (d) as well. The answers to these requirements are as follows:

(c) The selling price charged would have to cover the incremental costs of $166,000. For 808 litres that would mean the price would have to be

$$\frac{(\$166{,}000 + \$319{,}840)}{808\,\text{ltrs}} = \$601.29/\text{ltr}$$

or about $60.13 per 100 ml.

This represents an increase of only 1.05% on the price given and so clearly there may be scope for further consideration of this proposal.

(d) Outsourcing involves consideration of many factors, the main ones being:

Cost. Outsourcing often involves a reduction in the costs of a business. Cost savings can be made if the outsourcer has a lower cost base than, in this case, Sniff. Labour savings are common when outsourcing takes place.

Quality. Sniff would need to be sure that the quality of the perfume would not reduce. The fragrance must not change at all given the product is branded. Equally Sniff should be concerned about the health and safety of its customers since its perfume is 'worn' by its customers

Confidentiality. We are told that the blend of aromatic oils used in the production process is 'secret. This may not remain so if an outsourcer is employed. Strict confidentiality should be maintained and be made a contractual obligation.

Reliability of supply. Sniff should consider the implications of late delivery on its customers.

Primary Function. Sniff is apparently considering outsourcing its primary function. This is not always advisable as it removes Sniff's reason for existence. It is more common to outsource a secondary function, like payroll processing for example.

Access to expertise. Sniff may find the outsourcer has considerable skills in fragrance manufacturing and hence could benefit from that.

ACCA marking scheme		Marks
(a)	Per factor outlined	1
		5
(b)	Hormone costs	2
	Supervisor excluded	1
	Direct labour	3
	Fixed cost allocation excluded	1
	Market research	1
	Incremental revenue	3
	Net benefit	2
	Concluding comment	2
		15
Total		20

Examiner's comments (extract)

Part (a) was fairly well done with most mentioning incremental costs and health concerns. Rather fewer mentioned incremental revenue, which was rather worrying.

Part (b) was very mixed with poor layout undermining many efforts. The numbers, including blatantly non relevant costs, was disappointing. This was a decision-making question, so existing fixed costs; the existing supervisor cost and the market research were all correctly excluded as sunk cost. I would prefer in future that sunk costs that are correctly omitted from calculations be mentioned as sunk rather than simply ignored. The marking team will then be able to tell whether the sunk cost treatment has been understood or merely forgotten.

25   FURNIVAL

Key answer tips

Approach the question one step at a time, applying fundamental decision-making principles

(a)   Identify incremental revenues and incremental costs including opportunity costs.

(b)   Ignore fixed costs.

(c)   Ignore costs incurred prior to the split off point.

(i)   Process R further if incremental revenues are greater than incremental costs.

Incremental revenues

	$
Selling price at split off point (per gallon)	1.50
Selling price after mixing	10.00
Increase per gallon	8.50
∴ Total for 500 gallons $8.50 × 500	$4,250

Incremental costs

Variable costs + Opportunity costs

	$
90% of process costs 0.90 × $3,000	2,700
Other separable costs	500
Total	3,200

Opportunity costs

Mixing hours are limited and scarce. If R is not produced, the 'other work' could earn a contribution – this is foregone by processing R further.

Contribution = Profit + Fixed costs

Product R requires 10 hours work.

	$
Therefore, total profit from other work = $200 × 10 hours =	2,000
Fixed cost element 10% of $3,000 ($30 per hour × 10 hours) =	300
Total contribution	2,300
∴ Total incremental costs $3,200 + $2,300	5,500

Therefore do not process further. R should be sold at the split off point.

Tutorial note : The joint process costs are ignored as they are incurred prior to the separation point.

(ii)

Tutorial note

R is sold at the split off point and production remains at 500 gallons. Therefore, R is not relevant to the decision at hand and it may be ignored.

Consider new output from the distillation plant.

P :	700 gallons
Q :	800 gallons
R :	500 gallons
Production of P falls by (1,000 – 700)	300 gallons
Production of Q increases by (800 – 500)	300 gallons

Joint process costs will not change as total production remains at 2,000 gallons. Relevant costs only arise in the mixing plant.

		Product P		Product Q
Revenue per gallon		$12.50		$20.00
Variable costs:				
Process costs	$\frac{\$2,700}{1,000g}$	($2.70)	$\frac{\$2,700}{500g}$	($5.40)
Other	$\frac{\$2,000}{1,000g}$	($2.00)	$\frac{\$500}{500g}$	($1.00)
Contribution per gallon		$7.80		$13.60

Loss in contribution from P = 300 × $7.80 =	($2,340)
Gain in contribution from Q = 300 × $13.60 =	$4,080
Net gain	$1,740
Extra cost of Q = 300 × $1 =	($300)
Total	$1,440

However, this change in output will require additional machine hours:

Production of P: Hours used falls by $\dfrac{10}{1,000} \times 300$ = 3 hours

Production of Q: Hours used rise by $\dfrac{10}{500} \times 300$ = 6 hours

Therefore, additional hours required 3 hours

Thus 3 hours' contribution from 'other work' is forgone.

Contribution per hour from other work = $230 (see earlier).

Lost contribution with new plan = $230 × 3 hours = $690

Overall effect of new plan = $1,440 − $690 = $750 gain

Recommendations – Produce P : Q : R ratio of 7 : 8 : 5 and sell R at the split off point.

26   ELECTRONIC CONTROL SYSTEM

Key answer tips

This is a straightforward 'make or buy' problem emphasising rational decision-making. The main problem is to sort out from the mass of percentages for costs and profits, what incremental cash-flows will arise from each of the three alternative supply sources. Diagrams may be useful.

(a)   **Buy from external company A:** Relevant cost = **($33,200)**

(b)   **Buy from external company B**

		$
Cash paid to B		(35,000)
Cash received from B		13,000
Purchase of parts from Ilk		(7,500)
Relevant costs of RS:		
(125% × own costs) + 7,500	= 13,000	
∴ own costs = $\dfrac{5,500}{1.25}$	= 4,400	
∴ Variable cost to group	= 4,400 × 70% =	(3,080)
Relevant cost =		**(32,580)**

(c) **Buy from RS**

		$
Opportunity cost of external sales forgone by RR (production costs incurred anyway)	8,000 + 11,000 =	(19,000)
Relevant costs of RT:		
Total costs = $30,000 ÷ 120% =	25,000	
Less: transferred cost from RR	(11,000)	
∴ own costs	14,000	
∴ variable cost to group	= 14,000 × 65% =	(9,100)
Relevant costs of RS:		
own costs = 42,000 − ($30,000 + 8,000) =	4,000	
Therefore, variable cost to group	= 70% × $4,000	(2,800)
Relevant cost =		**(30,900)**

Advice: on economic grounds the order should be placed internally with RS.

27 RECYC

(a) **Payoff table**

		Level of waste		
		High	Medium	Low
Advance	High	962.5	636.5	397.5
order of	Medium	912.5	655.5	442.5
chemical	Low	837.5	617.5	457.5

(W1)

Advance order of chemical X	Level of waste	Prob.	Contrib. (excl. X) (W2) $000	Chemical X cost (W3) $000	Net contribution $000
High	High	0.30	1,462.5	500	962.5
	Medium	0.50	1,111.5	475	636.5
	Low	0.20	877.5	480	397.5
Medium	High	0.30	1,462.5	550	912.5
	Medium	0.50	1,111.5	456	655.5
	Low	0.20	877.5	435	442.5
Low	High	0.30	1,462.5	625	837.5
	Medium	0.50	1,111.5	494	617.5
	Low	0.20	877.5	420	457.5

(W2) **Waste available**

	High	Medium	Low
Aluminium extracted (000 kg)	7,500	5,700	4,500
	$000	$000	$000
Sales revenue (at $0.65 per kg)	4,875.0	3,705.0	2,925.0
Variable cost (at 70%)	3,412.5	2,593.5	2,047.5
Contribution	1,462.5	1,111.5	877.5

(W3) **Examples of workings for chemical X cost**

- High advance level of order for chemical X and low actual requirement: The price of $1.00 is subject to a penalty of $0.60 per kg. The cost of chemical X is, therefore, 300,000 kg × $1.60 = $480,000

- Low advance level of order for chemical X and medium actual requirement: The price is subject to a discount of $0.10 per kg. The cost of chemical X is, therefore, 380,000 × $1.30 = $494,000.

(b) Maximax suggests that the decision maker should look for the largest possible profit from all the outcomes. In this case this is a high advance order of chemical X where there is a possibility of a contribution of $962,500. This indicates a risk seeking preference by management. Although it offers the possibility of the highest contribution, there is also a 20% likelihood that the worst outcome of $397,500 will occur.

Maximin suggests that the decision maker should look for the strategy which maximises the minimum possible contribution. In this case this is a low advance order of chemical X where the lowest contribution is $457,500. This is better than the worst possible outcomes from high or medium advance orders of chemical X. This indicates a risk-averse management posture.

28 TICKET AGENT *Walk in the footsteps of a top tutor*

Key answer tips

It would be easy to get absorbed in the detail of this question and to spend too much time trying to perfect the calculations. However, to pass the exam, focus on the easy marks. If mistakes are made in earlier calculations, carry forward marks will be available.

(a) The question specifies that a long-run perspective is being taken so decisions can be made by reference to expected values.

Expected sales demand

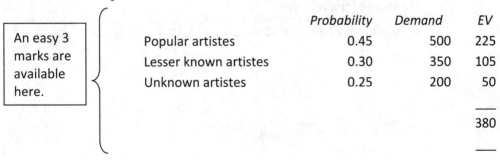

	Probability	Demand	EV
Popular artistes	0.45	500	225
Lesser known artistes	0.30	350	105
Unknown artistes	0.25	200	50
			380

An easy 3 marks are available here.

Expected demand = 380 tickets per concert

This part is harder but there are 20 minutes available for this requirement and therefore enough time to understand the scenario and to set out clear workings.

Maximising profit

To determine the best decision, the expected profits for each possible order level need to be calculated.

- Payoff table showing profit (W1, W2)

		Actual sales demand		
		200	350	500
	200	1,200	1,200	1,200
Purchase	300	(570)	2,250	2,250
Level	400	(2,040)	2,190	3,600
	500	(2,460)	1,770	6,000

There are 12 calculations to complete. Show the workings for at least one, so that the marker can follow the approach

- Expected values

		EV
200 tickets	$1,200 \times 1$	1,200
300 tickets	$(570) \times 0.25 + 2,250 \times 0.75$	1,545
400 tickets	$(2,040) \times 0.25 + 2,190 \times 0.3 + 3,600 \times 0.45$	1,767
500 tickets	$(2,460) \times 0.25 + 1,770 \times 0.3 + 6,000 \times 0.45$	2,616

Don't forget to conclude. Another easy mark available.

The optimum purchase level is 500 tickets per concert, which will give an expected profit of $2,616 per concert.

Workings

(W1) The gross profit made per ticket is the discount received on the selling price of $30.

Purchase level	Discount			Profit per ticket sold
200	20%	$20\% \times \$30$	=	$6.00
300	25%	$25\% \times \$30$	=	$7.50
400	30%	$30\% \times \$30$	=	$9.00
500	40%	$40\% \times \$30$	=	$12.00

(W2) Each net profit calculation consists of up to three elements:

1   the profit on the units sold;

2   the cost of the units which are unsold and returned;

3   the value of the returns

EV of returns = $30.00 \times 60\% \times 10\% = \$1.80$ per return.

Example calculation:

Buy 300 tickets but can only sell 200 $\Rightarrow$ Sell 200 tickets and return 100 tickets

	$
This part is relatively easy.	
Sales 200 tickets × 7.50 (W1)	1,500
EV of returns 100 tickets × $1.80	180
	1,680
Cost of returns 100 tickets × $22.50 (25% discount)	(2,250)
	(570)

This part is relatively easy.

This part is harder. Take a guess if unsure and move on.

(b) **Maximax**

An easy 2 marks.

The agent should order 500 tickets as this gives a maximum possible gain of $6,000 per concert

Maximin

The agent should buy 200 tickets to maximise the minimum possible pay-off ($1,200).

Minimax regret

A regret table is found by comparing the actual profit with what could have been made given the level of demand that occurred:

This is harder. Even if you can't do the calculation, explain what minimax regret is. This will gain 1 easy mark.

		Actual sales demand		
		200	350	500
	200	0	1,050	4,800
Purchase	300	1,770	0	3,750
Level	400	3,240	60	2,400
	500	3,660	480	0

The agent would thus order 400 tickets as this limits the maximum regret to $3,240.

This level of order would give an average profit of $1,767 per concert.

(c) The advice depends on the risk perspective of the agent

More easy marks available. The advice should be linked back to parts (a) and (b). Points should be separate and succinct.

- If he is willing to take a long term perspective and accept short-term uncertainty, then the expected value calculations in part (a) should be adopted, giving an order of 500 tickets

- If he is an optimist, then the maximax criteria would suggest ordering 500 tickets

- If he is a pessimist, then the maximin criteria would suggest ordering 200 tickets

- If he is a sore loser, then the minimax regret approach would suggest buying 400 tickets.

In reality the agent may be best advised to insist on knowing who the artists are before having to place an order.

29 SHIFTERS HAULAGE (DEC 08 EXAM)

(a) Maximax stands for maximising the maximum return an investor might expect. An investor that subscribes to the maximax philosophy would generally select the strategy that could give him the best possible return. He will ignore all other possible returns and only focus on the biggest, hence this type of investor is often accused of being an optimist or a risk-taker.

Maximin stands for maximising the minimum return an investor might expect. This type of investor will focus only on the potential minimum returns and seek to select the strategy that will give the best worst case result. This type of investor could be said to be being cautious or pessimistic in his outlook and a risk-avoider.

Expected value averages all possible returns in a weighted average calculation.

For example if an investor could expect $100 with a 0.3 probability and $300 with a 0.7 probability then on average the return would be:

$(0.3 \times \$100) + (0.7 \times \$300) = \$240$

This figure would then be used as a basis of the investment decision. The principle here is that if this decision was repeated again and again then the investor would get the EV as a return. Its use is more questionable for use on one-off decisions.

Key answer tips

Easy marks were available here. This is a core knowledge area and no application of knowledge was required. There will be easy marks for knowledge in each exam.

(b) **Profit calculations**

	Small Van		Medium Van		Large Van	
Capacity	100		150		200	
Low Demand (120)	300 (W1)		468 (W3)		368 (W5)	
High Demand (190)	300 (W2)		500 (W4)		816 (W6)	
Workings	(W1)	(W2)	(W3)	(W4)	(W5)	(W6)
Sales	1,000	1,000	1,200	1,500	1,200	1,900
VC	(400)	(400)	(480)	(600)	(480)	(760)
Goodwill	(100)	(100)		(100)		
VC adjustment			48		48	76
Depreciation	(200)	(200)	(300)	(300)	(400)	(400)
Profit	300	300	468	500	368	816

Tutorial note

Some candidates were confused about which level of demand should be used. The only levels of demand mentioned were 120 and 190 units and therefore these should have been used. Other candidates were confused about the appropriate adjustments that should have been made for variable costs, goodwill and depreciation.

Profit tables are a key part of risk and uncertainty. The approach to preparing them will always be similar and therefore candidates should practice a number of questions before sitting the exam.

(c)   **Which type of van to buy?**

This depends on the risk attitude of the investor. If they are optimistic about the future then the maximax criteria would suggest that they choose the large van as this has the potentially greatest profit.

If they are more pessimistic then they would focus on the minimum expected returns and choose the medium van as the worst possible result is $468, which is better than the other options. We are also told that the business managers are becoming more cautious and so a maximin criterion may be preferred by them.

Expected values could be calculated thus:

Small van	$300
Medium van ($468 × 0.4) + ($500 × 0.6) =	$487
Large van ($368 × 0.4) + ($816 × 0.6) =	$637

Given SH is considering replacing a number of vans you could argue that an EV approach has merit (not being a one-off decision – assuming individual booking sizes are independent of each other).

The final decision lies with the managers, but given what we know about their cautiousness a medium sized van would seem the logical choice. The small van could never be the correct choice.

Key answer tips

Good candidates discussed the results for the small, medium and large van in turn. Candidates linked their discussion back to the information provided in the scenario and expanded on the points made in part (a) of the answer.

Note: The original question asked for a discussion of three methods that coud be used to analyse and assess the risk in decision making. The suggested answer is given below:

Market research: This can be desk-based (secondary) or field-based (primary). Desk-based is cheap but can lack focus. Field-based research is better in that you can target your customers and your product area but can be time consuming and expensive. The internet is bringing down the cost and speeding up this type of research, email is being used to gather information quickly on the promise of free gifts etc.

Simulation: Computer models can be built to simulate real life scenarios. The model will predict what range of returns an investor could expect from a given decision without having risked any actual cash. The models use random number tables to generate possible values for the uncertainty the business is subject to. Again computer technology is assisting in bringing down the cost of such risk analysis.

Sensitivity analysis: This can be used to assess the range of values that would still give the investor a positive return. The uncertainty may still be there but the affect that it has on the investor's returns will be better understood. Sensitivity calculates the % change required in individual values before a change of decision results. If only a (say) 2% change is required in selling price before losses result an investor may think twice before proceeding. Risk is therefore better understood.

Calculation of worst and best case figures: An investor will often be interested in range. It enables a better understanding of risk. An accountant could calculate the worst case scenario, including poor demand and high costs whilst being sensible about it. He could also calculate best case scenarios including good sales and minimum running costs. This analysis can often reassure an investor. The production of a probability distribution to show an investor the range of possible results is also useful to explain risks involved. A calculation of standard deviation is also possible.

ACCA marking scheme		
		Marks
(a)	Maximax explanation	2.0
	Maximin explanation	2.0
	Expected value explanation	2.0
		———
	Maximum	5.0
		———
(b)	Small van sales	0.5
	Small van VC	0.5
	Small van goodwill or VC adjustment	1.0
	Small van depreciation	1.0
	Medium van – as above for small van	3.0
	Large van as above for small van	3.0
		———
		9.0
		———
(c)	Optimist view	2.0
	Pessimist view	2.0
	Expected value calculation	1.0
	Expected value discussion	1.0
		———
		6.0
		———
Total		20
		———

Examiner's comments (extract)

Part (a) was well done by most. The biggest issue was that some did not mention risk attitudes at all (an optimist would naturally favour maximax for example) this omission meant that 0.5 less marks were scored each time by failing to collect the allocated mark.

Part (b) was also reasonably done by many. There were problems here though:

- A surprising number of candidates did not seem to understand that if the capacity of a van is 150 and demand is 190 then sales must be restricted to 150. A large number of candidates still put down sales at the 190 level. This indicates a lack of understanding of the question (I assume that they do not read it properly).

- Many candidates did not include the goodwill adjustment in the profit calculation. This was not entirely unexpected. More than half marks were still available even if this adjustment were ignored.

- A common mistake was to try and calculate expected sales first and then work out some sort of answer accordingly.

Part (c) was more mixed. I expected that each potential risk attitude be taken in turn and applied to the figures. Where this was done good marks were earned. A surprising number failed to apply themselves to this. Some clearly knew what maximax, maximin and expected value were but could not then apply this knowledge to the question. The step up from F2 is significant and surely an element of application is part of that step.

Part (d) (i.e. the additional requirement) was poorly done by many. Those that had revised the area of risk in decision making did well and scored good marks. Many clearly did not have the knowledge required. Minimax regret was not a valid answer despite what about 50% of candidates thought. Sensitivity, simulation and market research comments all scored good marks.

30   THEATRE

(a)

Ticket sales ($)	Confectionary sales ($)	Total sales ($)	Joint xprobability	Sales xprobability ($)
7,500	900	8,400	.5 × .3 = .15	960
7,500	1,500	9,000	.5 × .5 = .25	2,250
7,500	3,000	10,500	.5 × .2 = .10	1,050
10,000	1,200	11,200	.3 × .3 = .09	1,008
10,000	2,000	12,000	.3 × .5 = .15	1,800
10,000	4,000	14,000	.3 × .2 = .06	840
12,500	1,500	14,000	.2 × .3 = .06	840
12,500	2,500	15,000	.2 × .5 = .10	1,500
12,500	5,000	17,500	.2 × .2 = .04	700
Total			1.00	11,248

The expected value is $11,248 − $10,000 = $1,248. Therefore it is worthwhile engaging MS for the concert.

(b) The data table shows profit values from each combination of ticket sales and contribution from confectionary sales. So, for example, for 300 people and $3 per person total sales are $8,400 (from (a)) – $10,000 fee = $1,600 loss.

Confectionary sales	$3 per person	$5 per person	$10 per person
Ticket sales			
300 people	(1,600)	(1,000)	500
400 people	1,200	2,000	4,000
500 people	4,000	5,000	7,500

(c) The probabilities can be applied to the data in the table to calculate expected values for each combination of outcomes.

People/contribution	Profit/loss ($)	Joint probability	Profit $\times$ probability ($)
300/$3	(3,600)	.5 × .3 = .15	(240)
300/$5	(1,000)	.5 × .5 = .25	(250)
300/$10	500	.5 × .2 = .10	50
400/$3	1,200	.3 × .3 = .09	108
400/$5	2,000	.3 × .5 = .15	300
400/$10	4,000	.3 × .2 = .06	240
500/$3	4,000	.2 × .3 = .06	240
500/$5	5,000	.2 × .5 = .10	500
500/$10	7,500	.2 × .2 = .04	300
		1.00	1,248

It can be seen that the expected value of the decision is $1,248 but the actual possible outcomes range from a loss of $1,600 to a profit of $7,500. The probability of making a loss is 0.4 and the probability of making a profit is 0.6. There is a probability of 0.26 of making a profit above $2,000.

Depending on the management's attitude to risk the decision may be different. A risk averse management may choose not to proceed as there is a substantial risk of making a loss. If management are risk seekers or risk neutral then they are likely to proceed despite this risk of loss as there is the opportunity to make a good profit and the expected value is positive.

(d) The value of perfect information is given by the expected value of the best strategy when the information is possessed less the expected value of the best strategy when the information is not possessed.

If it were known that ticket sales were for 300 people and contribution from confectionery sales were $3 or $5, then the management would choose not to proceed. Otherwise the management would proceed. The expected value would be $490 higher ($240 + $250) with perfect information and this is its value.

31   RY DECISION TREE

(a) and (b)

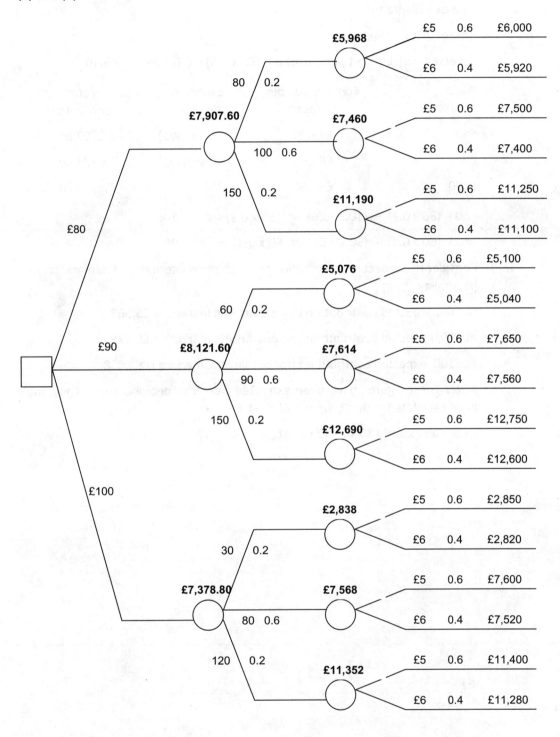

(b)   continued

The optimum price to set is £90. The answer can be calculated from the decision tree (see diagram).

Alternative working:

Expected variable cost per customer; (£5 x 0.6) + (£6 x 0.4) = £5.40

Price	Contribution per customer	Expected demand	Total contribution
£80	£74.60	106 (W1)	£7,907.60
£90	£84.60	96 (W2)	£8,121.60
£100	£94.60	78	£7,378.80

(W1) (80 x 0.2) + (100 x 0.6) + (150 x 0.2)=   106

(W2) (60 x 0.2) + (90 x 0.6) + (150 x 0.2) =   96

(c)   Consider the expected contribution for each price alternative if demand is pessimistic;

At £80, expected contribution (for pessimistic market) is £5,968

At £90, expected contribution (for pessimistic market) is £5,076

At £100, expected contribution (for pessimistic market) is £2,838.

Note: These figures have been extracted from the decision tree. They could have been calculated without the use of the tree.

Hence a price of £80 should be set

BUDGETING

32   NORTHLAND (JUNE 09 EXAM)

(a)   Overhead costs for the 2010 budget:

Property cost = $120,000 × 1.05 = $126,000

Central wages = ($150,000 × 1.03) + $12,000 = $166,500

Stationery = $25,000 × 0.6 = $15,000

(b)   The road repair budget will be based on 2,200 metres of road repairs; it is common to include a contingency in case roads unexpectedly need repair (see part (c)).

The weather conditions could add an extra cost to the budget if poor or bad conditions exist. The adjustment needed is based on an expected value calculation:

(0.7 × 0%) + (0.1 × 10%) + (0.2 × 25%) = 6%

Hence the budget (after allowing for a 5% inflation adjustment) will be:

2,200 × $15,000 × 1.06 × 1.05 = $36,729,000

This could be shown as:

(2,200 × 15,000 × 1.0 × 0.7) + (2,200 × 15,000 × 1.1 × 0.1) + (2,200 × 15,000 × 1.25 × 0.2) = $34,980,000

The $34,980,000 could then be adjusted for inflation at 5% to give $36,729,000 as above.

Tutorial note

Parts (a) and (b) were a straightforward test of budgeting. Most students should have been able to deal with the extected value calculation.

(c)   An expected value calculation used in budgeting has the following problems associated with it:

- It is often difficult to estimate the probabilities associated with different (in this case) weather conditions. The weather in one year may not reflect the weather in the following year leading to wildly inaccurate estimates and hence budgeting errors.

- It is difficult to estimate the precise monetary value attaching to each of the outcomes. 'Bad' weather can presumably take many forms (extreme cold, heat or water); the effect of each of these could be difficult to assess. Whilst using expected values it is common to group the events together and have one probability estimate. This may prove inadequate or inaccurate.

- The expected value that is calculated might not reflect the true cost leading to over or under spends on budget.

- The managers will have an easy fallback position should the budgets turn out to be incorrect. It would probably be accepted that the weather (and hence the probability of it) is outside their control and over spends could not then be blamed on them.

A contingency is often added to a budget in the event that there is uncertainty on the likely spend. In this case there would be much uncertainty over the level and indeed type of road repairs required. Roads could be damaged by weather conditions (extreme cold or heat) or unexpected land movements (earthquakes). Public safety could be at risk meaning that a repair is essential. This could result in a higher spend.

Equally the type of repair needed would vary and be unpredictable. Small holes might be simply filled in but larger holes or cracks might involve repairs to the foundations of the road. The costs could differ considerably between the different types of repairs.

Key answer tips

Plan your answer to ensure you have enough separate points. Aim for 8 points (4 for each area) and separate each point out using headings or individual paragraphs.

(d)   Zero based budgeting involves three main steps:

- **Define decision packages.** These are detailed descriptions of the activities to be carried out. There will be some standardisation within the data to allow comparison with other activities (costs, time taken and so on). A cost-benefit analysis is often carried out at this stage to ensure the most cost effective and beneficial approach to the activity is taken.

- **Evaluation and ranking of activities.** Each activity is assessed; those that are perhaps part of a legal obligation become 'must do' activities; others may be viewed as discretionary. The LGO will have to decide which of the activities offer the greatest value for money (VFM) or the greatest benefit for the lowest cost.

- **Allocation of resource.** The budget will then be created for the accepted activities.

Tutorial note

Easy marks were available here for this straightforward test of knowledge.

			Marks
	ACCA marking scheme		
(a)	Property cost		1.0
	Central wages		1.0
	Stationery		1.0
			———
		Maximum	3.0
(b)	Basic budget		2.0
	Contingency included		2.0
	Expected value adjustment		2.0
			———
		Maximum	6.0
(c)	Probability estimates difficult		1.0
	Monetary values uncertain		1.0
	EV not an actual value		1.0
	Easy fall back for managers		1.0
	Contingency		
	Uncertainty issue		1.0
	Weather		1.0
	Other outside influences		1.0
	Type of repairs variable		1.0
			———
		Maximum	8.0
(d)	Explanation of ZBB process		3.0
			———
Total			20
			———

Examiner's comments

This was probably the easiest question on the paper. Part (a) was very well done as expected. Part (b) was a little more mixed with candidates getting into a tangle with the EV calculations. Most candidates scored at least 4 out of 6 here.

Part (c) was less well done. I did not ask for the advantages and disadvantages of EVs I asked for the problems in using them in a budgeting context. I got very many text book descriptions of the issues surrounding EV in a decision making context. This was close to my question but that's all. Credit was given where possible here. As expected the practical aspects behind including a contingency in a budget eluded many. Candidates can do the calculations but seem to have little idea as to why!

Part (d) was poorly done, which surprised me as I considered it 3 easy marks. An average mark was only 1. There is a process for ZBB (involving decision packages, ranking and resource allocation and so on) but all candidates could remember often was that with ZBB you 'start from scratch' each year.

33 EFFECTIVE BUDGETING

(a)   Effective budgeting involves devising optimum sales/production/resource usage plans, and the setting of appropriate standards and targets that will encourage their achievement.

Plans must be devised based upon the current and expected future business and economic environments, with the organisation's reactions to known opportunities and threats built in. Alternative short- and medium-term strategies must be considered, and standards must be set taking account of expected variations from past data.

(b)   Whilst much of the data required to make budgeting decisions can be collected, computed and analysed from various software packages, many decisions must be made by the managers themselves. Indeed, the managers will initially have to decide the relevant data that the computer should be given to work on.

The impact of alternative strategies on profits, cash flow, resource availability etc. can be calculated by the computer, but the choice of the optimum strategy, probably incorporating multiple objectives with varying priorities, is down to management.

Certainly the budget number-crunching can now be a routine, automatic process, but the use of the numbers produced in decision making by management will determine the effectiveness of the budgeting system itself.

(c)   **A periodic budget** is one that is drawn up for a full budget period, such as one year. A new budget will not be introduced until the start of the next budget period, although the existing budget may be revised if circumstances deviate markedly from those assumed during the budget preparation period.

A **continuous, or rolling budget** is one that is revised at regular intervals by adding a new budget period to the full budget as each budget period expires. A budget for one year, for example, could have a new quarter added to it as each quarter expires. In this way, the budget will continue to look one year forward. Cash budgets are often prepared on a continuous basis.

The advantages of periodic budgeting are that it involves less time, money and effort than continuous budgeting. For example, frequent revisions of standards could be avoided and the budget-setting process would require managerial attention only on an annual basis.

A major advantage of continuous budgeting is that the budget remains both relevant and up to date. As it takes account of significant changes in economic activity and other key elements of the organisation's environment, it will be a realistic budget and hence is likely to be more motivating to responsible staff. Another major advantage is that there will always be a budget available that shows the expected financial performance for several future budget periods.

It has been suggested that if a periodic budget is updated whenever significant change is expected, a continuous budget would not be necessary. Continuous budgeting could be used where regular change is expected, or where forward planning and control are essential, such as in a cash budget.

(d)   **Budget bias (budgetary slack)** occurs when managers aim to give themselves easier budget targets by understating budgeted sales revenue or overstating budgeted costs.

Cost control using budgets is achieved by comparing actual costs for a budget period with budgeted or planned costs. Significant differences between planned and actual costs can then be investigated and corrective action taken where appropriate.

Budget bias will lead to more favourable results when actual and budgeted costs are compared. Corrective action may not be taken in cases where costs could have been reduced and in consequence inefficiency will be perpetuated and overall profitability reduced.

Managers may incur unnecessary expenditure in order to protect existing budget bias with the aim of making their jobs easier in future periods, since if the bias were detected and removed, future budget targets would be more difficult to achieve. Unnecessary costs will reduce the effectiveness of cost control in supporting the achievement of financial objectives such as value for money or profitability.

Where budget bias exists, managers will be less motivated to look for ways of reducing costs and inefficiency in those parts of the organisation for which they bear responsibility. The organisation's costs will consequently be higher than necessary for the level of performance being budgeted for.

34 NN

(a) **The adoption of zero-based budgeting within NN Ltd.**

During recent years the management of NN Ltd has used the traditional approach to incremental budgeting. The approach entails the use of the previous year's budget being rolled forward into the next year's budget purely budget.

Zero-based budgeting was developed to overcome the shortcomings of the technique of incremental budgeting. The implementation of a zero-based budgeting would require each manager within NN Ltd to effectively start with a blank sheet of paper and a budget allowance of zero. The managers would be required to defend their budget levels at the beginning of each and every year.

The implementation of a system of zero-based budgeting will require a consideration of the following:

- The need for major input by management
- The fact that it will prove extremely time consuming
- The need for a very high level of data capture and processing
- The subjective judgement inherent in its application
- The fact that it might be perceived as a threat by staff
- Whether its adoption may encourage a greater focus upon the short-term to the detriment of longer-term planning.

(b) The implementation of zero-based budgeting will require a major planning effort by our personnel. It is through the planning process that important guidelines and directions are provided for the development and ranking of the decision packages. Also, the planning process will enable managers to prepare for the uncertainty of the future. Long-range planning allows managers to consider the potential consequences of current decisions over an extended timeframe.

Zero-based budgeting addresses and supports comprehensive planning, shared decision-making, the development and application of strategies and allocation of resources as a way of achieving established goals and objectives. In addition, zero-based budgeting supports the added processes of monitoring and evaluation.

Zero-based budgeting, when properly implemented, has the potential to assist the personnel of an organisation to plan and make decisions about the most efficient and effective ways to use their available resources to achieve their defined mission, goals and objectives.

There is no doubt that the process of zero-based budgeting will consume a great deal more management time than the current system of budgeting does. This will certainly be the case in implementation of the system because managers will need to learn what is required of them. Managers may object that it is too time-consuming to introduce zero-based budgeting, however, it could be introduced on a piece-meal basis. As regards the imposition upon management time, managers may object that they simply do not have the necessary time in order to undertake an in-depth examination of every activity each year. However, if this proves to be the case then we could consider the establishment of a review cycle aimed at ensuring that each activity is reviewed on at least one occasion during every two or three years.

I propose that we hold a series of training seminars for our management to help in the transition to a system of zero-based budgeting. We must also ensure that we 'sell the benefits' that would arise from a successful implementation. A zero-based budgeting system would assist our managers to:

- Develop and/or modify the organisation's mission and goals
- Establish broad policies based on the mission and goals
- Efficiently identify the most desirable programs to be placed in operation
- Allocate the appropriate level of resources to each program
- Monitor and evaluate each program during and at the end of its operation and report the effectiveness of each program.

Thus, as a consequence of the adoption of zero-based budgeting our managers should be able to make decisions on the basis of an improved reporting system.

It is quite possible that zero-based budgeting would help identify and eliminate any budget bias or 'budget slack' that may be present. Budgetary slack is 'a universal behavioural problem' which involves deliberately overstating cost budgets and/or understating revenue budgets to allow some leeway in actual performance. We must acknowledge that in organisations such as ours where reward structures are based on comparisons of actual with budget results, bias can help to influence the amount paid to managers under incentive schemes. However, we should emphasise that if managers are to earn incentives as a consequence of incentive schemes that are based upon a comparison of actual outcomes with budgeted outcomes, then a zero-based budget would provide a fair yardstick for comparison.

It is important to provide reassurance to our managers that we do not intend to operate a system of zero-based budgeting against the backdrop of a blame-culture. This will help to gain their most positive acceptance of the change from a long established work practice that they may perceive afforded them a degree of 'insurance'.

(c)   The finance director is probably aware that the application of zero-based budgeting within NN Ltd might prove most fruitful in the management of discretionary costs where it is difficult to establish standards of efficiency and where such costs can increase rapidly due to the absence of such standards. A large proportion of the total costs incurred by NN Ltd will comprise direct production and service costs where the existence of input: output relationships that can be measured render them more appropriate to traditional budgeting methods utilising standard costs. Since the predominant costs incurred by a not for profit health organisation will be of a discretionary nature, one might conclude that the application of zero-based budgeting techniques is more appropriate for service organisations such as the not for profit health organisation than for a profit-seeking manufacturer of electronic office equipment. A further difference lies in the fact that the ranking of decision packages is likely to prove less problematic within an organisation such as NN Ltd which is only involved in the manufacture and marketing of electronic office equipment. By way of contrast, there is likely to be a much greater number of decision packages of a disparate nature, competing for an allocation of available resources within a not for profit health organisation.

35   BUDGETING SYSTEMS (JUNE 06 EXAM)

(a)   Incremental budgeting uses the previous year's budget as the starting point for the preparation of the next year's budget. It is assumed that the basic structure of the budget is acceptable and that adjustments will be made to allow for changes in volume, efficiency and price levels. The focus, therefore, tends to be on the existing use of resources rather than on identifying objectives and alternative strategies for the future budget period. It is argued that incremental budgeting does not question sufficiently the costs and benefits of operating a particular resource allocation structure.

Incremental budgeting may, therefore, be argued to have weaknesses in that:

- The resource allocation is not clearly linked to a strategic plan and the consideration of alternative strategies
- There is a tendency to constrain new high priority activities
- There is insufficient focus on efficiency and effectiveness and the alternative methods by which they may be achieved
- It often leads to arbitrary cuts being made in order to meet overall financial targets
- It tends not to lead to management commitment to the budget process.

(b)   The main features and potential advantages of activity based budgeting are:

(i)   The major focus is on strategically based resource allocation which aims at efficiency, effectiveness and continuous improvement. Features include:

- Minimum and incremental levels are identified for each activity
- The probability of significant change from the strategy is anticipated
- Key processes and constraints are identified and resource requirements quantified
- Efforts are made to identify critical success factors and the performance indicators which are most relevant for such factors.

(ii)   Activities are seen as the key to effective planning and control.

(iii)   It is argued that activities consume resources and that efforts should be focused on the control of the cause of costs not the point of incidence.

(iv)   Costs are traced to activities with the creation of 'cost pools' which relate to an activity.

(v)   Positive efforts are made to eliminate non-value added activities.

(vi)   Focus is on total quality management with concentration on:

- Emphasis on process control through identification of cost drivers

- The implementation of a 'right first time' philosophy aiming at zero defects

- Measurement of total performance including cost, efficiency and effectiveness

- Involvement of all members of the workforce.

(c)   **Participation in the budget-setting process**

A 'top-down' approach to budget setting leads to budgets that are imposed on managers. Where managers within an organisation are believed to want to avoid responsibility and avoid work, then imposed budgets may improve performance.

It is also possible that acceptance of imposed budgets by managers who are responsible for their implementation and achievement is diminished because they feel they have not been able to influence budget targets. Such a view is consistent with the perspective that managers naturally seek responsibility and do not need to be tightly controlled. According to this view, managers respond well to participation in the budget-setting process, since being able to influence the budget targets for which they will be responsible encourages their acceptance. A participative approach to budget-setting is also referred to as a 'bottom-up' approach.

In practice, many organisations adopt a budget-setting process that contains elements of both approaches, with senior management providing strategic leadership of the budget-setting process and other managers providing input in terms of identifying what is practical and offering knowledge of their area.

36   BIG CHEESE CHAIRS (DEC 09 EXAM)

(a)   The average cost of the first 128 chairs is as follows:

		$
Frame and massage mechanism		51.00
Leather	2 metres × $10/mtr × 100/80	25.00
Labour	(W1)	20.95
Total		96.95

Target selling price is $120.

Target cost of the chair is therefore $120 × 80% = $96

The cost gap is $96.95 − $96.00 = $0.95 per chair

(W1) The cost of the labour can be calculated using learning curve principles. The formula can be used or a tabular approach would also give the average cost of 128 chairs. Both methods are acceptable and shown here.

Tabulation:

Cumulative output (units)	Average time per unit (hrs)	Total time (hrs)	Average cost per chair at $15 per hour
1	2		
2	1.9		
4	1.805		
8	1.71475		
16	1.6290125		
32	1.54756188		
64	1.47018378		
128	1.39667459	178.77	20.95

Formula:

$$Y = ax^b$$

$$Y = 2 \times 128^{-0.074000581}$$

$$Y = 1.396674592$$

The average cost per chair is $1.396674592 \times \$15 = \$20.95$

(b) To reduce the cost gap various methods are possible (only four are needed for full marks)

– Re-design the chair to remove unnecessary features and hence cost

– Negotiate with the frame supplier for a better cost. This may be easier as the volume of sales improve as suppliers often are willing to give discounts for bulk buying. Alternatively a different frame supplier could be found that offers a better price. Care would be needed here to maintain the required quality

– Leather can be bought from different suppliers or at a better price also. Reducing the level of waste would save on cost. Even a small reduction in waste rates would remove much of the cost gap that exists

– Improve the rate of learning by better training and supervision

– Employ cheaper labour by reducing the skill level expected. Care would also be needed here not to sacrifice quality or push up waste rates.

(c) The cost of the 128th chair will be:

		$
Frame and massage mechanism		51.00
Leather	2 metres × $10/mtr × 100/80	25.00
Labour	1.29 hours × $15 per hour (W2)	19.35
Total		95.35

Against a target cost of $96 the production manager is correct in his assertion that the required return is now being achieved.

(W2) Using the formula, we need to calculate the cost of the first 127 chairs and deduct that cost from the cost of the first 128 chairs.

$Y = ax^b$

$Y = 2 \times 127^{-0.074000581}$

$Y = 1.39748546$

Total time is $127 \times 1.39748546 = 177.48$ hours

Time for the 128th chair is $178.77 - 177.48 = 1.29$ hours

ACCA marking scheme		
		Marks
(a)	Frame cost	1.0
	Leather cost	2.0
	Labour average time for 128 units	1.0
	Labour total time for 128 units	1.0
	Average cost per chair	1.0
	Target cost	1.0
	Cost gap	1.0
	Maximum	8.0
(b)	Per suggestion	1.5
	Maximum	6.0
(c)	Frame	0.5
	Leather	0.5
	Average time per unit	2.0
	Total time	1.0
	Time for 128th chair	1.0
	Conclusion	1.0
	Maximum	6.0
Total		20

37 HENRY COMPANY (DEC 08 EXAM)

(a) There are various issues that HC should consider in making the bid. (Only five are required for two marks each.)

Contingency allowance. HC should consider the extent to which its estimates are accurate and hence the degree of uncertainty it is subjected to. It may be sensible to allow for these uncertainties by adding a contingency to the bid.

Competition. HC must consider which other businesses are likely to bid and recognise that the builder may be able to choose between suppliers. Moreover HC has not worked for this builder before and so they will probably find the competition stiff and the lack of reputation a problem.

Inclusion of fixed overhead. In the long run fixed overhead must be covered by sales revenue in order to make a profit. In the short run it is often correctly argued that the level of fixed cost in a business may not be affected by a new contract and therefore could be ignored in bid calculation. HC needs to consider to what extent the fixed costs of its business will change if it wins this new contract. It is these incremental fixed costs that are relevant to a bid calculation.

Materials and loose tools. No allowance has been made for the use of tools and the various fixings (screws etc) that will be needed to assemble and fit the kitchens. It is possible that most fixings would be provided with the kitchen units but HC should at least consider this.

Supervision of labour. The time given in the question is 24 hours to 'fit' the first kitchen. There seems no allowance for supervision of the labour force. It could of course be included within the overhead figures but no detail is shown.

Idle time. It is common for building works to be delayed by lack of materials for example. The labour time figure needs to reflect this.

Likelihood of repeat business. Some businesses consider it worthwhile to accept a low price for a new contract if it establishes a reputation with a new buyer. HC could offer to do this work cheaper in the hope of more profitable work later on.

The risk of non-payment. HC may decide not to bid at all if it feels that the builder may struggle to pay.

Opportunity costs of alternative work.

Possibility of working in overtime.

Key answer tips

Easy marks were available here for discussing any sensible and relevant factors that should be taken into account. Good candidates related their discussion back to the information provided in the scenario and used short paragraphs to explain each factor, with the aim of scoring one mark for each of the factors explained.

(b)   Bid calculations for HC to use as a basis for the apartment contract.

Cost	Hours		Rate per hour		Total $
Labour	9,247	(W1)	$15		138,705
Variable Overhead	9,247		$ 8	(W2)	73,976
Fixed Overhead	9,247		$ 4	(W2)	36,988
Total Cost					249,669

(W1) Need to calculate the time for the 200th kitchen by taking the total time for the 199 kitchens from the total time for 200 kitchens.

For the 199 Kitchens

Using

$y = ax^b$	OR	$y = ax^b$
$y = 24 \times 199^{-0.074}$		$y = (24 \times 15) \times 199^{-0.074}$
$y = 16.22169061$ hours		$y = 243.32536$
Total time $= 16.22169061 \times 199$		Total cost $= \$48,421.75$
Total time $= 3,228.12$ hours		

For the 200 Kitchens

$y = ax^b$	OR	$y = ax^b$
$y = 24 \times 200^{-0.074}$		$y = (24 \times 15) \times 200^{-0.074}$
$y = 16.21567465$ hours		Total cost $= \$48,647.02$
Total time $= 16.21567465 \times 200$		200th cost $= \$225.27$
Total time $= 3,243.13$ hours		

The 200th Kitchen took $3,243.13 - 3,228.12 = 15.01$ hours

Total time is therefore:

For first 200	3,243.13 hours
For next 400 (15.01 hours $\times$ 400)	6,004.00 hours
Total	9,247.13 hours (9,247 hours)

(W2) The overheads need to be analysed between variable and fixed cost elements.

Taking the highest and lowest figures from the information given:

	Hours	Cost $
Highest	9,600	116,800
Lowest	9,200	113,600
Difference	400	3,200

Variable cost per hours is $3,200/400$ hours $= \$8$ per hour

Total cost $=$ variable cost $+$ fixed cost

$116,800 = 9,600 \times 8 +$ fixed cost

Fixed cost $= \$40,000$ per month

Annual fixed cost $= \$40,000 \times 12 = \$480,000$

Fixed absorption rate is $480,000/120,000$ hours $= \$4$ per hour

Key answer tips

Requirements (b)and (c) Involved learning curve calculations. This is a core knowledge area and candidates who had practised learning curve calculations will have scored well.

(c)   A table is useful to show how the learning rate has been calculated.

Number of Kitchens	Time for Kitchen (hours)	Cumulative time (hours)	Average time (hours)
1	24.00	24.00	24.00
2	21.60	45.60	22.80

The learning rate is calculated by measuring the reduction in the average time per kitchen as cumulative production doubles (in this case from 1 to 2).

The learning rate is therefore 22.80/24.00 or 95%

ACCA marking scheme			
			Marks
(a)	1 mark for each description	Maximum	5.0
(b)	Average time for the 199th kitchen		1.0
	Total time for 199 kitchens		1.0
	Average time for the 200th kitchen		1.0
	Total time for 200 kitchens		1.0
	200th kitchen time		1.0
	Cost for the first 200		1.0
	Cost for the next 400		1.0
	Variable cost per hour		2.0
	Fixed cost per month		1.0
	Fixed cost per hour		1.0
	Cost for variable overhead		1.0
	Cost for fixed overhead		1.0
			13
(c)	Average time per unit and explanation		2
Total			20

38   SCIENTO

Key answer tips

For part (a) the question states that the learning curve applies to the labour time. Therefore as cumulative production doubles, average time per unit will change by a fixed percentage.

Once the standard cost card has been determined, variances can be calculated in the normal way.

(a)   Producing 1 unit takes an average of 200 hours.

Producing 2 units takes an average of 180 hours.

180 is 90% of 200, therefore the 90% learning curve applies. The remaining average times given for doubling confirms the fit i.e. 162 90% of 180, and 145.8 90% of 162.

Now the equation of the learning curve is $y = ax^b$

Where a = the time to produce the initial unit = 200

and $b = \dfrac{\log r}{\log 2} = \dfrac{\log(0.90)}{\log 2} = \dfrac{0.04576}{0.30103} = -0.152$

Cumulative production at end of period	=	$526 + 86$	=	612
Average hours per unit, at start	=	$200 \times 526^{-0.152}$	=	77.169
Therefore total hours, at start	=	77.169×526	=	40,591
Average hours per unit, at end	=	$200 \times 612^{-0.152}$	=	75.413
Therefore total hours at end	=	75.413×612	=	46,153

Therefore standard hours per batch of 86 = 5,562 hours (46,153 – 40,591)

Therefore average standard hours per unit = 5,562/86 = 64.67 hours

Standard overhead absorption rate = $\dfrac{\$150,903}{5,562}$ = $27 (approx)

Electronometers standard cost schedule

	Per unit $
Direct material	250
Direct labour 64.67 × $10 per hour	647
	897
Overheads 64.67 × $27 per hour	1,746
Total	2,643

(b) **Variance analysis**

A full variance analysis is advisable as it provides a check on numerical errors.

(i) *Total cost*

	$	$
Standard $2,643 × 86		227,298
Actual		$
Direct materials	20,850	
Direct labour	71,823	
Overheads	152,600	
		245,273
Total variance		17,975

(ii) *Direct labour cost variance*

	$
Standard $647 × 86	55,642
Actual	71,823
	16,181 A

(1) Direct labour rate variance
Actual hours paid (standard rate – actual rate)
(6,861 × $10) – 71,823 .... 3,213 A

(2) Direct labour efficiency variance
Standard rate
(standard hours worked – actual hours worked)
$10 (5,562 – 6,861) .... 12,990 A

16,203 A

There is a small error due to rounding.

(iii) *Direct materials cost variance*

	$
Standard $250 × 86	21,500
Actual	20,850
	650 F

(iv) *Overhead variance* $

Total
Standard $27 × 5,562   150,174
Actual   152,600
                           ─────────
                           2,426 A
                           ─────────

(1) Expenditure
Budgeted cost — actual cost
$150,174 – 152,600   2,426 A

(2) Capacity
Absorption rate (budgeted hours — actual hours worked)
= BC − (Overhead absorption rate × actual hours worked)
= $l50,174 – (27 × 6,86l)   35,073 F

(3) Efficiency
OAR(Standard hours worked – actual hours worked)
= $27 (5,562 — 6,861)   35,073 A

(c) Use of the learning curve in establishing labour standards

- Useful where work is labour intensive rather than capital intensive
- Useful when dealing with new products
- The use of the learning curve may lead to:
  - improved planning e.g. production planning,
  - improved standard setting and, therefore, control and motivation,
  - improved product pricing

39   THE WESTERN

(a) In 2010 the four quarters will be numbers 5–8, consequently the trend figures for waste to be collected will be:

Quarter 1 (Q = 5): 2,000 + 25(5) = 2,125 tonnes

Quarter 2 (Q = 6): 2,000 + 25(6) = 2,150 tonnes

Quarter 3 (Q = 7): 2,000 + 25(7) = 2,175 tonnes

Quarter 4 (Q = 8): 2,000 + 25(8) = 2,200 tonnes

Seasonal adjustments are needed thus:

Quarter 1: 2,125 – 200 = 1,925

Quarter 2: 2,150 + 250 = 2,400

Quarter 3: 2,175 + 150 = 2,325

Quarter 4: 2,200 – 100 = 2,100

Total tonnage is 1,925 + 2,400 + 2,325 + 2,100 = 8,750 tonnes for the year.

(b) Regression analysis can be used to calculate the variable operating and fixed operating costs in 2009.

	Tonnes (X)	Total Cost (Y) $000s	XY	X^2
	2,100	950	1,995,000	4,410,000
	2,500	1,010	2,525,000	6,250,000
	2,400	1,010	2,424,000	5,760,000
	2,300	990	2,277,000	5,290,000
Sum	9,300	3,960	9,221,000	21,710,000

$Y = a + bX$

Where 'a' is fixed operating cost and 'b' is variable operating cost in this context.

Using the formula given:

$b = (4 \times 9,221,000 - 9,300 \times 3,960)/(4 \times 21,710,000 - (9,300)2)$

b = 0.16 or $160 per tonne as the original data is in $000's. This was the variable operating cost per tonne for 2009.

$a = (3,960/4) - (0.16 \times 9,300/4)$

a = 618 or $618,000 as the original data is in $000's. This was the fixed operating cost in 2009.

Allowing for inflation:

The variable operating cost in 2010 will be $160 \times 1.05 = $168 per tonne

The fixed operating cost in 2010 will be $618,000 \times 1.05 = $648,900

(c) Advantages of an incremental budgeting approach:

– Local government organisations are often complex and incremental budgeting will be seen as a simple approach to a budget that will take little effort.

– Budget processes can be long ones, however incremental approaches do tend to be quicker than most. Complex local government organisations can suffer from very long budget processes and incremental budgeting can alleviate this a little.

Disadvantages of incremental budgeting:

– Public bodies, such as local governments, will be encouraged to use up all of this year's budget in order to ensure that *next* year's budget will be as high as possible to give themselves the flexibility they need to do whatever is needed. The public services required can be unpredictable and so local government organisations prefer to be able to be flexible.

– Overspends made in this year will be budgeted for again next year, this is hardly giving taxpayers value for money.

ACCA marking scheme		
		Marks
(a)	Calculation of trend figures	1.0
	Adjustment for seasonal variation	2.0
	Total tonnage for budget	1.0
		____
	Maximum	4.0
		____
(b)	Completion of table with X, Y, XY and X^2	4.0
	Calculation of (b)	2.0
	Calculation of (a)	2.0
	Allowance for inflation	2.0
		____
	Maximum	10.0
		____
(c)	Per advantage/disadvantage	1.5
		____
	Maximum	6.0
		____
Total		20
		____

40   PMF

Key answer tips

The trend calculations are very straightforward. The question tests your understanding of why trend analysis is used in forecasting and performance measurement.

(a)   Quarter 3 year 1 = period 3 = Q3

Quarter 3 year 2 = period 7 = Q7

Quarter 3 year 3 = period 11 = Q11

Trend values for quarter 3 of each year:

10,000 + 4,200 Q

Adjust the trend value for Year 3 Q3 (11):

$((10{,}000 + (4{,}200 \times 11)) \times 75\% = 42{,}150$ passengers to be carried in the third quarter of year 3.

(b)   The transit staff cost item is a semi-variable cost, comprising a fixed element of $32,000 and a variable element of $3 for each passenger. Hence the cost equation is in the form 32,000 + 3x. The reason for this is most likely that transit staff receive a fixed basic salary but are awarded bonuses according to how many passengers are carried as a motivational tool.

(c) x = 42,150

Cost item	Relationship	Cost ($)
Premises cost	y = 260,000	260,000
Premises staff	y = 65,000 + 0.5x	86,075
Power	y = 13,000 + 4x	181,600
Transit staff	y = 32,000 + 3x	158,450
Other	y = 9,100 + x	51,250
		————
Total costs expected in year 3 Q3		737,375
		————

(d) It is highly unlikely that the actual data for Year 3 Quarter 3 will be the same as that predicted by the calculations for the following reasons:

- The key variable is the number of passengers predicted. The relationships show that any change in the value of x will have an effect on all the cost items except for the premises costs. While trend value calculations are very useful they are necessarily based on historical data and it is always true that past events are not guaranteed to be replicated. It is therefore possible that the predicted growth in passenger numbers will not happen

- All the cost relationships apart from premises costs are related to the number of passengers. It may well be that, currently or in the future, other cost drivers might affect the costs. For instance, the number of transit units run on time might be the cost driver for penalties charged by the industry regulator

- It is also possible that the historical seasonal variation from the trend value of 75% in quarter 3 will also not be replicated. This seasonal variation could have been due to factors that happened in Years 1 and 2 and which might fail to recur in Year 3

- The derivation of the cost relationships may be flawed, either by particular events that will not be repeated or by failure to include some relationships or the inclusion of others that actually are not true

- All the cost relationships are linear which, while being a useful approximation for reality, rarely reflect real life. For instance, it may be that once a certain level of passengers is reached there may need to be a step change in the number of staff employed, or the amount of power used as more transit units are run

- The effect of cost increases unrelated to the number of passengers has not been taken into account. Penalties and staff costs have already been mentioned. Another possibility is that the unit cost of power might change.

(e) A spreadsheet is a matrix, or table, comprising rows and columns which intersect to form cells. Each cell may be used to store a description, a value, or a formula.

A sales budget shows the quantity of each product to be sold, the selling price per unit, and the consequent sales value. These values may be analysed in many ways, for example by sales person, geographical region, etc.

When using a spreadsheet for complex budgets of large organisations it is important to create a formalised structure comprising an input area, a working area, and an output area.

As its name suggests an input area is the area of the spreadsheet which is used to receive the data upon which the sales budget is to be based. The basic data for a sales budget are the volume of sales and the selling price. However the volume may be analysed over sales persons, geographical areas, products, accounting periods. Selling prices will be different for each product and may be different in different geographical areas and at different times of the year.

The working area will be used to store the results of intermediate calculations based upon the data entered. These calculations will be the subject of formulae which act on the data values.

The output area will be the part of the spreadsheet that provides the final sales budget report. This can be in the form of a table of values and/or a graphical output.

Spreadsheets are used for these tasks because they can calculate and re-calculate values very quickly and any change made in the input area of the spreadsheet (assumptions) will automatically update the values in the output area.

Furthermore, actual values may be exported from the general ledger accounting system into the spreadsheet. Here they may be linked to the budget data and a variance report prepared.

41 BUDGETING (JUNE 07 EXAM)

(a) The key stages in the planning process that links long-term objectives and budgetary control can be divided between long-term planning and the budgeting process. Long-term planning involves identifying objectives, and identifying, evaluating and selecting alternative courses of action. The budgeting process involves implementing the long-term plan in the annual budget, monitoring actual results and responding to divergences from plan.

Identifying objectives

The planning process cannot take place unless organisational objectives are identified, since these determine what the organisation is seeking to accomplish through its operations and activities. These objectives will be long-term or strategic in nature and will give direction to the organisation's operational activities.

Identifying alternative courses of action

Once organisational objectives have been identified, alternative courses of action that may lead to achieving those objectives can be identified. Strategic analysis of the organisation and its environment can indicate potential courses of action. For example, a company may look at its existing products and markets and decide that a key objective is the development of new products to replace existing products

Evaluating alternative courses of action

At this stage the various alternative courses of action are considered from the point of view of suitability, feasibility and acceptability. In order for this to be done, detailed information about each alternative course of action needs to be gathered and analysed.

Selecting alternative courses of action

Once the most appropriate alternative courses of action have been selected, long-term plans to implement them are formulated. Because these plans are long-term in nature, they will of necessity be less detailed than short-term plans.

A budget is a short-term plan formulated in financial terms and will show in detail the short-term actions the organisation will take in working towards its long-term objectives. Once the budget has been formulated, finalised and agreed it can be implemented.

Monitoring actual results

In order to achieve the long-term objectives that are reflected in the budget, the organisation must ensure that actual performance is proceeding according to plan. It will therefore need to monitor actual performance and results.

Responding to divergences from plan

Divergences from planned activity, as measured by variances from budget, can lead to action if they are deemed to be significant. This action may be corrective in nature, in order to bring actual activity back into line with planned activity, or may entail revision of the budget if one of its underlying assumptions is seen as being in error.

(b)   A fixed budget is one prepared in advance of the relevant budget period which is not changed or amended as the budget period progresses. This budget represents a periodic approach to budgeting, since a new budget is prepared towards the end of the budget period for the subsequent budget period. In this way, an organisation may set a new budget on an annual basis.

A rolling budget, sometimes called a continuous budget, represents an alternative approach to periodic budgeting. Here, a portion of the budget period is replaced on a regular basis so that the overall budget period remains unchanged. For example, with a budget period of one year, at the end of each quarter a new quarter could be added to the end of the budget period and the elapsed quarter could be deleted, so that the budget was always looking one year ahead. Continuous budgeting continues to increase in popularity.

A zero-based budget is a periodic budget which seeks to dispose of the incremental approach to budgeting. In the incremental approach, an increment is added to the relevant figure from last year's budget, for example to take account of inflation. In this way, inefficiency can become embedded in the annual budget and profitability may suffer as a result. With the zero-based approach, each element of planned activity is required to be justified in terms of its contribution towards achieving organisational objectives. This involves the formulation of decision packages, which describe particular activities in such a way that managers can compare them in terms of their competing claims on organisational resources, and then rank them from a cost-benefit point of view. In this way, zero-based budgeting looks at each budget period with a new perspective.

A fixed budget is likely to be useful in circumstances where the organisational environment is relatively stable and can be predicted with a reasonable degree of certainty.

A rolling budget is likely to be useful in circumstances where the future is less certain and more flexibility is needed in the organisational response to its changing environment. For this reason, rolling budgets are popular with new organisations. A cash budget is often a rolling budget because of the need to keep tight control of this area of financial management. A rolling budget is also supported by the availability of cheap and powerful information processing via personal computers and computer networks.

A zero-based budgeting approach tends to be most beneficial when used with services and with discretionary activities, and so is most widely used in the public sector.

(c) Linear regression is a powerful way of analysing past information in order to derive linear relationships and so is ideally suited to deriving cost equations from past accounts. Sales volume, however, is unlikely to follow a linear relationship alone. Linear regression could be used to determine the overall trend being followed by sales volume on, for example, an annual basis, but inspection of historic sales volumes is likely to show variations about the trend. These could be due to seasonal variations, or longer-term cyclical variations. Time-series analysis can extract these seasonal and cyclical variations and therefore produce forecasts of sales volumes that are likely to be more accurate in a given period than forecasts based on the underlying trend alone. In forecasting future sales volumes, therefore, both quantitative methods have their place in increasing forecasting accuracy.

STANDARD COSTING AND VARIANCE ANALYSIS

42 STANDARD COSTING

(a)   Standard costing has been employed for many years in situations where there is a **significant degree of repetition** in the production process or the service supplied. Repetition is a condition, since standards presuppose that averages, as expected values, are accurate to a fair degree.

The main uses of standard costing relate to:

- **Valuation of inventories** and costs of production for reporting purposes, either internally or for statutory reasons.

- Providing an excellent device which enables **costs to be monitored**, reviewed and controlled by management.

- Enabling **exception reporting** through the use of variance analysis. Exception reporting allows management to exercise control with a lower degree of effort and less time than otherwise would be the case.

- Assisting in the **budgeting** process. Standards, once established in a business, become the common language by which performance is discussed and measured.

- Evaluating managerial performance.

- **Motivation** of staff by setting standards at levels to which staff feel able to respond. In this respect, standards have been characterised as 'ideal', 'attainable', 'current' and 'basic' as a way of categorising the different ways standards may be viewed in terms of their motivational impact.

- **Improving efficiency.** Standard setting is often viewed as a way of understanding the detail of a process through monitoring its important components. If standards are an accurate reflection of a process, then they can be used to highlight ways of improving efficiency and act as signals when the process becomes inefficient.

Once standards have been set, they cannot be assumed to be accurate over long periods of time. **Standards have to be reviewed** to enable the benefits of standard costing to continue. In this respect, standards must change with the changing practices of an organisation. For example, in environments which continuously seek greater efficiency and reduced costs of production, standards have to change to reflect such improvements. In fact, under such circumstances, standards can very quickly become out of date. In order to review standards, they must be continually assessed to ensure that the basis of their calculation still applies. Moreover, other purposes of standards are undermined, if they are not continually reviewed.

Thus, for example:

- The motivational impact of standards may no longer be effective if standards are out of date.

- Assessment of managerial performance becomes inaccurate.

- Reporting procedures are undermined.

- The credibility of standards in their role in assisting with the budget setting process is called into question.

- The fate of standard costing as a management tool is put at risk if management do not trust the standards. Alternative mechanisms for management control inevitably emerge which may be undesirable, untested and lack organisational approval.

(b) Financial statements of any sort are only an expression of organisational activities that can be measured. Many of the activities of an organisation cannot be easily measured, nor can its relations with various stakeholder groups who may have a non-financial interest in the organisation.

Non-finance objectives that may be difficult to measure or express in financial terms include:

1 Welfare of employees and management
- Health
- Safety
- Leisure and other services.

2 Welfare in the broader community
- Minimisation of intrusion into the community (e.g. traffic).

3 The provision of a service for which no charge is made, for example:
- Public hospitals
- Local or regional government services
- Housing
- Education.

4 The effective supply of goods or services (in addition to costs/efficiency issued) such as:
- Product or service quality
- Ensuring product or service supply (e.g. vital services)
- Timeliness
- After-sales support
- Customer/user satisfaction.

5 Fulfilment of product or services responsibilities: this is a very broad area and would cover many of the core activities of a business such as:
- Leadership in research and development
- Product development
- Maintenance of standards in goods or service provision
- Maintenance of good business and community relationships
- Employee training and support.

6 Support for community activities.

7 Minimisation of externalities (e.g. pollution and other socially responsible objectives).

8 Fulfilment of statutory or regulatory responsibilities.

Note: Only THREE objectives are required.

Whilst it may be argued that many of the objectives expressed have an impact on profitability or costs, they only do so in an indirect manner. Moreover, as with most organisational activities, non-financial objectives crystallises into financial issues given enough time. Thus, for example, poor service provision will ultimately lead to loss of customers in a competitive environment.

The range of stakeholders that may have an interest in an organisation's activities are wide and, because organisations have to respond to stakeholder interests, the non-financial responsibilities and hence range of objectives, is extended. In this respect, stakeholders create for organisations a range of non-financial issues that have to be addressed. If organisations are responsive then these issues become part of the culture of an organisation and hence part of its broader purposes. Interest in the organisation's activities from a non-financial perspective can arise even if the stake holder has a financial relationship with the organisation. Thus, the stakeholders who may have an interest might include the following:

- Shareholders
- Suppliers and trade payables
- Debt holders
- Customers
- Employees
- Pensioners and ex-employees
- Competitors
- Local community
- Broader national and international interests
- Government
- Regulatory authorities
- Tax authorities
- Special interest groups concerned with pollution, for example

Moreover, many of the stakeholders have common interests and hence stakeholders groupings can emerge.

43 PERSEUS CO – REVISION OF BASIC VARIANCES

Key answer tips

It is unlikely that a question in the F5 exam will just include variances covered in F2. The purpose of this question is to allow you to revise these 'basic variances'.

(a) **Workings**

Standard variable cost per unit		$
Materials:		
007	6 kilos at $12.25 per kilo	73.50
XL90	3 kilos at $3.20 per kilo	9.60
		83.10
Labour	4.5 hours at $8.40 per hour	37.80
		120.90

Standard usages:

Material 007	15,400 units should use (× 6)	92,400 kilos
Material XL90	15,400 units should use (× 3)	46,200 kilos
Labour	15,400 units should take (× 4.5)	69,300 hours

15,400 units of production and sale

	Actual		Standard	
	$	$	$	$
Sales	(at $138.25)	2,129,050	(at $140)	2,156,000
Costs				
Materials				
007		1,256,640	(15,400 × $73.50)	1,131,900
XL90		132,979	(15,400 × $9.60)	147,840
Labour		612,766	(15,400 × $37.80)	582,120
Fixed overheads		96,840		86,400
Total costs		2,099,225		1,948,260
Profit		29,825		207,740

(b)   **Reconciliation**

Workings

Sales price	$	
15,400 units should sell for	2,156,000	
They did sell for	2,129,050	
Sales price variance	26,950	(A)

Materials 007	kg	
15,400 units should use	92,400	
They did use	98,560	
Material 007 usage variance (kg)	6,160	(A)

Standard price/kg	$12.25	
Usage variance in $	$75,460	(A)

Materials 007	$	
98,560 kg should cost (× $12.25)	1,207,360	
They did cost	1,256,640	
Material price variance	49,280	(A)

Materials XL90	kg	
15,400 units should use	46,200	
They did use	42,350	
Material 007 usage variance (kg)	3,850	(F)

Standard price/kg	$3.20	
Usage variance in $	$12,320	(F)

Materials XL90	$	
42,350 kg should cost (× $3.20)	135,520	
They did cost	132,979	
Material price variance	2,541	(F)

Actual hours worked = $612,766 ÷ $8.65 = 70,840 hours

Labour efficiency	Hours	
15,400 units should take	69,300	
They did take	70,840	
Labour efficiency variance (hrs)	1,540	(A)

Standard rate/hour	$8.40	
Efficiency variance in $	$12,396	(A)

Labour rate	$	
70,840 hours should cost		
(× $8.40)	595,056	
They did cost	612,766	
Material price variance	17,710	(A)

	$	
Fixed overhead expenditure		
Budgeted fixed overhead costs	86,400	
Actual fixed overhead costs	96,840	
Expenditure variance	10,440	(A)

Reconciliation

			$
Standard profit on 15,400 units of sale, on previous page			207,740

	Fav	Adverse	
	$	$	
Variances:			
Sales price		26,950	
Materials 007 usage		75,460	
Materials XL90 usage	12,320		
Materials 007 price		49,280	
Materials XL90 price	2,541		
Labour efficiency		12,936	
Labour rate		17,710	
Fixed overhead expenditure variance		10,440	
	14,861	192,776	
Total variances			177,915 A
Actual profit			29,825

(c)   The causes of variances might be inter-related, and the reason why one variance is favourable could also help explain why another variance is adverse.

Using poor quality materials could result in a favourable price variance because of paying a lower price. The poor quality material could be the cause of both an adverse material usage variance and an adverse labour efficiency variance, because cheaper materials might be more difficult to work with, resulting in more rejects/spoilt work, or more waste.

If a higher grade of labour was used, compared with that which was planned, there would most certainly be an adverse labour rate variance. The higher skill level employed could well be the reason for a favourable labour efficiency variance and a favourable material usage variance, for example due to a lower number of rejects and less waste of materials.

(d)   Possible causes of an adverse labour rate variance include the following:

- The standard labour rate per hour may have been set too low.
- Employees may have been of a higher grade than standard, with a consequent increase in the hourly rate paid.
- There may have been an unexpected increase in the prevailing market rate of pay for employees with appropriate skills.
- Where bonuses are included as a part of direct labour costs, increased bonus payments may have been made, above the standard level expected.
- There may have been a change in the composition of the work force, which resulted in an increase in the average rate of pay.

Note: Only TWO possible causes are required.

44   CRUMBLY CAKES (JUNE 09 EXAM)

(a)

Tutorial note

The concept of 'controllability' is important for the exam. A common theme in exam questions is that a manager's bonus is linked to a number of variances. However, on analysis it often becomes apparent that the manager is not being assessed on the variances which they control, i.e. their assessment is unfair.

Production manager

Assessing the performance of the two managers is difficult in this situation. In a traditional sense the production manager has seriously over spent in March following the move to organic ingredients. He has a net adverse variance against his department of $2,300 in one month. No adjustment to the standards has been made to allow for the change to organic.

The manager has not only bought organically he has also changed the mix, increasing the input proportion of the more expensive ingredients. This may have contributed to the increased sales of cakes.

However, the decision to go organic has seen the sales of the business improve. We are told that the taste of the cakes should be better and that customers could perceive a health benefit. However, the production manager is allocated none of the favourable sales variances that result. If we assume that the improved sales are entirely as a result of the production manager's decision to change the ingredients then the overall net favourable variance is $7,700.

The production manager did appear to be operating within the original standard in February, indicating a well performing department. Indeed he will have earned a small bonus in that month.

Sales manager

A change to organic idea would need to be 'sold' to customers. It would presumably require a change of marketing and proper communication to customers. The sales manager would probably feel he has done a good job in March. It is debatable, however, whether he is entirely responsible for all of the favourable variances.

The move to organic certainly helped the sales manager as in February he seems to have failed to meet his targets.

Bonus scheme

The problem here is that the variances have to be allocated to one individual. The good sales variances have been allocated to the sales manager when in truth the production manager's decision to go organic appears to have been a good one and the driver of the business success. Responsibility accounting systems struggle to cope with 'joint' success stories, refuting in general a collective responsibility.

Under the current standards the production manager has seemingly no chance to make a bonus. The main problems appear to be the out-of-date standards and the fact that all sales variances are allocated to the sales manager, despite the root cause of the improved performance being at least in part the production manager's decision to go organic. The system does not appear fair.

General comments

It would appear that some sharing of the total variances is appropriate. This would be an inexact science and some negotiation would be needed.

One problem seems to be that the original standards were not changed following the decision to go organic. In this sense the variances reported are not really 'fair'. Standards should reflect achievable current targets and this is not the case here.

Key answer tips

The normal loss of 10% will only impact the material yield variance. The standard ingredients to make a cake must be adjusted from 0.36kg to 0.4kg. However, even if the normal loss had been ignored a good mark could still have been obtained in this exam question.

(b)
Flour

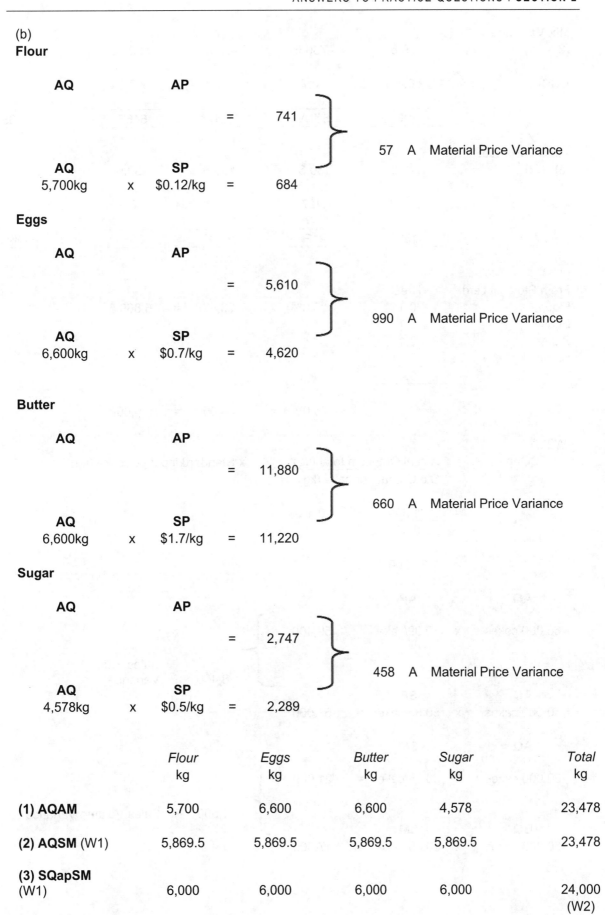

	AQ		AP			
			=	741		
					57	A	Material Price Variance
	AQ		**SP**			
	5,700kg	x	$0.12/kg	=	684	

Eggs

	AQ		AP			
			=	5,610		
					990	A	Material Price Variance
	AQ		**SP**			
	6,600kg	x	$0.7/kg	=	4,620	

Butter

	AQ		AP			
			=	11,880		
					660	A	Material Price Variance
	AQ		**SP**			
	6,600kg	x	$1.7/kg	=	11,220	

Sugar

	AQ		AP			
			=	2,747		
					458	A	Material Price Variance
	AQ		**SP**			
	4,578kg	x	$0.5/kg	=	2,289	

	Flour kg	Eggs kg	Butter kg	Sugar kg	Total kg
(1) AQAM	5,700	6,600	6,600	4,578	23,478
(2) AQSM (W1)	5,869.5	5,869.5	5,869.5	5,869.5	23,478
(3) SQapSM (W1)	6,000	6,000	6,000	6,000	24,000 (W2)

Mix Variance:

(2) – (1)	169.5	–730.5	–730.5	1,291.5	
x SP	x 0.12	x 0.7	x 1.7	x 0.5	
	20F	511A	1,242A	646F	1,087A

Yield Variance:

(3) – (2)	130.5	130.5	130.5	130.5	
x SP	x 0.12	x 0.7	x 1.7	x 0.5	
	16F	91F	222F	65F	394F

(W1)

From Std cost card:	litres				
Flour	0.1	25.0%	x	23,478	= 5,869.5
Eggs	0.1	"			
Butter	0.1	"			
Sugar	0.1	"			
	0.4				

	25.0%	x	24,000	=	6,000

(W2)

$$\text{SQap} = \frac{\text{Actual Output in total (kg)}}{\text{Std Output per cake (kg)}} \times \text{Standard input per cake (kg)}$$

$$= \frac{21,600}{0.36} \times 0.4$$

$$= 24,000$$

AQ		**AP**			
60,000 cakes	x	$0.99/cake	59,400		
				8,400 F	Sales Price Variance
AQ		**SP**			
60,000 cakes	x	$0.85/cake	=	51,000	

AQ		**SM**			
60,000 cakes	x	$0.35/cake	=	21,000	
				3,500 F	Sales Volume Variance
BQ		**SM**			
50,000 cakes	x	$0.35/cake	=	17,500	

Alternative variance calculations

Material price variances

Ingredient	Act price /kg	Std price /kg	Actual quantity kg	(AP – SP) × AQ MPV
Flour	0.13	0.12	5,700	57 (A)
Eggs	0.85	0.70	6,600	990 (A)
Butter	1.80	1.70	6,600	660 (A)
Sugar	0.60	0.50	4,578	458 (A)
Total				2,165 (A)

Material mix variance

Ingredient	Act mix	Std mix	Std price	Variance
Flour	5,700	5,870	0.12	20 (F)
Eggs	6,600	5,870	0.70	511 (A)
Butter	6,600	5,870	1.70	1,241 (A)
Sugar	4,578	5,870	0.50	646 (F)
Totals	23,478	23,478		1,086 (A)

Material yield variance

Actual yield	60,000 cakes
Standard yield (23,478/0.4)	58,695 cakes
Difference	1,305 cakes
Standard cost of a cake (W1)	$0.302
Yield variance (1,305 * 0.302)	394 Fav

Sales price variance

	Act price	Std price	Act volume	(AP – SP) * Act Vol variable	Adv or Fav
Cake	0.99	0.85	60,000	8,400	Fav

Sales volume contribution variance

Actual volume	60,000 cakes
Budget volume	50,000 cakes
Standard contribution	0.35
Variance (60,000 – 50,000) * 0.35 =	$3,500 Fav

(W1) Standard cost of a cake

Ingredients	Kg	$	Cost
Flour	0.10	$0.12 per kg	0.012
Eggs	0.10	$0.70 per kg	0.070
Butter	0.10	$1.70 per kg	0.170
Sugar	0.10	$0.50 per kg	0.050
Total input	0.40		0.302
Normal loss (10%)	(0.04)		
Standard weight/cost of a cake	0.36		0.302

ACCA marking scheme			
			Marks
(a)	Production manager assessment		2.0
	Sales manager assessment		2.0
	Bonus scheme comment		3.0
		Maximum	7.0
(b)	Price variance		3.0
	Mix variance		3.0
	Yield variance		3.0
	Sales price variance		2.0
	Sales volume variance		2.0
		Maximum	13
Total			20

Examiner's comments (extract)

This question should have had a familiar feel to it for many candidates as the pilot paper contained a question on the same topic.

Many candidates completely missed the point in part (a). If a business fundamentally changes its business process without altering the standard costs of the process it renders the variances that are produced meaningless.

Some candidates tried to discuss each variance in turn rather than carry out a performance assessment of each manager. This is not as effective a method. Some provided detailed definitions of each variance which I am afraid was not asked for and gained no marks.

Surprisingly a significant number of candidates thought the bonus scheme was fair, despite the fact that the production manager (who had the idea for the organic ingredients resulting in increased sales and margin)) lost all hope of a bonus. Motivation is a complex topic and credit was given for any sensible comments.

Part (b) was well done with many of the candidates scoring good marks. There are many methods of calculating these variances and the marking team gave credit for all consistently applied approaches.

45   MATERIAL VARIANCES

Key answer tips

Given that mix and yield variances are some of the few new variances in F5 compared to F2, you should expect them to feature regularly in the real exam. Ensure you learn the steps required.

(a)   **Standard cost per tonne of input**

			$
Material X:	60%	at $30 per tonne	18
Material Y:	40%	at $45 per tonne	18
	100%		36
Standard loss	10%		
Standard yield	90%		

Standard cost per standard tonne of output = $36/90% = $40.

Material price variance

	January $	February $	March $
Material Y:			
Actual price of $45 = standard price so material price variance =	Nil	Nil	Nil
Material X:			
Total cost of all materials	32,400	31,560	38,600
Less cost of material Y (360 × $45)	16,200	16,200	16,200
Actual cost of material X	16,200	15,360	22,400
Standard price of material X used:			
January: 540 tonnes should cost (× $30)	16,200		
February: 480 tonnes should cost (× $30)		14,400	
March: 700 tonnes should cost (× $30)			21,000
Material X price variance	Nil	960 (A)	1,400 (A)

Mix variances

January	Actual mix tonnes		Standard mix tonnes	Mix variance tonnes
Material X	540	(60%)	540	0
Material Y	360	(40%)	360	0
	900		900	0

February	Actual mix tonnes		Standard mix tonnes	Mix variance tonnes	Standard price $	Mix variance $
Material X	480	(60%)	504	24 (F)	30	720 (F)
Material Y	360	(40%)	336	24 (A)	45	1,080 (A)
	840		840			360 (A)

March	Actual mix tonnes		Standard mix tonnes	Mix variance tonnes	Standard price $	Mix variance $
Material X	700	(60%)	636	64 (A)	30	1,920 (A)
Material Y	360	(40%)	424	64 (F)	45	2,880 (F)
	1,060		1,060			960 (F)

Yield variances

January

810 tonnes of output	should use (× 10/9)	900	tonnes
	did use (540 + 360)	900	tonnes
Yield variance		0	tonnes

February

765 tonnes of output	should use (× 10/9)	850	tonnes
	did use (480 + 360)	840	tonnes
Yield variance		10	tonnes (F)
Standard price per tonne of input		$36	
Yield variance in $		$360	(F)

March

900 tonnes of output	should use (× 10/9)	1,000	tonnes
	did use (700 + 360)	1,060	tonnes
Yield variance		60	tonnes (A)
Standard price per tonne of input		$36	
Yield variance in $		$2,160	(A)

Summary

	January		February		March	
	$	$	$	$	$	$
Material price variance						
Material X		0		960 (A)		1,400 (A)
Material Y		0		0		0
Materials mix variance	0		360 (A)		960 (F)	
Materials yield variance	0		360 (F)		2,160 (A)	
Materials usage variance		0		0		1,200 (A)
Total materials variances		0		960 (A)		2,600 (A)

Tutorial note

In the time available, it should be permissible to calculate the usage variance as the sum of the mix and yield variances. Alternatively you could calculate the usage variances from first principles.

(b)   Production in January is exactly according to standard. The price of Y has remained at standard for the whole period. The price of X is $2 ($960/480) in excess of standard in February and $2 ($1,400/700) in excess of standard in March. If this continues, the standard price of X will need to be increased. The proportion of X in the mix changed to 57% (480/840) and 66% (700/1,060) in February and March respectively. The cost increase in February, shown as an adverse mix variance of $360, is caused by dearer Y being used instead of cheaper X. There is an improvement in yield in February. The increased yield could be viewed as an abnormal gain of 9 tonnes [(840 × 90% – 765)] with a standard value of (× $40 =) $360. There is also a reduction in volume produced in February.

In March, the significant increase in the usage proportion of X (which is cheaper) has caused a favourable mix variance but may also have contributed to the large adverse yield variance. Production in March is considerably higher than for January and February – this may be a reason for the adverse yield variance.

Overall, there appears to be a link between mix and yield. If the proportion of Y is increased, causing an adverse mix variance since Y is more expensive, the yield is improved – as occurred in February. The opposite took place in March.

There could also be a link between yield and the volume of production – in February production is low and yield is high, whereas in March production is high and yield is low.

46 CARAT

Key answer tips

This question is largely a straightforward test of your ability to calculate variances, including material mix and yield variances, and labour variances when idle time is recorded. However, do not overlook part (c) of the question: there are 7 marks available for a description of the different types of standard cost. The answer here describes a basic, current, attainable and ideal standard. It would also be relevant to answer the question by discussing 'ex post' and 'ex ante' standards, as a means of separating planning and operational variances.

(a)   **Standard cost and standard contribution**

	$	$
Standard sales price		12.00
Material A: (2.5 × $1.70)	4.25	
Material B: (1.5 × $1.20)	1.80	
Labour: (0.45 × $6.00)	2.70	
		8.75
Contribution per unit		3.25

Calculation of variances

(i)   **Sales variances**

	$	
48,000 units should sell for (× $12)	576,000	
They did sell for	580,800	
Sales price variance	**4,800**	**(F)**

	Units	
Budgeted sales volume	50,000	
Actual sales volume	48,000	
Sales volume variance	2,000	(A)

Standard contribution/unit	$3.25	
Sales volume contribution variance	**$6,500**	**(A)**

(ii) **Materials variances**

Material A price variance	$
121,951 kg should cost (× $1.70)	207,317
They did cost	200,000
Material A price variance	**7,317** (F)

Material B price variance	$
67,200 kg should cost (× $1.20)	80,640
They did cost	84,000
Material A price variance	**3,360** (A)

Mix variance

The standard mix is 2.5kg of A for each 1.5kg of B, i.e. 62.5% Material A and 37.5% Material B.

	Actual quantities used		Actual quantities in standard mix	Mix variance	Std price	Mix variance
	kg		kg	kg	$	$
Material A	121,951	(62.5%)	118,219	3,732 (A)	1.70	6,344 (A)
Material B	67,200	(37.5%)	70,932	3,732 (F)	1.20	4,478 (F)
	189,151		189,151			**1,866 (A)**

Yield variance

The standard cost per kg of material for A and B together is:

($4.25 + $1.80)/(2.5kg + 1.5kg) = $6.05/4kg = $1.5125 per kg.

	kg
48,000 units of ZP should use (× 4kg)	192,000
They did use	189,151
Total yield variance	2,849 (F)

Standard cost per kg	$1.5125
Material yield variance	$4,309 **(F)**

(iii) **Labour variances**

	$
19,200 hours should cost (× $6.00)	115,200
They did cost	117,120
Labour rate variance	1,920 (A)

Idle time variance = (19,200 − 18,900) hours = 300 hours (A).

At the standard rate per hour, the idle time variance =

300 hours (A) × $6.00 = **$1,800 (A).**

Labour efficiency variance	Hours	
48,000 units of ZP should take (× 0.45 hours)	21,600	
They did use	18,900	
Total yield variance	2,700	(F)
Standard rate/hour	$6	
Labour efficiency variance	$16,200	**(F)**

(b)   The **favourable material A price variance** indicates that the actual price per kilogram was less than standard. Possible explanations include buying lower quality material, buying larger quantities of material A and thereby gaining bulk purchase discounts, a change of supplier, and using an out-of-date standard.

The **adverse material B price variance** indicates that the actual price per kilogram was higher than standard. Possible explanations include buying higher quality material, buying smaller quantities of material B and thereby losing bulk purchase discounts, a change of supplier, and using an out-of-date standard.

The **adverse materials mix variance** indicates that more of the more expensive material A was used in the actual input than indicated by the standard mix. The favourable material A price variance suggests this may be due to the use of poorer quality material (hence more was needed than in the standard mix), or it might be that more material A was used because it was cheaper than expected. It could also be due to deciding to use less material B due to its increase in price (adverse price variance).

The **favourable material yield variance** indicates that more output was produced from the quantity of material used than expected by the standard. This increase in yield is unlikely to be due to the use of poorer quality material A but could be due to better quality material B. It is more likely, however, to be the result of employing more skilled labour, or introducing more efficient working practices.

It is only appropriate to calculate and interpret material mix and yield variances if quantities in the standard mix can be varied.

The **unfavourable labour rate variance** indicates that the actual hourly rate paid was higher than standard. Possible explanations for this include hiring staff with more experience and paying them more (this is consistent with the favourable overall direct material variance), or implementing an unexpected pay increase. The **favourable labour efficiency variance** shows that fewer hours were worked than standard. Possible explanations include the effect of staff training, the use of better quality material (possibly on Material B rather than on Material A), employees gaining experience of the production process, and introducing more efficient production methods. The **adverse idle time variance** may be due to machine breakdowns; or a higher rate of production arising from more efficient working (assuming employees are paid a fixed number of hours per week).

(c)   The **theory of motivation** suggests that having a clearly defined target results in better performance than having no target at all, that targets need to be accepted by the staff involved, and that more demanding targets increase motivation provided they remain accepted. It is against this background that basic, ideal, current and attainable standards can be discussed.

A **basic standard** is one that remains unchanged for several years and is used to show trends over time. Basic standards may become increasingly easy to achieve as time passes and hence, being undemanding, may have a negative impact on motivation. Standards that are easy to achieve will give employees little to aim at.

Ideal standards represent the outcome that can be achieved under perfect operating conditions, with no wastage, inefficiency or machine breakdowns. Since perfect operating conditions are unlikely to occur for any significant period, ideal standards will be very demanding and are unlikely to be accepted as targets by the staff involved as they are unlikely to be achieved. Using ideal standards as targets is therefore likely to have a negative effect on employee motivation.

Current standards are based on current operating conditions and incorporate current levels of wastage, inefficiency and machine breakdown. If used as targets, current standards will not improve performance beyond its current level and their impact on motivation will be a neutral one or a negative one since employees may feel unmotivated due to the lack of challenge.

Attainable standards are those that can be achieved if operating conditions conform to the best that can be practically achieved in terms of material use, efficiency and machine performance. Attainable standards are likely to be more demanding than current standards and so will have a positive effect on employee motivation, provided that employees accept them as achievable.

47   CHAFF CO (JUNE 08 EXAM)

Key answer tips

This is typical of the examiner's approach. Where possible, he intends to separate calculations from discussion. This is not a difficult question but a planned structure is required to score a good mark.

In part (a) use a heading for each manager and aim for 2 to 4 separate and succinct points for each manager. Discuss each of the variances that the manager may have impacted. An overall assessment of each individual manager could have been made by adding together each of the individual variances impacted.

In part (b) ensure you show your workings clearly, in particular to show how you have dealt with the expected idle time

(a)   When assessing variances it is important to consider the whole picture and the interrelationships that exist. In Chaff there appears to be doubt about the wisdom of some of the decisions that have been made. Favourable variances have been applauded and adverse variances criticised and the managers in charge dispute the challenge to their actions.

Purchasing manager.

The purchasing manager has clearly bought a cheaper product, saving $48,000. The cause of this is not specified and it could be due to good buying or negotiation, reductions in quality or changes in overall market conditions. We are told the market for buying seeds is stable, so there is more likely to be an internal reason for the problem. The material usage variance is significantly adverse, indicating much more waste than is normal has occurred in month 1. This suggests that the quality of the seed bought was poor and as a result a $52,000 excess loss has occurred. It is possible that the waste was caused by the labour force working poorly or too quickly and this has to be considered.

The sales price achieved is also well down on standard with the sales price variance showing an $85,000 loss of revenue and (therefore) profit. We are told that the market for sales of brown rice is stable and so it is reasonable to presume that the fall in sales price achieved is as a result of internal quality issues rather than general price falls. The purchasing manager of the only ingredient may well be responsible for this fall in quality. This may have also led to a fall in the volume of sales, another $21,000 of adverse variance.

In conclusion the purchasing manager appears mainly responsible for a loss of $110,000* taking the four variances above together.

* ($85,000 + $52,000 + $21,000 − $48,000)

Production director.

The production director has increased wage rates and this has cost an extra $15,000 in month 1. However one could argue that this wage increase has had a motivational effect on the labour force. The labour efficiency variance is $18,000 favourable; and so it is possible that a wage rise has encouraged the labour force to work harder. Academic evidence suggests that this effect might only be temporary as workers get used to the new level of wages.

Equally the amount of idle time has reduced considerably, with a favourable variance of $12,000 resulting. Again it is possible that the better motivated labour force has been more willing to work than before. Idle time can have many causes, including, material shortages or machine breakdowns. However, we are told the machines are running well and the buyer has bought enough rice seeds.

In conclusion the increase in the wage rate did cost more money but it may have improved morale and enhanced productivity. The total of the three variances above is $15,000* Fav. *($18,000 + $12,000 − $15,000)

Maintenance manager.

The maintenance manager has decided to delay the annual maintenance of the machines and this has saved $8,000. This will increase profits in the short term but could have disastrous consequences later. In this case only time will tell. If the machines breakdown before the next maintenance then lost production and sales could result.

The maintenance manager has only *delayed* the spend and not prevented it altogether. A saving of $8,000 as suggested by the variance has not been made. It is also possible that the adverse variable overhead expenditure variance has been at least partly caused by poor machine maintenance.

The variance calculated is not the saving made as it represents a timing difference only. The calculation also ignores the risks involved.

(b)   The standard contribution is given, but could be calculated as follows (not required by the question but shown as a proof):

	$	$
Sales price		240
Less:		
Rice seed (1.4 Tonnes × $60/tonne)	84	
Labour (2 hours × $20/hr)	40	
Variable overhead (2 hours × $30/hr)	60	
Marginal costs of production		184
Standard contribution		56

The standard labour charge needs to be adjusted to reflect the cost to the business of the idle time. It is possible to adjust the time spent per unit or the rate per hour. In both cases the adjustment would be to multiply by 10/9 – a 10% adjustment. In the case above the rate per hour has been adjusted to $18 × 10/9 = $20/hr. (Both approaches would gain full marks.)

Variances

1   Sales price: (225 – 240)8,000 = 120,000 Adv

2   Sales volume: (8,000 – 8,400)56 = 22,400 Adv

3   Material price: $\frac{660,000}{12,000} \times 60 \ \times 12,000 = 60,000$ Fav

4   Material usage: (12,000 – 11,200*)60 = 48,000 Adv

     *(8,000 × 1.4 = 11,200)

5   Labour rate: (19.20 – 18)15,800 = 18,960 Adv

6   Labour efficiency: (15,000 – 16,000)20 = 20,000 Fav

7   Idle time: (800 – 1,580*)20 = 15,600 Fav

     *10% of 15,800

8   Variable overhead expenditure: $\frac{480,000}{15,000} \times \ 30 \ \times 15,000 = 30,000$ Adv

9   Variable overhead efficiency variance: (15,000 – 16,000)30 = 30,000 Fav

Alternative calculations if standard **hours** adjusted for expected idle time and not the rate.

Standard cost (2 hours × 10/9) × $18 = $40 per tonne

Or 2.222 hours × $18 = $40 per tonne

Rate variance as above = 18,960 Adv

Idle time: (800 – 1,580)18 = 14,040 Fav

Efficiency variance: (15,000 – 16,197.77777*)18 = 21,560 Fav

* (standard time allowed less standard idle time)

Standard time is 8,000 tonnes × 2.222 hours = 17,777.777 hours

Standard idle time is 10% of 15,800 = 1,580 hours

Therefore expected working hours is 17,777.777 – 1,580 = 16,197.777 hours

	AQ		AP						
					1,800,000				
							120,000	A	Sales Price Variance
	AQ		**SP**						
	8,000 tonnes	x	$240/t	=	1,920,000				
	AQ		**SM**						
	8,000 tonnes	x	$56/t	=	448,000				
							22,400	A	Sales Volume Variance
	BQ		**SM**						
	8,400 tonnes	x	$56/t	=	470,400				
	AQ		**AP**						
				=	660,000				
							60,000	F	Material Price Variance
	AQ		**SP**						
	12,000 tonnes	x	$60/t	=	720,000				
							48,000	A	Material Usage Variance
	SQap		**SP**						
	1.4t x 8,000t	x	$60/t	=	672,000				
	AH		**AR**						
				=	303,360				
							18,960	A	Labour Rate Variance
	AH paid		**SR**						
	15,800 hrs	x	$18/hr	=	284,400				
							15,600	F	Excess Idle Time Variance
	AH worked		**SGR**						
	15,000 hrs	x	18/0.9	=	300,000				
							20,000	F	Labour Productive Efficiency Variance
	SHap		**SGR**						
	2hrs x 8,000t	x	18/0.9	=	320,000				
	AH		**AR**						
		x		=	480,000				
							30,000	A	Variable Overhead Expenditure Variance
	AH		**SR**						
	15,000 hrs	x	$30/hr	=	450,000				
							30,000	F	Variable Overhead Efficiency Variance
	SHap		**SR**						

2hrs x 8,000t   x $30/hr   =   480,000

Actual Cost   200,000   }   10,000   F   Fixed Overhead Expenditure Variance

Budgeted Cost   210,000

> *Note:* The original question also included the requirement to reconcile actual and budgeted profit.
>
> In order to reconcile the budget profit to the actual profit, both these profits need to be calculated and an operating statement prepared (see workings below). This would have required the following additional work.

Budgeted profit statement for month 2

	$	$
Sales (8400u × $240/u)		2,016,000
Less:		
Rice seed (1.4 tonnes × $60/tonne × 8,400 tonnes)	705,600	
Labour (2 hours × $20/hr × 8,400 tonnes)	336,000	
Variable overhead (2 hours × $30/hr × 8,400 tonnes)	504,000	
Marginal costs of production		1,545,600
Contribution		470,400
Less Fixed costs		210,000
Budget profit		260,400

Actual profit for month 2

	$	$
Sales		1,800,000
Less:		
Rice seed	660,000	
Labour	303,360	
Variable overhead	480,000	
Marginal costs of production		1,443,360
Contribution		356,640
Less Fixed costs		200,000
Actual profit		156,640

Operating statement for month 2

	$	$	$
Budget contribution			470,400
Variances:	*Adverse*	*Favourable*	
Sales price	120,000		
Sales volume	22,400		
			142,400
			328,000
Material price		60,000	
Material usage	48,000		
Labour rate	18,960		
Labour efficiency		20,000	
Idle time		15,600	
Variable overhead efficiency		30,000	
Variable overhead expenditure	30,000		
	96,960	125,600	28,640
Actual contribution			356,640
Budget fixed cost		210,000	
Less: Fixed cost expenditure variance		10,000	
Actual fixed cost			200,000
Actual profit			156,640

ACCA marking scheme		
		Marks
(a)	Buyer (poor quality, usage, sales issue)	3
	Production director (motivation, efficiency and idle time issue)	3
	Administration manager (short-termism, timing only)	3
		9
(b)	Sales price/ volume variance (1mark each)	2
	Material price/ usage variance (1 mark each)	2
	Labour rate variance	1
	Labour efficiency variance	2
	Idle time variance	2
	Variable overhead expenditure variance	1
	Variable overhead efficiency variance	1
	Fixed overhead expenditure variance	1
	maximum	11
	Total	20

Walk in the footsteps of a top tutor

(a)

Key answer tips

For part (a) there are only 16 minutes available. By the time the question has been read, annotated and the answer planned, there will probably only be 10 minutes remaining. However, all the hard thinking work has been done during the planning stage. All that is left to do is to write up a succinct and relevant answer. Below is an example of what could be achieved in the ten minutes remaining.

Purchasing manager

Comment on performance:

- The purchasing manager has purchased cheaper seeds from another supplier. This has resulted in a favourable material price variance.

- However, although the new supplier is cheaper, quality may have been impacted. Poor quality may have resulted in more wastage and hence an adverse material usage variance.

- In addition, the quality of the final product may have been lower and as a result lower sales volumes (adverse sales price variance) and lower sales prices achieved (adverse sales volume variance).

Conclusion on performance:

- Based on the analysis above the total of the variances under the control of the purchasing manager is $110,000 adv. Therefore, his performance has been poor and his decision has not benefited the company.

Note: Total variance of $110,000 adv = material price $48,000 fav + material usage $52,000 adv + sales price variance $85,000 adv + sales volume variance $21,000 adv.

Production manager

Comment on performance:

- The production manager's decision to increase wage rates has resulted in an adverse labour rate variance of $15,000.

- However, the driving force for the wage increase was to increase employee morale. This appears to have worked since employees are more efficient (labour efficiency variance $18,000 fav) and have been taking fewer breaks from work (labour idle time variance of $12,000 fav).

- Variable overhead efficiency is linked to labour efficiency and as a result of improved labour efficiency the variable overhead efficiency variance is $30,000 fav.

Conclusion on performance:

- Based on the analysis above the total of the variances under the control of the purchasing manager is $45,000 fav. It appears that the director has performed well and that his decision to increase wages was a good one.

Note: Total variance of $45,000 fav = labour rate of $15,000 adv + labour efficiency of $18,000 fav + labour idle time $12,000 fav + variable overhead efficiency $30,000 fav.

Maintenance manager

Comment on performance:

- The maintenance manager took the decision to delay machine maintenance for another month. This resulted in a favourable fixed overhead expenditure variance of $8,000.

- However, this variance represents a timing difference only and delaying the maintenance may have resulted in the adverse variable overhead expenditure variance of $18,000.

Conclusion on performance:

- Based on the analysis above the total of the variances under the control of the purchasing manager is $10,000 adv. The manager's decision was poor and he has not performed well.

Note: Total variance of $10,000 adv = Fixed overhead expenditure of $8,000 fav + variable overhead expenditure of $18,000 adv.

(b)

Key answer tips

In part (b) you need to work methodically through each variance, setting up clear workings. Don't get stuck on one variance but move on if unsure. The aim is to complete the question and get most of it right.

(W1) **Sales price variance**

	$
Actual sales of 8,000 tonnes should sell for $240 each	1,920,000
Actual sales of 8,000 tonnes did sell for	1,800,000
Variance	120,000 A

(W2) **Sales volume variance**

	Tonnes
Budgeted sales	8,400
Actual sales	8,000
Variance	400 A

400A tonnes × standard contribution of $56 per tonne = <u>$22,400 A</u>

Note: Standard contribution =   Selling price $240

Less material of $84 ($60 × 1.4 tonnes)

Less labour of $40 ($18 × 2 hours × 100/90)

Less variable overhead of $60 ($30 × 2 hours)

(W3) Material price variance

	$
Actual material of 12,000 tonnes should cost $60 per tonne	720,000
Actual material of 12,000 tonnes did cost	660,000
Variance	60,000 F

(W4) Material usage variance

	Tonnes
Actual production of 8,000 tonnes should use 1.4 tonnes of rice seed/ tonne rice	11,200
Actual production of 8,000 tonnes did use	12,000
Variance	800 A

800A tonnes × standard cost per tonne of $60 = $48,000 A

(W5) Labour rate variance

	$
Actual hours of 15,800 should cost $18 per hour	284,400
Actual hours of 15,800 did cost	303,360
Variance	18,960 A

(W6) Labour efficiency variance (labour productive efficiency)

	Hours
Actual production of 8,000 tonnes should take 2 hours per tonne	16,000
Actual production of 8,000 tonnes did take	15,000
Variance	1,000 F

1,000 F hours × standard cost per hour of $20 (i.e. $18 × 100/90) = $20,000 F

(W7) Labour idle time variance (labour excess idle time)

	Hours
Expected idle time is 10% of 15,800 hours	1,580
Actual idle time is 15,800 hours paid – 15,000 hours worked	800
Variance	780 F

780F × standard cost per hour of $20 (include idle time) = <u>$15,600 F</u>

Note: there are other ways to deal with the idle time.

(W8) Variable overhead expenditure variance

	$
Actual labour hours worked of 15,000 should cost $30 per hour	450,000
Actual labour hours of 15,000 did cost	480,000
Variance	30,000 A

(W9) Variable overhead efficiency variance

Labour efficiency variance of 1,000F hours × standard cost of $30 per hour = <u>$30,000 F</u>

(W10) Fixed overhead expenditure variance

	$
Budgeted fixed cost	210,000
Actual fixed cost	200,000
Variance	10,000 F

Alternative answer

Sales Volume Variance

	Actual	8000
	Standard	8400
		400 A x 240 sales price = 96,000 A

Sales Price Variance

	Actual	240
	Standard	225
		15 A x 8000 = 120,000 A

Rice Seeds

AA 12000 x price	= 660,000	
		60,000 F material Price
AS 12000 x 60	= 720,000	
		48,000 A material Usage
SS (1.4 x 8000) x 60	= 672,000	

Labour

AA 15,800 x price	= 303,360	
		18,960 A Labour Rate
AS 15,800 x 18	= 284,400	
		15,600 F Idle time
AS 15,000 x 18/0.9	= 300,000	
		20,000 F Labour efficiency
SS (8000 x 2) x18/0.9	= 320,000	

Variable overhead

AA 15,000 x actual	= 480,000	
		30,000 A Variable expenditure
AS 15,000 x 30	= 450.000	
		30,000 F Variable efficiency
SS (8000 x 2) x 30	= 480,000	

Fixed Overhead

Expenditure	actual	200,000
	Budget	210,000
		10,000 F

48 WC

Tutorial note

For part (a): The information given in the question suggests that an OAR of $2,500 per job is used to absorb central services costs. This means that there is under absorbed central services cost of 17.5 – 6.5 – 6.25 = $4.75m. There is no indication that this is charged to profit centres but total costs must be shown to arrive at total profit.

(a)

Budget	Kitchens	Bathrooms	Total
	$	$	$
Sales	40	14	54
Direct costs	(22)	(6)	(28)
Central services	(10)	(5)	(15)
Budget profit	8	3	11

Actual	Kitchens	Bathrooms	Total
	$	$	$
Sales	33.8	15.25	49.05
Direct costs	(20.8)	(6.75)	(27.55)
Central services	(6.5)	(6.25)	(17.5)
Actual profit	6.5	2.25	4

(b)

	Kitchens	Bathrooms	Total
	$	$	$
Standard selling price	10,000	7,000	
Actual selling price	13,000	6,100	
	3,000 F	900 A	
× Actual no. of units sold	× 2,600	× 2,500	
	7,800,000 F	2,250,000 A	5,550,000 F

Sales mix profit variances

	Actual Sales	Standard Mix of Actual sales	Difference	Value at standard profit	Mix Variance $m
Kitchens	2,600	3,400	800 A	$2,000	1.6 A
Bathrooms	2,500	1,700	800 F	$1,500	1.2 F
	5,100	5,100			0.4 A

Sales quantity profit variances

	Budget Sales	Standard Mix of Actual sales	Quantity Variance	Value at standard profit	Mix Variance $
Kitchens	4,000	3,400	600 A	$2,000	1.20 A
Bathrooms	2,000	1,700	300 A	$1,500	0.45 A
	6,000	5,100			1.65 A

Check

Sales volume variances

Kitchens $(4,000 - 2,600) \times \$2,000 = \$2.8m$ A

Bathrooms $(2,000 - 2,500) \times \$1,500 = \$0.75m$ F   Total $2.05m

Sales volume variance   = mix variance + quantity variance

    $= \$0.4m$ A $+ \$1.65m$ A $= \$2.05$ m

(c)

			$m
Budgeted profit (from part a)			11
	F	A	
	($m)	($m)	
Sales mix variance (from part b)			
– kitchens		1.6	
– bathrooms	1.2		
Sales quantity variance (part b)			
– kitchens		1.2	
– bathrooms		0.45	
Sales price variances (part b)			
– kitchens	7.8		
– bathrooms		2.25	
Direct costs (W1)			
– kitchens		6.5	
– bathrooms	0.75		
Central services (W2)			
– volume (kitchens)		3.5	
– volume (bathrooms)	1.25		
– expenditure		2.5	
	11	18	7 A
Actual profit (from part a)			4

Workings

(W1) Direct cost variances

Kitchens   2,600 × (5,500 – 8,000) = $6.5m A

Bathrooms 2,500 × (3,000 – 2,700) = $0.75m F

(W2) Central services volume variances

Kitchens (4,000 – 2,600) × $2,500 = $3.5m A

Bathrooms (2,500 – 2,000) × $2,500 = $1.25m F

Central services expenditure variance = $15m – $17.5m = $2.5m A

(d)   (Actual profit at $4m is $7m below budgeted profit, a shortfall of 64%). The main causes are as follows:

–   an overall fall in the total volume of sales resulting in a sales quantity variance of $1.65m A. The lower than expected volume has also resulted in central services costs being under absorbed as shown by the volume variances (net impact $2.25A).

–   the sales mix has also switched from more profitable kitchens to less profitable bathrooms and this is reflected in the sales mix variance of $0.4m A.

–   the impact of the lower volume of kitchen sales has been partially offset by the favourable price variance for kitchens. It is possible that a higher proportion of jobs are of the highly customised category rather than the 'off the shelf' packages. This has led to higher average prices being charged but also higher direct costs being incurred. The opposite seems to have occurred with bathrooms.

–   Central services costs have exceeded budget by $2.5m. This may be due to higher costs incurred designing customised jobs.

It would be worth investigating whether the extra price charged for customised designs is covering all of the additional costs incurred. Higher prices may be necessary or better control of costs.

49   STICKY WICKET (JUNE 10 EXAM)

(a)   The performance of the production director could be looked at considering each decision in turn.

The new wood supplier: The wood was certainly cheaper than the standard saving $5,100 on the standard the concern though might be poor quality. The usage variance shows that the waste levels of wood are worse than standard. It is possible that the lower grade labour could have contributed to the waste level but since both decisions rest with the same person the performance consequences are the same. The overall effect of this is an adverse variance of $2,400, so taking the two variances together it looks like a poor decision. As the new labour is trained it could be that the wood usage improves and so we will have to wait to be sure.

The impact that the new wood might have had on sales cannot be ignored. No one department within a business can be viewed in isolation to another. Sales are down and returns are up. This could easily be due to poor quality wood inputs. If SW operates at the high quality end of the market then sourcing cheaper wood is risky if the quality reduces as a result.

The lower grade of labour used: SW uses traditional manual techniques and this would normally require skilled labour. The labour was certainly paid less, saving the company $43,600 in wages. However, with adverse efficiency and idle time of a total of $54,200 they actually cost the business money overall in the first month. The efficiency variance tells us that it took longer to produce the bats than expected. The new labour was being trained in April 2010 and so it is possible that the situation will improve next month. The learning curve principle would probably apply here and so we could expect the average time per bat to be less in May 2010 than it was in April 2010.

(b) Variance for May 2010:

Material price variance ($196,000/40,000 – 5) × 40,000 = $4,000 Fav

Material usage variance (40,000 – (19,200 × 2)) × $5/kg = $8,000 Adv

Labour rate variance ($694,000/62,000 – 12) × 62,000 = 50,000 Fav

Labour efficiency variance (61,500 – 57,600) × 12 = 46,800 Adv

Labour idle time variance 500 × 12 = 6,000 Adv

Sales price variance (68 – 65) × 18,000 = 54,000 Adv

Sales volume contribution variance (18,000 – 19,000) × 22 = 22,000 Adv

ACCA marking scheme		Marks
(a)	Assessment of wood decision	2·5
	Assessment of labour decision	2·5
	Sales consequences	2
	Total	7
(b)	MPV	2
	MUV	2
	LRV	2
	LEV	2
	LIT	1
	SPV	2
	SVCV	2
		13
	Total	20

50   SPIKE CO (DEC 07 EXAM)

Key answer tips

In part (a) eight marks may seem overwhelming at first but a good plan should make this more manageable. There are two separate areas to discuss, namely labour and materials. The eight marks can therefore be split into four marks for each area. Within each four mark section it should be possible to discuss three arguments for/ against budget revision (3 marks) and to conclude (1 mark). Breaking the question down like this makes it much more manageable and increases the chance of success.

In part (b) there are four marks available for the calculation of basic variances. This is core knowledge and candidates must be able to score well here.

Part (c) is trickier but candidates will not fail if they can't answer this requirement. However, the examiner will continue to test some of the more advanced variances and so practice these before the exam.

In part (d) four marks will be available for discussing each variance in terms of business performance. Four variances were calculated in parts (b) and (c) and so there will be one mark for discussing each variance.

(a)   **Materials**

Arguments in favour of allowing a revision:

- The nature of the problem is outside the control of the organisation. The supplier went in to liquidation; it is doubtful that Spike Limited could have expected this or prevented it from happening.

- The buyer, knowing that budget revisions are common, is likely to see the liquidation as outside his control and hence expect a revision to be allowed. He may see it as unjust if this is not the case and this can be demoralising.

Arguments against allowing a budget revision:

- There is evidence that the buyer panicked a little in response to the liquidation. He may have accepted the first offer that became available (without negotiation) and therefore incurred more cost than was necessary.

- A cheaper, more local supplier may well have been available, so it could be argued that the extra delivery cost need not have been incurred. This could be said to have been an operational error.

Conclusion:

The cause of this problem (liquidation) is outside the control of the organisation and this is the prime cause of the overspend. Urgent problems need urgent solutions and a buyer should not be penalised in this case. A budget revision should be allowed.

Labour

Arguments in favour of allowing a revision:

- The board made this decision, not the departmental manager. It could be argued that the extra cost on the department's budget is outside their control.

Arguments against allowing a budget revision:

- This decision is entirely within the control of the organisation as a whole. As such, it would fall under the definition of an operational decision. It is not usual to allow a revision in these circumstances.
- It is stated in the question that the departmental manager complained in his board report that the staff level needed improving. It appears that he got his wish and the board could be said to have merely approved the change.
- The department will have benefited from the productivity increases that may have resulted in the change of policy. If the department takes the benefit then perhaps they should take the increased costs as well.

Conclusion:

This is primarily an operational decision that the departmental manager agreed with and indeed suggested in his board report. No budget revision should be allowed.

An alternative view is that the board made the final decision and as such the policy change was outside the direct control of the departmental manager. In this case a budget revision would be allowed.

(b)   **Total sales variances**

Sales price variance	= (Actual SP – Std SP) × Act sales volume
	= (16.40 – 17.00) × 176,000
	= $105,600 (Adverse)
Sales volume variance	= (Actual sales volume – Budget sales volume) × Std contribution
	= (176,000 – 180,000) × 7
	= $28,000 (Adverse)

(c)   **Market size and share variances**

Market size variance	= (Revised sales volume – budget sales volume) × Std contribution
	= (160,000 – 180,000) × 7
	= $140,000 (Adverse)
Market share variance	= (Actual sales volume – revised sales volume) × Std contribution
	= (176,000 – 160,000) × 7
	= $112,000 (Favourable)

(d)   **Comment on sales performance**

Sales price

The biggest issue seems to be the decision to reduce the sales price from $17.00 down to $16.40. This 'lost' $105,600 of revenue on sales made compared to the standard price.

It seems likely that the business is under pressure on sales due to the increased popularity of electronic diaries. As such, they may have felt that they had to reduce prices to sustain sales at even the level they achieved.

Volume

The analysis of sales volume into market size and share shows the usefulness of planning and operational variances. Overall, the sales level of the business is down by 4,000 units, losing the business $28,000 of contribution or profit. This calculation does not in itself explain how the sales department of the business has performed.

In the face of a shrinking market they seem to have performed well. The revised level of sales (allowing for the shrinking market) is 160,000 units and the business managed to beat this level comfortably by selling 176,000 units in the period.

As mentioned above, the reducing price could have contributed to the maintenance of the sales level. Additionally, the improved quality of support staff may have helped maintain the sales level. Equally the actions of competitors are relevant to how the business has performed. If competitors have been active then merely maintaining sales could be seen as an achievement.

Spike should be concerned that its market is shrinking.

Note: The original question also asked for a general discussion regarding when budget revisions were allowable. The suggested answer to this requirement was as follows:

A budget forms the basis of many performance management systems. Once set, it can be compared to the actual results of an organisation to assess performance. A change to the budget can be allowed in some circumstances but these must be carefully controlled if abuse is to be prevented.

Allow budget revisions when something has happened that is beyond the control of the organisation which renders the original budget inappropriate for use as a performance management tool.

These adjustments should be approved by senior management who should attempt to take an objective and independent view.

Disallow budget revisions for operational issues. Any item that is within the operational control of an organisation should not be adjusted.

This type of decision is often complicated and each case should be viewed on its merits.

The direction of any variance (adverse or favourable) is not relevant in this decision.

ACCA marking scheme

		Marks
(a)	Materials discussion	3
	Conclusion	1
	Labour discussion	3
	Conclusion	1
		8
(b)	Sales price variance	2
	Sales volume variance	2
		4
(c)	Market size variance	2
	Market share variance	2
		4
(d)	Comment on sales price	2
	Comment on sales volume	2
		4
Total		20

Examiner's comments (extract)

This question required an understanding of budget revisions. Budgets, once set, can be altered if planning errors have been made. The critical point is that if something happens that is outside the control of the organisation which renders the budget inappropriate as a means of control then the budget can be changed to reflect the change. In the real world things are rarely as clear as in the classroom and whether or not to allow a budget revision is a subjective choice. The potential for abuse should be clear, where poor operational performance is passed off as a planning error.

Part (a) of this question was often very poorly done. It appeared that, where candidates had studied planning and operational variances, they had confined themselves to the mechanics and avoided any understanding of the practical problems involved. I would encourage all to briefly consider the ideas behind calculations before mastering the calculations themselves.

The basic variances in part (b) were well done by most candidates. In part (c) I often got a discussion rather than the analysis I asked for. I did give some credit for a general comment on the implications of a falling market and the apparent increase in market share.

In part (d) the better candidates realised that the sales performance was not as bad as it looked. This was, after all, my intention. A business that fails to meet its sales budget by only 2.2% in the face of a market that has shrank by 11% could hardly be totally criticised. However, the weaker candidates seemed totally unaware of the meaning and implications of the data. Performance management is not only about the calculations. Candidates must understand what the numbers tell them about the businesses performance.

51 SECURE NET

> **Tutorial Note** *The method above is in line with the article previously written by the examiner and published in the ACCA student newsletter. Other methods, such as the one presented here, would score full marks.*

(a) The total variances are as follows:

Total price variance = ($5.25 – $4) 3,500kg = $4,375 Adverse

Total usage variance = (3,500 – 4,000) 4 = $2,000 Favourable

This makes a total of $2,375 Adverse

(b) The planning variances are calculated by comparing the original budget and the revised standards after adjustment for factors outside the control of the organisation. On this basis the revised standards would be a price of $4·80 per kg with revised usage at 42g per card.

Planning price variance = ($4·80 – $4) 4,200 = $3,360 Adverse

Planning Usage variance = (4,200 – 4,000) $4 = $800 Adverse

The total planning error (variance) is $4,160 Adverse

The operational variances compare the actual spend with the revised budget figures.

Operational price variance = ($5·25 – $4.80) 3,500kg = $1,575 Adverse

Operational usage variance = (3,500 – 4,200) $4.80 = $3,360 Favourable

The total operational variance is $1,785 Favourable

(c) The production manager is subject to external pressures which appear beyond his control. The size of the security card has to fit the reader of that card and if the industry specification changes there is nothing that he can do about that. This is, then, a 'planning' error and should not form part of any assessment of his performance.

Equally if world-wide oil prices increase (and hence plastic prices) then the production manager cannot control that. This would be allocated as a planning error and ignored in an assessment of his performance.

The performance of the production manager should be based on the operational variances (and any relevant qualitative factors). The decision to use a new supplier 'cost' an extra $1,575 in price terms. On the face of it this is, at least potentially, a poor performance. However, the manager seems to have agreed to the higher price on the promise of better quality and reliability. If this promise was delivered then this could be seen as a good decision (and performance). The savings in waste (partly represented by the usage variance) amount to $3,360 favourable. This would seem to suggest better quality. The fact that the production level jumped from 60,000 to 100,000 also suggests that suppliers' reliability was good (in that they were able to deliver so much). The net variance position is relevant at a saving of $1,785.

It is also possible that such a large increase in volume of sales and production should have yielded a volume based discount from suppliers. This should also be reflected in any performance assessment in that if this has not been secured it could be seen as a poor performance.

This is backed up by the lack of obvious quality problems since we are told that 100,000 cards were produced and sold in the period, a huge increase on budget. The ability of a production manager to react and be flexible can often form a part of a performance assessment.

In conclusion the manager could be said to have performed well.

Alternative answer :

(a)

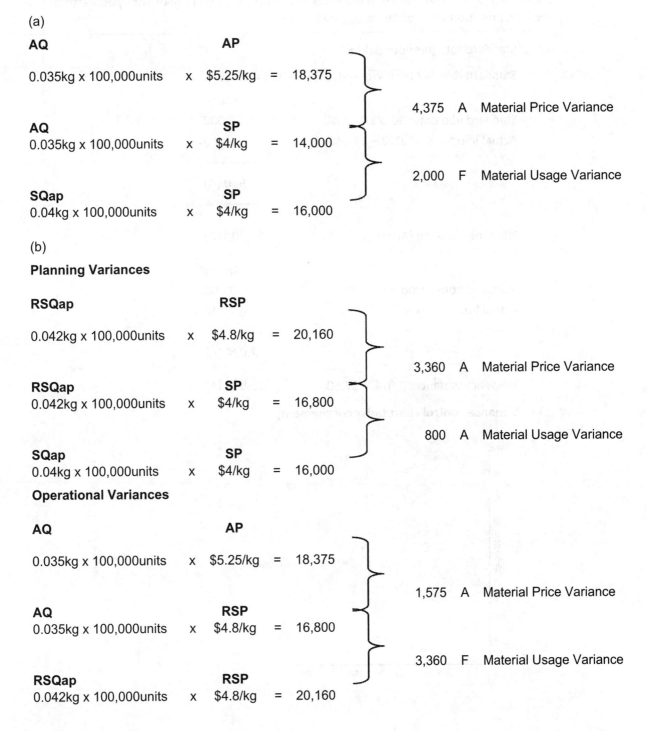

AQ   **AP**

0.035kg x 100,000units   x $5.25/kg   =   18,375

                                                              4,375   A   Material Price Variance

AQ   **SP**
0.035kg x 100,000units   x $4/kg   =   14,000

                                                              2,000   F   Material Usage Variance

SQap   **SP**
0.04kg x 100,000units   x $4/kg   =   16,000

(b)

Planning Variances

RSQap   **RSP**

0.042kg x 100,000units   x $4.8/kg   =   20,160

                                                              3,360   A   Material Price Variance

RSQap   **SP**
0.042kg x 100,000units   x $4/kg   =   16,800

                                                              800   A   Material Usage Variance

SQap   **SP**
0.04kg x 100,000units   x $4/kg   =   16,000

Operational Variances

AQ   **AP**

0.035kg x 100,000units   x $5.25/kg   =   18,375

                                                              1,575   A   Material Price Variance

AQ   **RSP**
0.035kg x 100,000units   x $4.8/kg   =   16,800

                                                              3,360   F   Material Usage Variance

RSQap   **RSP**
0.042kg x 100,000units   x $4.8/kg   =   20,160

---

52 PH

Key answer tips

Provided you remember to 'gross up' the hourly rate from that paid to that worked, part (a) should not present any problems. In part (b) however, there are quite a lot of workings to perform before the control chart can even be prepared, so you may well have experienced time pressure here. Don't let this be an excuse for poor presentation of the chart. Part (c) offers easy marks and you should always make sure that you make very good attempts at the interpretation parts of questions such as this.

(a)   Standard rate per hour paid $6

Standard rate per hour worked: $6/(1 − 0.2) = $7.50

	Hours
Standard idle time: 30,000 × 20%	6,000
Actual idle time: 30,000 − 23,040	6,960
	960 (A)

Idle time variance (April): 960 × $7.50	$7,200 (A)

	Hours
Standard hours produced	20,966
Actual hours worked	23,040
	2,074 (A)

Efficiency variance: 2,074 × $7.50	$15,555 (A)

(b)   **Variance control chart (adverse segment)**

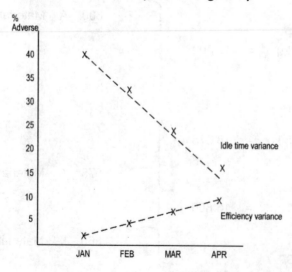

Workings

		Standard cost of standard idle time	Actual idle time variance	
		$	$	%
January	10,000 × $7.50 × 20%	15,000	6,000 (A)	40 (A)
February	14,000 × $7.50 × 20%	21,000	6,720 (A)	32 (A)
March	17,000 × $7.50 × 20%	25,500	6,120 (A)	24 (A)
April	30,000 × $7.50 × 20%	45,000	7,200 (A)	16 (A)

		Standard cost of standard hours produced	Actual efficiency variance	
		$	$	%
January	6,984 × $7.50	52,380	1,620 (A)	3 (A)
February	9,789 × $7.50	73,418	3,863 (A)	5 (A)
March	11,889 × $7.50	89,168	6,713 (A)	7.5 (A)
April	20,966 × $7.50	157,245	15,555 (A)	10 (A)

Information presented in a graphical format is often well received by managers for whom the actual numbers per month are of less interest. The presentation of this information on labour variances over time highlights the trends in the two sets of figures, and the fact that they are heading in opposite directions. In a very clear way, therefore, the presentation points to a possible connection between the trends, which would not immediately be obvious from a table of figures alone, and suggests the need for control action to be taken.

Since the percentages in this chart are taken of standard rather than actual costs, the underlying trend is highlighted. If actual costs had been used then the percentages would have reflected changing activity levels (PH is a seasonal business) and so the real trends over time would have been obscured.

(c)   The fact that the idle time variances are improving at the same time as the efficiency variances are deteriorating suggests that they are correlated.

The two variances are actually breakdowns of the overall labour efficiency (as opposed to rate) variance. This has improved slightly from ($6,000 + $1,620) $7,620 adverse on a labour spend of $60,000 in January (12.7%) to ($7,200 + $15,555) $22,755 adverse on a labour spend of $180,000 (12.6%). Overall labour efficiency is not deteriorating, therefore, and less of the workers' time is being spent on official idle time – but the number of hours that they take to produce items is higher. This suggests that, instead of being 'idle', the workers may deliberately be working slowly so as not to be so bored. Alternatively, quality standards may have been increased without a commensurate alteration to standard times.

53 MARSHALL

Key answer tips

The actual costs to date can be derived by calculating the standard cost of 29,600 services, then adjusting for the variances. The budget figure for 29,600 services should be shown, for a valid comparison.

(a) **Summary statement for six months to 30 September**

	Cumulative actual to date	Cumulative budget to date	Total variance	Price/ expenditure variance	Efficiency variance
Production (units)	29,600	30,000	400		
Costs:	$	$	$	$	$
Materials	1,207,100	1,184,000	(23,100)	(1,100)	(22,000)
Labour	846,129	976,800	130,671	130,671	0
Variable overheads	455,000	444,000	(11,000)	(11,000)	0
Fixed overheads	738,000	710,400	(27,600)	(18,000)	(9,600)
Total costs	3,246,229	3,315,200	68,971	100,571	(31,600)

() = Adverse variance

Note: Alternative statements that summarise the performance of the Service Department would be acceptable.

(b) **Report to the operations director of Marshall regarding the performance of the service department for six months to 30 September 20X3**

A summary performance statement is attached to this report. The main features are set out below, along with issues that require further explanation or information.

- There has been a rise, then fall in volumes. Is this a seasonal variation, such as fewer services required during the summer, or the result of other factors, such as action from competitors in months 4 to 6? If the trend in the last three months continues, this could be a serious problem that needs to be addressed promptly

- A favourable material usage variance, as occurred in month 2, must mean that some parts were not replaced during the service. Is this acceptable? There seems to be a general inefficiency in material usage. Is this caused by a lack of care by service engineers, or by poor quality sets? The price variance – see below – does not indicate cheap parts are being purchased

- Material prices are on a general upward path. Is there a general drift in material prices or is there a material shortage? Are there other suppliers offering a better price?

- Labour price is massively out of line with budget yielding large favourable variances. Is this caused by a mistake in the budget or an unexpected change in the price, for example, using different grades/mix of labour. This variance is more than 13% of budgeted cost and thus must be investigated quickly and thoroughly

- Labour efficiency gets much worse after month 4. Has something unusual happened to labour during this month, perhaps a dispute? Is this significantly worse labour efficiency linked to the fall in output over the same months?

- Month 4 is significantly out of line with other months. What happened? Was production disrupted; was there a labour dispute or supplier problems or did another factor affect the result? It is important to find satisfactory explanations for the results in this month and attempt to ensure this performance is not repeated

- Only total variable overhead variance has meaning and reveals a worsening position after the disaster in month 4, giving further evidence for some unusual circumstances

- Fixed overhead spending seems to come under control from month 5, but what caused the problems in the early months? Has management acted to remedy matters?

- The fixed overhead volume variance is purely technical and represents differences between planned and actual production

- Overall costs are 2% below budget, but this apparently satisfactory position masks considerable variation. Nevertheless, the general performance of the Service Department has been close to budget.

PERFORMANCE MEASUREMENT AND CONTROL

54   JUMP PERFORMANCE APPRAISAL (JUNE 10 EXAM)

(a)   Bonus calculation:

	Qtr to 30 June 2009	Qtr to 30 September 2009	Qtr to 31 December 2009	Qtr to 31 March 2010	Bonus; hits'
Staff on time?					
On-time %	430/450 = 95.5%	452/480 = 94.2%	442/470 = 94.0%	460/480 = 95.8%	
Bonus earned?	Yes	No	No	Yes	2
Members visits					
Target visits	60% × 3,000 × 12 = 21,600	60% × 3,200 × 12 = 23,040	60% × 3,300 × 12 = 23,760	60% × 3,400 × 12 = 24,480	
Actual visits	20,000	24,000	26,000	24,000	
Bonus earned?	No	Yes	Yes	No	2

	Qtr to 30 June 2009	Qtr to 30 September 2009	Qtr to 31 December 2009	Qtr to 31 March 2010	Bonus; hits'
Personal training					
Target	10% × 3,000 = 300	10% × 3,200 = 320	10% × 3,300 = 330	10% × 3,400 = 340	
Actual sessions	310	325	310	339	
Bonus earned	Yes	Yes	No	No	2
Total					6

The bonus earned by the manager would be 6 × $400 = $2,400, which is 50% of the total bonus available.

(b)   An important principle of any target based bonus system is that the targets must be based on controllable aspects of the manager's role.

Staff on time

The way in which a manager manages staff can have a big bearing on whether or not an individual staff member is keen to work and arrive on time. We are told that the local manager has the power to vary employment contracts so he should be able to agree acceptable shift patterns with staff and reward them for compliance. In this respect the lateness of staff is controllable by the manager.

On the other hand an individual staff member may be subject to home pressures or problems with public or other transport meaning that even they cannot control the time of arrival at work on some days. The manager cannot control these events either. If this problem became regular for a member of staff then the local manager could vary the contract of employment accordingly.

Overall, lateness to work is controllable by the local manager.

Member use of facilities

The local manager controls the staff and hence the level of customer service. Good quality customer services would probably encourage members to use the facilities more often. Equally, by maintaining the club to a high standard then the local manager can remove another potential reason for a member not to use the facilities regularly.

On the other hand customers are influenced by many factors outside of the club. Their state of health or their own work pressures can prevent members being able to come to the club.

Overall, the local manager can only partly control the number of member visits.

Personal training sessions

Again, the local manager controls the level of customer service and the standard of maintenance in the personal training department. He also has control over prices so, if the bookings fall, he is able to reduce price or make special offers to encourage use of the facilities.

On the other hand, personal training sessions may be seen as a luxury by customers and in times of financial difficulty they are expendable by them. Personal training sessions are often available from other sources and competition can force down the sales of the club. The manager can respond to that by improving services. He cannot, however, make significant investment in improving the facilities without board approval.

Overall, the local manager can only partly control the number of personal training sessions booked.

(c)   There are a variety of methods that the performance data can be manipulated:

Cut off

The unethical manager could record visits in a different period than was actually the case. For example in quarter three the target for personal training sessions was not met by 20 sessions. This was probably obvious to the manager in the last few days of that quarter. He could have therefore recorded some sessions as having taken place in the next quarter. Indeed, only one session would have to be moved in this way in order for the manager to meet the target in the final quarter and gain another $400 of bonus.

Reduce prices to below economic levels to encourage use

The targets that the manager is subject to are mainly volume driven. A reduction in prices would harm profitability but would not damage the manager's bonus potential. More sessions are bound to follow if the price is set low enough.

(Other ideas would be acceptable including advising staff to take the day off if they were going to be late. This would damage service levels admittedly, but would potentially gain a bonus for lateness.)

ACCA marking scheme		
		Marks
(a)	Per target	2
	Total	6
(b)	For each target – supporting controllability	1·5
	For each target – denying controllability	1·5
	Target	9
(c)	For each idea of manipulation up to	2·5
		5
	Total	20

55 PACE COMPANY (DEC 08 EXAM)

(a)   Performance statistics

	2005	2006	2007	2008
ROI	13%	17.5%	16.7%	20%
Bonus paid?	No	Yes	Yes	Yes
Sales Growth	–	0%	–10%	–5.6%
Gross margin	40%	35%	35%	30%
Overheads	$67,000	$56,000	$53,000	$43,000
Net profit % on Sales	6.5%	7%	5.6%	4.7%

The performance of store W can be assessed in various ways:

Sales Growth

Sales revenue growth is most unimpressive. We are told that the market in which PC operates is steadily growing and yet store W has shrunk in terms of sales over the last four years. This could be poor volumes or poor prices achieved. Given the reducing gross margin (see below) then a reducing sales price is likely. It is possible that W is subject to higher than normal levels of competition.

Gross Margin

The gross margins have also shrunk. Reducing margins can result from sales price pressure or increases in the cost of sales levels being incurred. Suppliers might have increased prices or labour could have got more expensive. The level of margin has only reached the normal level once in the last four years. Clearly W is under performing.

Overhead Control

The one area that is impressive is the apparent ability of the business to reduce overheads as sales and margin have shrunk. This is often difficult to do. It is possible that reducing these overheads could have contributed to the poor sales performance, if (for example) quality has been affected, or one could say it reflects flexible management.

Net Margin

The net margin has also fallen, primarily due to falling gross margins as overheads have reduced. Clearly a disappointing performance.

ROI

The ROI has improved in most years and has exceeded the 15% target in all but one year (year 1). This is simply due to the reducing asset base as the stores assets have gradually been depreciated. Net profit levels have fallen overall and yet ROI has increased.

It is hard to argue that the ROI figures properly reflect the performance of the store. The ROI will tend to increase as assets get older and this will distort the financial performance picture. In a period of falling sales and weaker margins the manager of W has been awarded bonuses in three out of four years. This is hard to justify.

Key answer tips

Easy marks were available for the calculation of the ROI for each of the four years. There were no complicated numbers here. Good candidates carried out a number of other calculations, such as gross margin or sales growth.

Many candidates spent the majority of their time carrying out detailed calculations. Some calculations were required but it was important to leave sufficient time to interpret the calculations completed.

(b)   The unethical manager would have needed to move profits out of 2006 and in to 2005. One immediate problem here is having the information in good time to respond. The manager would have to be able to anticipate the 2005 poor result and the improvement in 2006. It is likely that such a manager would have to gamble at the end of 2005 and make an adjustment in the hope of a better year in 2006.

The manager need only move $2,000 of profit from 2006 to 2005 to achieve a 15% return in both years.

Possible methods of adjustment include:

Accelerate revenue: Sales made early in 2006 could be wrongly included in 2005. He could, for example, raise an invoice before is normal, perhaps on the receipt of an order and before actual delivery. The invoice itself would not have to be sent to the customer, merely filed until the second year had begun and delivery made.

Delay the recording of 2005 cost: A supplier's invoice could be left unrecorded at the end of 2005, including it in 2006 expenses instead.

Understate a provision or accrual in 2005: This has the effect of moving cost from 2005 to 2006 (assuming that by the end of 2006 the provision is correctly stated).

Manipulate accounting policy: Inventory values (for example) are easy targets for the unethical manager. If inventory in 2005 could be overstated this would have the effect of increasing 2005 profits at the expense 2006 profits.

Key answer tips

Good candidates were able to apply their knowledge of performance management to the scenario and came up with a number of relevant ideas.

Good exam technique - aim for four separate points and use sub-headings or paragraphs to separate each point. A brief explanation of each point, one to two sentences, is sufficient to gain four marks.

(c)   The forecast for store S is as follows:

		2009 ($)	2010 ($)	2011 ($)	2012 ($)
Sales	(W1)	216,000	237,600	248,292	235,877
Gross Profit	(W2)	86,400	95,040	91,476	79,061
Overheads		70,000	70,000	80,000	80,000
Net Profit		16,400	25,040	11,476	(939)
Investment		100,000	75,000	50,000	25,000
ROI		16.4%	33.39%	22.95%	−3.8%

(W1)

	2009	2010	2011	2012
Sales Volume (units)	18,000	19,800a	21,780b	21,780
Sales Price ($)	12.00	12.00	11.40c	10.83d
Revenue ($)				
(Volume × Price)	216,000	237,600	248,292	235,877

a: 18,000 (1.1) = 19,800

b: 19,800 (1.1) = 21,780

c: 12.00 (0.95) = 11.40

d: 11.40 (0.95) = 10.83

(W2)

Gross Profit

2009 40% (given). Total gross profit = $216,000 × 0.4 = $86,400

2010 40% (given). Total gross profit = $237,600 × 0.4 = $95,040

2011(40 − 5)/100(0.95) = 36.8421052%

Total gross profit = $248,292 × 0.368421052 = $91,476

2012 (40 − 5 − 4.75)/(100(0.95)(0.95)) = 33.5180055%

Total gross profit = $235,877 × 0·335180055 = $79,061

Alternatively, given that variable costs are said to be constant over the four years, could calculate the variable cost in year one and hold for the four years. Gross profit is then simply sales revenue less variable costs.

Variable costs in 2005:

$216,000 – 18,000 × VC = $86,400

VC per unit = $7.20

So year two gross profit will be:

$237,600 – 19,800 × 7.2 = $95,040

Key answer tips

Easy marks were available here. There were no difficult calculations. Good candidates presented their answer in columnar format. This method of presentation is quick, looks professional and any workings can simply be referenced in.

Note: The original question included an additional requirement. The suggested solution is as follows:

In order for a bonus to be paid in 2012 an ROI of 15% is needed. This implies a net profit of $25,000 × 15% = $3,750.

Adding overheads of $80,000 to this net profit means that $83,750 of gross profit is needed. At a gross profit % of 33.518% this implies sales of $249,866.

At a price of $10.83 this suggests sales volumes of 23,072 units.

ACCA marking scheme		
		Marks
(a)	Calculations of performance statistics (0.5 each max 2.5)	2.5
	Sales comment	1.0
	Gross margin comment	1.0
	Overheads comment	1.0
	Net margin comment	1.0
	ROI discussion	3.0
		———
	Maximum	7.0
(b)	Timing of decision problem	1.0
	Revenue acceleration	1.0
	Delay of cost	1.0
	Manipulation of accounting policy	1.0
		———
	Maximum	4
(c)	Sales volume	1.5
	Sales price	1.5
	Gross profit for year 1	0.5
	Gross profit for year 2	0.5
	Gross profit for year 3	0.5
	Gross profit for year 4	0.5
	Overhead included	1.0
	Investment values	2.0
	ROI calculations	1.0
		———
		9.0
		———
Total		20
		———

56   PROPOSALS FOR DIVISION X

(a)   The calculations of manager's bonus are shown in the following table.

	Year 1	Year 2	Year 3	Total
Original draft	$15,625	$13,500	Nil	$29,125
Project (i) – W1	$15,625	$13,250	$20,375	$49,250
Project (ii) –W2	Nil	Nil	$25,000	$25,000
Project (iii) – W3	$12,500	$16,000	$16,875	$45,375

Workings

For each 1% by which ROI exceeds 10%, the bonus is increased by 2.5% of $50,000, i.e. by $1,250.

(W1) **Project (i)**

	Year 1	Year 2	Year 3
PBIT	$3.0m	$2.7m	$4.4m
Asset base	$24m	$25.5m	$27m
ROI	12.5%	10.6%	16.3%
	$	$	$
Basic bonus @ 25% of salary	12,500	12,500	12,500
Additional bonus	3,125	750	7,875
Total bonus	15,625	13,250	20,375

Note:

Additional bonus Year 1 = 2.5 × $1,250 = $3,125

Additional bonus Year 2 = 0.6 × $1,250 = $750

Additional bonus Year 3 = 6.3 × $1,250 = $7,875

(W2) **Project (ii)**

	Year 1	Year 2	Year 3
PBIT	$2.0m	$1.7m	$6.4m
Asset base	$24m	$25m	$26m
ROI	8.3%	6.8%	24.6%
	$	$	$
Basic bonus @ 25% of salary	0	0	12,500
Additional bonus	0	0	12,500
Total bonus	0	0	25,000

Note: Additional bonus Year 3 = (ignoring the bonus cap) 14.6 × $1,250 = $18,250, but total bonus capped at 50% of $50,000 = $25,000.

(W3) **Project (iii)**

	Year 1	Year 2	Year 3
PBIT	$2.4m	$3.2m	$3.5m
Asset base	$24m	$25m	$26m
ROI	10.0%	12.8%	13.5%
	$	$	$
Basic bonus @ 25% of salary	12,500	12,500	12,500
Additional bonus	0	3,500	4,375
Total bonus	12,500	16,000	16,875

Note:

Additional bonus Year 2 = 2.8 × $1,250 = $3,500

Additional bonus Year 3 = 3.5 × $1,250 = $4,375

The manager is likely to be influenced in his choice of projects by the personal rewards he can expect from them. In this case, he would favour Project (i) with total bonuses of $49,250, and Project (iii) with total bonuses of $45,375 over the three-year period. Both the first draft plan and adoption of Project (ii) are less attractive from this perspective. Moreover, this view is reinforced by the fact that most weight is likely to be given to bonuses achievable in the short term: on this basis Project (ii) is easily the least attractive, since no bonuses will arise until Year 3.

These considerations illustrate a common problem of bonus systems, namely that they may not achieve goal congruence. In the present case, Project (ii) is the most attractive from the organisation's point of view because its NPV is higher than the alternatives. However, because of its impact on the manager's own bonus Project (ii) is unlikely to be favoured. Indeed, from the manager's point of view it is the project with the lowest NPV that appears most attractive.

(b) The calculations of the manager's bonuses are shown in the following table.

	Year 1	Year 2	Year 3	Total
Original draft (W1)	$12,000	$4,000	Nil	$16,000
Project (i)	$12,000	$3,000	$25,000	$40,000
Project (ii) – W2	Nil	Nil	$25,000	$25,000
Project (iii) – W3	Nil	$14,000	$18,000	$32,000

Workings

(W1) **Original draft**

	Year 1	Year 2	Year 3
PBIT	$3.0m	$2.7m	$2.4m
Interest at 10% on asset base	$2.4m	$2.5m	$2.6m
Residual income	$0.6m	$0.2m	Nil
Bonus at 2%	$12,000	$4,000	Nil

(W2) **Project (ii)**

	Year 1	Year 2	Year 3
PBIT	$2.0m	$1.7m	$6.4m
Interest at 10% on asset base	$2.4m	$2.5m	$2.6m
Residual income	Nil	Nil	$3.8m
Bonus at 2% (limited to $25,000)	Nil	Nil	$25,000

(W3) **Project (iii)**

	Year 1	Year 2	Year 3
PBIT	$2.4m	$3.2m	$3.5m
Interest at 10% on asset base	$2.4m	$2.5m	$2.6m
Residual income	Nil	$0.7m	$0.9m
Bonus at 2%	Nil	$14,000	$18,000

Overall, the bonuses work out less generously under this scheme. However, the manager's preference is unaffected: he still benefits most from Project (i), followed by Project (iii). Once again, Project (ii) is the least attractive from his point of view.

57   TIP (DEC 09 EXAM)

Tutorial note *: one of the key areas of the Paper F5 syllabus is that of perfromance measurement and control. Ann Irons, your Examiner, has selected this very question to illustrate her suggested approach to that topic in an article published in the July 2010 edition of 'Student Accountant magazine'. Find it here:*
http://www.accaglobal.com/pubs/students/publications/student_accountant/archive/sa_j ul10_f5_perf_meas.pdf

(a)   TIPs Financial performance can be assessed in a number of ways:

Sales growth

Sales are up about 1.3% (W1) which is a little above the rate of inflation and therefore a move in the right direction. However, with average admission prices jumping about 8.6% (W2) and numbers of visitors falling there are clearly problems. Large increases in admission prices reduce the value proposition for the customer, it is unlikely that the rate of increase is sustainable or even justifiable. Indeed with volumes falling (down by 6.7%, (W6)) it appears that some customers are being put off and price could be one of the reasons.

Maintenance and repairs

There appears to be continuing drift way from routine maintenance with management preferring to repair equipment as required. This does not appear to be saving any money as the combined cost of maintenance and repair is higher in 2009 than in 2008 (possible risks are dealt with in part (b)).

Directors pay

Absolute salary levels are up 6.7% (W3) well above the modest inflation rate. It appears that the shareholders are happy with the financial performance of the business and are prepared to reward the directors accordingly. Bonus levels are also well up, it may be that the directors have some form of profit related pay scheme and are being rewarded for the improved profit performance. The directors are likely to be very pleased with the increases to pay.

Wages

Wages are down by 12% (W5). This may partly reflect the loss of customers (down by 6.7% (W6) if we assume that at least part of the wages cost is variable. It could also be that the directors are reducing staff levels beyond the fall in the level of customers to enhance short-term profit and personal bonus. Customer service and indeed safety can be compromised here.

Net profit

Net profit is up a huge 31.3% (W7) and most shareholders would be pleased with that. Net profit is a very traditional measure of performance and most would say this was a sign of good performance.

Return on assets

The profitability can be measured relative to the asset base that is being used to generate it. This is sometimes referred to as ROI or return on investment. The return on assets is up considerably to 11.4% from 8% (W8). This is partly due to the significant rise in profit and partly due to the fall in asset value. We are told that TIP has cut back on new development so the fall in asset value is probably due to depreciation being charged with little being spent during the year on assets. In this regard it is inevitable that return on assets is up but it is more questionable whether this is a good performance. A theme park (and thrill rides in particular) must be updated to keep customers coming back. The directors on TIP are risking the future of the park.

(b)   **Quality provision**

Reliability of the rides

The hours lost has increased significantly. Equally the % of capacity lost due to breakdowns is now approaching 17.8% (W9).

This would appear to be a very high number of hours lost. This would surely increase the risk that customers are disappointed being unable to ride. Given the fixed admission price system this is bound to irritate some customers as they have effectively paid to ride already.

Average queuing time

Queuing will be seen by customers as dead time. They may see some waiting as inevitable and hence acceptable. However TIP should be careful to maintain waiting times at a minimum. An increase of 10 minutes (or 50%) is likely to be noticeable by customers and is unlikely to enhance the quality of the TIP experience for them. The increase in waiting times is probably due to the high number of hours lost due to breakdown with customers being forced to queue for a fewer number of ride options.

Safety

The clear reduction in maintenance could easily damage the safety record of the park and is an obvious quality issue.

Risks

If TIP continues with current policies then they will expose themselves to the following risks:

–   The lack of routine maintenance could easily lead to an accident or injury to a customer. This could lead to compensation being paid or reputational damage

–   Increased competition. The continuous raising of admission prices increases the likelihood of a new competitor entering the market (although there are significant barriers to entry in this market e.g. capital cost, land and so on).

–   Loss of customers. The value for money that customers see when coming to TIP is clearly reducing (higher prices, less reliability of rides and longer queues). Regardless of the existence of competition customers could simply chose not to come, substituting another leisure activity instead

–   Profit fall. In the end if customers' numbers fall then so will profit. The shareholders, although well rewarded at the moment could suffer a loss of dividend. Directors job security could then be threatened.

Workings:

(W1)   Sales growth is $5,320,000/$5,250,000 = 1.01333 or 1.3%

(W2)   Average admission prices were:

2008: $5,250,000/150,000 = $35 per person
2009: $5,320,000/140,000 = $38 per person

An increase of $38/$35 = 1.0857 or 8.57%

(W3)   Directors pay up by $160,000/$150,000 = 1.0667 or 6.7%

(W4)   Directors bonuses levels up from $15,000/$150,000 or 10% to $18,000/$160,000 or 12.5% of turnover. This is an increase of 3/15 or 20%

(W5)   Wages are down by (1 – $2,200,000/$2,500,000) or 12%

(W6)   Loss of customers is (1 – 140,000/150,000) or 6.7%

(W7)   Profits up by $1,372,000/$1,045,000 = 1.3129 or 31.3%

(W8)   Return on assets: 2008: $1,045,000/$13,000,000 = 1.0803 or 8.03%

2009: $1,372,000/$12,000,000 = 1.114 or 11.4%

(W9)   Capacity of rides in hours is 360 days x 50 rides x 10 hours per day = 180,000

2008 lost capacity is 9,000/180,000 = 0.05 or 5%; 2009 lost capacity is 32,000/180,000 = 0.177 or 17.8%

58   Y AND Z

(a)   Return on Investment (ROI) = $\dfrac{\text{Profit}}{\text{Investment}}$

Unfortunately, both the top and the bottom of the equation can be calculated in different ways. There is no ambiguity, here. For the value of the investment, we shall use the $9.76m and the $1.26m. The profit figure, here, involves a choice – should we use the controllable income of $460,000 and $201,000 or should we use the $122,000 and $21,000 that are the net income before tax figures? If you think a question is ambiguous, you must state your assumption and choose whichever figures you think are appropriate.

One trick, here, is that whichever profit figure you choose it is expressed per month and has to be annualised as made clear in the requirement.

	Division Y	Division Z
Net income before tax ($000)		
(122 × 12 and 21 × 12)	1,464	252
Investment ($000)	÷ 9,760	÷ 1,260
ROI	15%	20%

On the basis of ROI, division Z is performing better than division Y.

Division Y's net income before tax is almost six times as much as division Z's, and its ROI does exceed the target, so division Y does increase the wealth of the shareholders to a greater extent than division Z. This is not reflected in the ROI, and indeed is a well-known flaw of the method, in that it is only a measure of relative profitability, not absolute profitability.

If the target return on capital of 12% is raised, then division Z has the greater margin of safety, whereas division Y's performance with its ROI of 15% would quickly become less and less attractive.

The net income before tax figures are very much affected by the apportioned central costs. It would be nice to know on what basis the apportionment has been made. Indeed a very convincing argument could be made that, if we are trying to judge performance in the two divisions, then we should only be looking at controllable profit as it would be unfair to judge managers on factors over which they have no control.

If there are unlimited funds available for investment, then both divisions earn above the target return and, provided they can find projects with similar returns to their existing projects, then they should seek additional funds. If there are limited funds available and division Z can find new projects with returns similar to its existing projects, then division Z will be the more attractive destination for funds.

	Division Y	Division Z
Controllable income ($000)		
(460 × 12 and 201 × 12	5,520	2,412
Investment ($000)	÷ 9,760	÷ 1,260
	56.6%	191.4%

The controllable income return on net assets is very much higher for Z than for Y and, compared to the ROIs calculated on the basis of net income before tax, show Z to be performing better than Y to a much greater extent. This is an indication than Z is earning its income with much less use of divisional net assets.

(b)

	Division Y	Division Z
	$000	$000
Net income before tax	1,464.0	252.0
Imputed interest		
12% × $9.76m	1,171.2	
12% × $1.26m		151.2
Residual income	292.8	100.8

Division Y has a better performance on the basis of residual income, but residual income is not a useful comparator when comparing divisions of different sizes. Division Y has a bigger residual income, but so it should, as it is a much bigger division.

All in all, division Y does increase the wealth of the shareholders to a greater extent than division Z, but division Z does earn its income at a better rate than division Y.

(c)   ROI is expressed as a percentage and is more easily understood by non-financial managers.

ROI can be used to compare performance between different sized divisions or companies.

It is not necessary to know the cost of capital in order to calculate ROI.

ROI may lead to dysfunctional decisions. For instance, if a division has a very high ROI of say, 40%, and is considering a project with an ROI of 30%, which is still well above the cost of capital of say 10%, then the project should be accepted as it provides a return well in excess of the cost of capital. The division may quite possibly reject the project, however, as when added to its existing operations it will reduce the ROI from 40%.

Using residual income as a performance measure should ensure that divisions make decisions which are in the best interests of the group as a whole and should eliminate the problem outlined in the previous paragraph.

Different divisions can use different rates to reflect different risk when calculating residual income.

Residual income is not useful for comparing divisions of different sizes.

Both residual income and ROI improve as the age of the assets increase and both provide an incentive to hang onto aged possibly inefficient machines.

Other methods of assessment that could be used in addition to ROI or RI include:

- Expected value added is similar to residual income except that, instead of using book values for profit and capital employed, the figures are adjusted to reflect the true economic value of the profit and of the capital employed

- the Balanced Scorecard, which still looks at financial performance, perhaps using residual income or ROI, but also encompasses three other perspectives: the customer perspective, the internal business process perspective, and the learning and innovation perspective.

59   FP

Key answer tips

A tricky question on transfer pricing.

In part (a) you need to ensure that all costs have been included, especially the impact of the transfer price.

(a)

	Per repair	Total cost for 500 repairs
	$	$
Parts	54	
Labour 3 hours @ $15 each	45	
Variable overhead 3 hours at $10 per hour	30	
Marginal cost	129	64,500
Fixed overhead 3 hours at $22 per hour	66	33,000
Total cost	195	97,500
Mark-up	78	39,000
Selling price	273	136,500

Transfers at 40% mark-up

	Sales	Service	FP
	$	$	$
	120,000	136,500	120,000
	136,500	97,500	97,500
Profit	(16,500)	39,000	22,500

Transfers at marginal cost

	Sales	Service	FP
	$	$	$
	120,000	64,500	120,000
	64,500	97,500	97,500
Profit	55,500	(33,000)	22,500

Repairs carried out by RS

	Sales	Service	FP
	$	$	$
	120,000	0	120,000
	90,000	33,000	123,000
Profit	30,000	(33,000)	(3,000)

(b)   (i)   Transfers at full cost plus may not be appropriate for FP because, at this price, the Sales Department can buy more cheaply from external suppliers and will not wish to purchase from the Service Department. This decision would be dysfunctional for the company as a whole as an overall loss is made.

           It would also lead to any inefficiencies of the Service Department being passed on to the Sales Department which would give no incentive to control costs.

     (ii)   Issues to consider include:

- Can RS guarantee the quality and reliability of the repairs?

- Is the offer by RS a short-term offer? Would the price rise in the longer term?

- Can the Service Department find other work to take up the capacity released if RS does the guarantee repairs?

- Can the Service Department find cost savings to reduce costs?

(c)   Operating the two departments as profit centres may have the following advantages:

- If managers are given autonomy to take decisions, this may lead to improved profitability owing to specialist knowledge and the ability to make decisions quickly

- If realistic targets are set which are within managers' control, then managers may be motivated to improve performance

- Head office time may be freed up to focus on strategic issues

- Profit centres may provide a training ground for senior management positions.

There could also be disadvantages as follows:

- Loss of control by head office

- Dysfunctional decision making

- Duplication of functions such as personnel and administration.

60 CTD

(a)   The current transfer price is ($40 + $20)) × 1.1 = $66.

		FD	FD	TM	TM
		$000	$000	$000	$000
Internal sales	15,000 × $66		990		
External sales	5,000 × $80		400		
	15,000 × $500				7,500
			1,390		7,500
Production – variable	20,000 × $40	(800)			
costs	15,000 × $366			(5,490)	
Selling/distribution –	5,000 × $4	(20)			
variable costs	15,000 × $25			(375)	
			(820)		(5,865)
			570		1,635
Production overheads	20,000 × $20	(400)			
	15,000 × $60				(900)
Administration	20,000 × $4	(80)			
overheads	15,000 × $25				(375)
Net profit			90		360
Interest charge	$750,000\$1,500,000 × 12%		(90)		(180)
Residual income (RI)			0		180
Target RI			85		105
Bonus	$180,000 × 5%		0		9

Implications of the current reward system

While the TM manager has received a bonus and presumably will be pleased about it, the FD manager has received nothing. This will not be very motivating and may lead to problems within the division as a whole, such as inefficiency, staff turnover and unreliability. Since the TM division relies so completely on the FD division, this situation is clearly unacceptable.

Key answer tips

The calculations involved in this question are very straightforward, but don't be deceived – the real thrust of this question is to make sure that you both understand the principles of different transfer pricing methods, and can apply them to a situation.

(b)   (i)   In order to achieve a 5% bonus, the manager of TM division will be willing to accept a decrease in residual income of $(180,000 – 105,000) = $75,000. This is an increase in transfer price of the 15,000 units transferred of $75,000/15,000 = $5. Thus the transfer price would rise to $66 + $5 = $71.

(ii)   In order to achieve a 5% bonus, the manager of FD division will want an increase in residual income of $85,000. This is an increase in transfer price of the 15,000 units transferred of $85,000/15,000 = $5.67. Thus the transfer price would have to rise to $66 + $5.67 = $71.67.

61   DIVISION A

Key answer tips

This is a demanding question linking transfer prices to performance targets. As with all transfer pricing questions the key aspects of discussion are linking transfer prices to managerial performance.

(a)   (i)   Profit required by division A to meet RI target:

	$
Cost of capital $3.2m @ 12%	384,000
Target RI	180,000
	————
Target profit	564,000
Add fixed costs	1,080,000
	————
Target contribution	1,644,000
	————
Contribution earned from external sales 90,000 @ ($35 – $22)	1,170,000
Contribution required from internal sales	474,000
Contribution per bit on internal sales ($474,000/ 60,000)	$7.90
Transfer price to division C $22.00 + $7.90	$29.90

(ii)   The two transfer prices based on opportunity costs:

40,000 units (150,000 – 110,000) at the marginal cost of $22.00

20,000 units (110,000 – 90,000) at the external selling price of $35.00

(b)   Where divisional managers are given total autonomy to purchase units at the cheapest price and where divisional performance is assessed on a measure based on profit, sub-optimal behaviour could occur i.e. divisional managers could make decisions that may not be in the overall interests of the group.

Impact of group's current transfer pricing policy

Division C's objective is to maximise its RI in order to achieve its target RI. It will therefore endeavour to find the cheapest source of supply for Bits. As C requires 60,000 Bits and X is willing to supply them at $28 each, C would prefer to buy them from X rather than division A. However this will not benefit the group, as division A will be unable to utilise its spare capacity of 40,000 Bits. The effect on the group's profit will be as follows:

	$
Additional payment by division C 60,000 Bits@ ($28 – $22)	(360,000)
Gain in contribution by Division A 20,000 Bits @ $13	260,000
	————
Net loss to group	(100,000)
	————

Impact of group's proposed transfer pricing policy

If division A were to set transfer prices based on opportunity costs the effect on its divisional profit would be as follows:

	$
Reduction in profit 40,000 Bits @ ($29.90 – $22.00)	(316,000)
Increase in profit 20,000 Bits @ ($35 – $29.90)	102,000
Net loss to division	(214,000)

Division C has the following two purchase options:

	$
Purchase from division A 40,000 Bits @ $22	880,000
Purchase from Z 20,000 Bits @ $33	660,000
Total cost of Bits	1,540,000
Or: Purchase 60,000 from X 60,000 Bits @ $28	1,680,000

As division C will opt to source the Bits from the cheapest supplier(s) it will choose to purchase 40,000 Bits from division A at $22 per Bit and the remaining 20,000 Bits from Z at $33 per Bit. This also benefits the group, as there is no opportunity cost to division A on the 40,000 units transferred to division C.

When marginal cost is used as the transfer price division C will make the correct decision and the group will maximise profits. However division A would suffer. This can be overcome by changing the way it measures the performance of its divisions – rather than using a single profit-based measure it needs to introduce a variety of quantitative and qualitative measures.

(c) **Purchase of 60,000 Bits from division A**

	Contribution $	Taxation $	Net effect $
A – external sales 90,000 Bits @ ($35 – $22)	1,170,000		
– internal sales 60,000 Bits @ ($30 – $22)	480,000		
Total contribution from A	1,650,000		
Taxation @ 55%		(907,500)	
C – purchases 60,000 Bits @ $30	(1,800,000)		
Taxation @ 25%		450,000	
Net effect	(150,000)	(457,500)	(607,500)

Purchase of 60,000 Bits from X

	Contribution $	Taxation $	Net effect $
A – external sales 110,000 Bits @ ($35 – $22)	1,430,000		
Taxation @ 55%		(786,500)	
C – purchases 60,000 Bits @ $28	(1,680,000)		
Taxation @ 25%		420,000	
Net effect	(250,000)	(366,500)	(616,500)

The group will maximise its profits if division C purchased the Bits from division A.

62 BRIDGEWATER CO (JUNE 08 EXAM)

Key answer tips

Part (a) is a relatively straightforward requirement but requires a systematic approach. Use four headings, i.e. one for each objective. Aim for two relevant and succinct points underneath each heading. One mark could be obtained for a reasoned discussion of performance for each quarter and for the year against target. Another mark could then be obtained for linking this back to the promotion prospects of the manager.

Part (b) requires some care as forecasted profit will be impacted by the first two proposals only. Delaying the payment of the trainers will impact cash flow only. There are thirteen minutes available to do this calculation and so there is no need to rush or revise the forecasts in one step. The best approach would be to work through each line of the proposals in turn and calculate any incremental costs and sales that would result from the proposals. The forecast can then be adjusted to take these changes into account

Part (c) was also relatively straightforward and there are plenty of relevant points that could be made. Divide the answer up using three headings (one for each change). Aim to discuss the benefits and drawbacks of each change and to link each change back to the promotion. The key mistake in written answers is to write too little or the other extreme is to write too much unstructured and irrelevant discussion. Planning your answer should not only help to score a higher mark but should also help with time management

(a)　The divisions of Bridgewater Co have been given very specific targets to meet it is reasonable to assume that performance will be assessed relative to them.

Sales Growth

The northwest division suffers from a slow start to the year, with falls in sales from quarter 1 to quarter 2. Overall sales growth looks better with an average growth of 14% achieved. We don't have quarterly budget sales to compare to but the low growth in budget profit suggests that much slower sales growth than that actually achieved was expected. Overall the sales budget has been exceeded, with big increases in sales in the last two quarters The manager's promotion could be damaged by the slow start. The 'good news' of better sales growth comes after the promotion decision is taken.

Cost control – trainer costs

The division spends slightly more (as a % of sales) than budgeted on trainers. It is spending 20% as opposed to 18% on trainers. Given the manager's attitude towards quality it appears he is trying to employ better trainers in the hope of more satisfied customers. This should, logically, build customer loyalty and improve local and brand reputation. This could possibly explain the better growth in the later quarters.

Again the problem for the promotion seeking manager, investing in the future in this way damages short term performance measures, in this case cost targets.

Cost control – room hire costs

The divisional manager is also spending more on room hire. He is spending 10% as opposed to the budgeted 9% of sales. He could be buying poorly, hence wasting money. Alternatively he could be hiring better quality rooms to improve the learning environment and enhance the training experience.

Again his focus on quality may be undermining his short term promotional prospects.

Profit

Annually, the divisional manager is beating the targets laid down for profit. His problem as far as his promotion is concerned is the profit targets laid down for the first two quarters are not met.

The promotion decision comes too early for his employers to see the benefit of a quality focus made earlier in the year.

Overall, promotional prospects do not look good. The manager has not met any of his targets in the first two quarters. His only hope is that his bosses look at future forecasts and take them in to consideration when making the decision.

(b)   **Revised forecasts**

	Q1	Q2	Q3	Q4	Total
	$000	$000	$000	$000	$000
Sales	42.5	38.5	62.5	74.5	218.0
Less:					
Trainers	8.0	7.2	12.0	14.4	41.6
Room hire	4.0	3.6	6.0	7.2	20.8
Staff training	1.5	1.5	1.0	1.0	5.0
Other costs	3.0	1.7	6.0	7.0	17.7
Software	1.8				1.8
Forecast Net profit	24.2	24.5	37.5	44.9	131.1
Original Budget profit	25.0	26.0	27.0	28.0	106.0

Incremental effects (as a working)

	Q1 $000	Q2 $000	Q3 $000	Q4 $000	Total $000
Extra sales:					
Voucher sales	2.5	2.5	2.5	2.5	10.0
Software sales			10.0	12.0	22.0
Extra costs:					
Trainers			2.0	2.4	4.4
Room hire			1.0	1.2	2.2
Staff training	0.5	0.5			1.0
Software	1.8				1.8
Change in forecast net profit	+0.2	+2.0	+9.5	+10.9	+22.6

(c)   **Voucher scheme**

At first glance of it the voucher scheme looks a good one. The manager is confident of a reasonable volume of sales and given that all the attendees will go on existing courses there will be no additional costs. The scheme seems to generate $10,000 of extra sales revenue in the year. One should question the assumption that no extra costs are incurred.

One potential concern would be that existing customers may object to the price reduction, particularly if they have already paid a higher price for a future course. However, most customers will probably not be aware of the price difference or will not bother complaining, those that do complain can be dealt with individually. It is common with promotions that the offer clearly states the terms and conditions that apply. In this way the manager can protect existing sales by excluding existing sales from the new offer.

From a promotion point of view the extra revenue and profit helps a little. If the revenue is spread evenly (as suggested) there will be $2,500 of extra revenue and profit in each of quarter 1 and 2. Unfortunately, in both cases the manager will still fall short of the target profit and the growth between quarter 1 and 2 will still be negative. He would need the take up rate of the sessions to be quicker to help his promotion prospects. Manipulation of the accounting figures should be resisted

Software upgrade

A software training company must stay in touch with modern software developments. From that point of view you could argue that this development is essential. Financially the proposal looks sound. The extra courses will generate a profit of $12,600 in this year alone, with, presumably, more courses to follow. A slower than expected take-up rate for the new course would reduce this year's effect.

The promotional aspects are not as good. The extra costs occur in quarter 1 and 2 but the revenue does not come in until after the promotion decision is made. Integrity is an issue here. Personal promotional prospects must come second to sound business decisions. The manager should show the revised forecasts to his bosses and hope this sways the decision.

Delayed payment to trainers

This is a poor idea. This will not affect profit, costs or any of the performance measures in question. It will affect cash flow in a positive manner. However, to delay payment without agreement can damage the relationships with the trainers, upon which he depends on for the quality of their presentations.

Overall the three proposals do improve the performance of the division. However most of the benefits accrue after quarter 2 and might therefore come too late for the promotion decision.

Note: The original question also had a requirement to discuss how to encourage a longer-term view. The suggested answer to this requirement is as follows:

To encourage a longer term view more emphasis should be placed on non-financial measures of performance.

This business is dependent amongst other things on the quality of its course provision. As a result an improvement could be to set targets for the quality of presentations given. Attendees could be asked to grade all trainers (or facilities) at the end of sessions. This would prevent cheap but weak presenters (and poor quality rooms) being employed by managers.

Equally, the senior managers have to take account of longer periods when assessing performance. Viewing a single quarter is too narrow and looking at the whole year is advisable. Wider issues should also be taken into consideration when making promotional decisions. Repurchase rates could be measured for client companies for example.

ACCA marking scheme		
		Marks
(a)	Per target discussed	2
		—
		8
		—
(b)	Revised forecasts	
	Voucher sales affect	1
	Vista sales affect	2
	Extra trainer cost	1
	Extra room hire cost	1
	Staff training increase	½
	Software cost	½
	Overall revised profit calculation	1
		—
	maximum	6
		—
(c)	2 marks per idea commented on maximum	6
		—
	Total	20
		—

Examiner's comments (extract)

For half marks in part (a) all that was expected was a statement (with simple supporting calculations) of whether or not the manager would meet each of the targets. Those that had a go at this invariably did well. Few, however, realised that the divisions improving performance in quarters 3 and 4 came too late for the promotion at the end of quarter 2. Many only commented on the profits of the division and ignored all the other targets. Many also assessed the performance more generally, calculating amongst other things % margins and ignored the targets altogether. This was very disappointing.

Part (b) was also poorly performed. Misreading the question was common. The extra revenue was clearly 80 vouchers x $125 = $10,000. It was not $10,000 per quarter despite many candidates belief. The revenue for the software upgrade should have begun in quarter 3 as stated in the question, but many candidates included extra revenue for all quarters. This, despite the clear indication in the question, that staff training would be needed in the first 2 quarters before course could be offered. Incremental room hire and trainer costs were missed by a large number of candidates. Candidates must learn to read performance management questions more carefully. The third suggestion by the manager to improve performance was to delay payment on trainer invoices. This is unethical and ineffective (since income statements are drawn up on an accrual basis). Remarkably few of the marginal candidates realised or commented on either of these points.

For part (c) candidates answers primarily consisted of a re-statement of the different steps being proposed with little or no comment at all. A comment requires opinion and anything sensible scored marks. For example stating that offering substantial discounts can upset existing customers is a valid point to make. Not one of all the marginal candidates I looked at made that point and very often any 'comment' at all.

This style of question was in the pilot paper, in the December 2007 paper. It is a core area. I cannot guarantee it will feature in every single exam in the future but candidates should prepare themselves to assess the performance of a business, both financially and non-financially if they want to pass.

63 OLIVER'S SALON (JUNE 09 EXAM)

(a) The average price for hairdressing per client is as follows:

2008: Female clients paid $200,000 for 8,000 visits. This is an average price per visit of $200,000/8,000 = $25.

In 2009 the female hairdressing prices did not increase and the mix of sales did not change so of the total revenue $170,000 (6,800 × $25) was from female clients. This means that the balance of $68,500 ($238,500 − $170,000) was from male clients at an average price of $20 per visit ($68,500/3,425).

(b) **Financial performance assessment**

Hairdressing sales growth: Oliver's Salon has grown significantly during the two years, with an increase of 19.25% (W1). This is impressive in a mature industry like hairdressing.

The increase has come from the launch of the new male hairdressing with a significant contraction in the core female business – down 15% (W1).

Hairdressing gross margin: Oliver's hairdressing overall gross margin has reduced significantly, down from 53% to 47.2% in 2009 (W2).

There has been an increase in staff numbers for the female part of the business and this, combined with the fall in the volume of sales from female clients, has significantly damaged margins from that customer type, with a fall from 53% to 40.5% (W2).

The margins from male clients in 2009 are 63·5% which is better than that achieved in 2008 from the female clients. This is probably mainly due to faster throughput, so that despite the lower average prices charged the overall margin was still quite good.

Staff costs: The staffing levels have had to increase to accommodate the new male market and the extra levels of business. The new hairdresser for the male clients is being paid slightly more than the previously employed staff (W3). This might encourage dissatisfaction. The addition of a junior will clearly reduce the overall average wage bill but increases costs overall whilst the volume of female clients is shrinking.

Advertising spend: This has increased by 150% in the year (W4). This is probably nothing to worry about as it is likely that the launching of the new product range (males!) will have required advertising. Indeed, given the increase in sales of male hair services it is fair to say that the money was well spent.

Rent is clearly a fixed cost and administrative expenses have gone up a mere 5.5%; these costs appear under control given the overall volume of clients is well up on 2008.

Electricity costs have jumped 14.3% which seems a lot but is probably a cost which Oliver would find hard to control. Energy companies are often very large organisations where competition is rarely significant. Small businesses have little choice but to pay the going rate for energy.

Net Profit: Overall net profit has worsened to 33.5% from 39% (W8). This is primarily due to the weakening gross margin and extra costs incurred for advertising. The advertising cost may not recur and so the net margin might improve next year.

Overall it is understandable that Oliver is disappointed with the financial results. With a 19.25% increase in overall sales he might have expected more net profit.

(c)   **Non-financial performance**

Quality: The number of complaints is up by 283% (W5) and is proportionately more frequent. This seems to be due to two main reasons. Firstly the switch away from a single gender salon has upset the existing customer base. It is possible that by trying to appeal to more customer types Oliver is failing to meet the needs of at least one group. It may be that the quality of hair services has not worsened but that the complaints are regarding the change towards a multi-gender business.

Secondly the wage rates paid to the new junior staff seem to be well below the wage rates of the existing staff (W3). This implies that they are in training and could be of poorer quality. It is stated that they are in a supporting role but if not properly supervised then mistakes could occur. This can easily lead to customer complaints.

Resource utilisation: The main resources that Oliver has are the staff and the rented property. As far as the property is concerned the asset is being used to a much higher degree with 27.8% more clients being serviced in the year (W6). However, as the overall margins are lower one might argue that just focusing solely on volume misses the point on asset utilisation.

As far as the staff usage is concerned it is a mixed scene. The female specialists are producing less per member of staff than in 2008 after the recruitment of one more staff member and a fall in volume of female clients. Each specialist served 2,000 female clients in 2008 and only 1,360 in 2009 (W9). Oliver may have been concerned with the complaints coming in and decided to do something about service levels by increasing resources for the female clients.

The specialist dealing with male clients has produced far more treatments than those serving the females. This is probably not unusual; we are told that the male customer requires only a simple service. Without comparative data we cannot say whether 3,425 customers per year is good. We also cannot say that this specialist is doing 'better' than the others. Cutting men's hair is quicker, so more output is inevitable.

Workings:

(W1) Sales growth overall is $238,500/$200,000 or +19.25%. The female hairdressing sales has though fallen by 15% ($200,000 − $170,000)/$200,000. This is entirely reflected in volume as there was no price increase in 2009 for female clients.

(W2) Gross margin overall is $106,000/$200,000 or 53% in 2008 and $112,500/238,500 or 47.2% in 2009. This can be analysed between the female and male clients:

	2008		*2009*	
	Female $	$	Female $	Male $
Sales	200,000		170,000	68,500
Less cost of sales:				
Hairdressing staff costs (W3)	(65,000)		(74,000)	(17,000)
Hair products – female	(29,000)		(27,000)	
Hair products – male				(8,000)
Gross profit	106,000		69,000	43,500
GP%	53%		40.5%	63.5%

(W3) Staff cost growth is $91,000/$65,000 or +40%. In absolute terms average staff costs were $65,000/4 = $16,250 in 2008.

Additional staff cost $26,000 ($91,000 − $65,000) in total for two people. The junior was paid $9,000 and so the new specialist for the male customers must have been paid $17,000

(W4) Advertising increased by $5,000/$2,000 or 150%

(W5) Number of complaints up by 46/12 or 283%. Complaints per customer visit up from 12/8,000 or 0.15% to 46/10,225 or 0.44%

(W6) Client growth is 10,225/8,000 or 27.8%

(W7) Number of female clients per specialist is 8,000/4 or 2,000 in 2008 and 6,800/5 or 1,360 in 2009. Number of male clients per specialist is 3,425 in 2009.

(W8) Net profit is $78,000/200,000 or 39% in 2008 and $80,000/238,500 or 33.5% in 2009.

ACCA marking scheme		
		Marks
(a)	Average price for female customers	1.0
	Average price for male customers	2.0
	Maximum	3.0
(b)	Sales growth	2.0
	Gross margin	2.0
	Rent	1.0
	Advertising spend	2.0
	Staff costs	2.0
	Electricity	1.0
	Overall comment	1.0
		11
(c)	Quality – single gender	1.5
	Quality – wage levels	1.5
	Quality – other	1.5
	Resource utilisation – property	1.0
	Resource utilisation – staff	2.0
	Resource utilisation – other	1.5
	Maximum	6.0
Total		20

Examiner's comments

This was a pure performance management question and the core of the paper. As is not uncommon with my papers the candidates were presented with two years of income based financial results. The last part of the question involved the use of non-financial indicators of success.

Astonishingly a significant number of candidates could not calculate the prices for female and male clients in the two years in question. An average price for the two client types was often the fall back. Basic numeracy is not an unreasonable expectation for accountants.

In part (b) there was some improvement in candidate's ability to assess performance. There were problems however:

Mathematical descriptions are not performance assessments. For example Sales are up 19%, but costs are up by 29% and so profits are only up by 3%.

Simply stating the % increases in numbers is not enough.

Indicating the absolute change in a cost is rarely that useful

Too narrow a range of figures considered, virtually all the numbers in the question carry marks

Surprisingly some were so desperate to calculate ROCE that they made up figures for assets values. Not surprisingly there were no marks for this.

I have written many times on this topic suggesting approaches that could be used. Without wishing to repeat myself too often candidates need to calculate a ratio (0.5 marks), make a qualitative statement (1 mark) and suggest a cause or some other comment (1 mark).

The non-financial indicators candidates were asked to consider were surrounding quality and resource utilisation.

Answers on quality dealt with the complaints issue well, but very few talked about the new members of staff and how their performance might be suspect. The lack of a pay rise can be de-motivating and so quality might suffer, this too was rarely picked up.

On resource utilisation candidates had a mixed result. The male throughput per specialist was very high but this was perhaps due to the fact that male hair tends to be easier (quicker) to cut. The female situation was different, with fewer clients for more staff. Many candidates recognised this. Very few talked about the property utilisation at all.

I did not ask for recommendations for Oliver. This is a higher skill level than required at F5. The marking team were instructed to give some credit for sensible advice but I would not recommend this as strategy to pass F5 in the future. Sticking to the question as set is the best advice.

64 TIES ONLY (DEC 07 EXAM)

Key answer tips

This is an in-depth question on performance appraisal where the key is to be able to discuss figures given or calculated. It is also an excellent example of how the examiner wants you to be able to discuss both financial and non-financial data. Non-financial performance is one of the examiner's key motivations. The examiner has stated that 'organisations seem obsessed with financial performance measures, but the future is determined more by non-financial performance. Both are important'.

In part (a) the simplest approach is to aim for eight points and try to use the key lines of table one as headings, e.g. sales, gross profit, website development. It is more meaningful to do some straightforward numerical analysis, e.g. calculate the percentage change in gross profit, than to just include the $ figure. Ensure a comment is made about each of the key figures included. Use the information in the scenario together with any other relevant knowledge.

In part (b) aim for four separate points and try to give a balanced answer pointing out the causes for concern, e.g. a falling gross profit percentage, in addition to the positive points.

In part (c) use each line of table two as a key heading. If you have time, include some straightforward calculations, e.g. calculate the percentage change between quarter 1 and 2 and compare to the industry average. This will make the data more meaningful and will make it easier to comment.

(a) **Financial performance of Ties Only Limited**

Sales growth

Ties Only Limited has had an excellent start to their business. From a standing start they have made $420,000 of sales and then grown that figure by over 61% to $680,000 in the following quarter. This is impressive particularly given that we know that the clothing industry is very competitive. Equally it is often the case that new businesses make slow starts, this does not look to be the case here.

Gross profit

The gross profit for the business is 52% for quarter 1 and 50% for quarter 2. We have no comparable industry data provided so no absolute comment can be made. However, we can see the gross profit has reduced by two points in one quarter. This is potentially serious and should not be allowed to continue.

The cause of this fall is unclear, price pressure from competitors is possible, who may be responding to the good start made by the business. If Ties Only Limited is reducing its prices, this would reflect on the gross profit margin produced.

It could also be that the supply side cost figures are rising disproportionately. As the business has grown so quickly, it may have had to resort to sourcing extra new supplies at short notice incurring higher purchase or shipping costs. These could all reduce gross margins achieved.

Website development

Website costs are being written off as incurred to the management accounting profit and loss account. They should be seen as an investment in the future and unlikely to continue in the long term. Website development has been made with the future in mind; we can assume that the future website costs will be lower than at present. Taking this into consideration the loss made by the business does not look as serious as it first appears.

Administration costs

These are 23.9% of sales in quarter 1 and only 22.1% of sales in quarter 2. This could be good cost control, impressive given the youth and inexperience of the management team.

Also any fixed costs included in the cost (directors' salaries are included) will be spread over greater volume. This would also reduce the percentage of cost against sales figure. This is an example of a business gaining critical mass. The bigger it gets the more it is able to absorb costs. Ties Only Limited may have some way to go in this regard, gaining a much greater size than at present.

Distribution costs

This is a relatively minor cost that again appears under control. Distribution costs are likely to be mainly variable (postage) and indeed the proportion of this cost to sales is constant at 4.9%.

Launch marketing

Another cost that although in this profit and loss account is unlikely to continue at this level. Once the 'launch' is complete this cost will be replaced by more general marketing of the website. Launch marketing will be more expensive than general marketing and so the profits of the business will improve over time. This is another good sign that the results of the first two quarters are not as bad as they seem.

Other costs

Another cost that appears under control in that it seems to have simply varied with volume.

(b)   Although the business has lost over $188,000 in the first two quarters of its life, this is not as disastrous as it looks. The reasons for this view are:

- New businesses rarely breakeven within six months of launch
- The profits are after charging the whole of the website development costs, these costs will not be incurred in the future
- Launch marketing is also deducted from the profits. This cost will not continue at such a high level in the future

The major threat concerns the fall in gross profit percentage which should be investigated.

The owners should be relatively pleased with the start that they have made. They are moving in the right direction and without website development and launch marketing they made a profit of $47,137 in quarter 1 and $75,360 in quarter 2.

If sales continue to grow at the rate seen thus far, then the business (given its ability to control costs) is well placed to return significant profits in the future.

The current profit (or loss) of a business does not always indicate a business's future performance.

(c)   **Non-financial indicators of success**

Website hits

This is a very impressive start. A new business can often find it difficult to make an impression in the market. Growth in hits is 25% between the two quarters. If this continued over a year the final quarter hits would be over 1.3m hits. The internet enables new businesses to impact the market quickly.

Number of ties sold

The conversion rates are 4% for quarter 1 and 4.5% for quarter 2. Both these figures may seem low but are ahead of the industry average data. (Industry acquired data must be carefully applied, although in this case the data seems consistent). It appears that the business has a product that the market is interested in. Ties Only Limited are indeed looking competitive.

We can use this statistic to calculate average price achieved for the ties

Quarter 1

$$\frac{\$420,000}{27,631} = \$15.20 \text{ per tie}$$

Quarter 2

$$\frac{\$680,000}{38,857} = \$17.50 \text{ per tie}$$

This suggests that the fall in gross profit has little to do with the sales price for the ties. The problem of the falling gross profit must lie elsewhere.

On time delivery

Clearly the business is beginning to struggle with delivery. As it expands, its systems and resources will become stretched. Customers' expectations will be governed by the terms on the website, but if expectations are not met then customers may not return. More attention will have to be placed on the delivery problem.

Sales returns

Returns are clearly common in this industry. Presumably, ties have to be seen and indeed worn before they are accepted as suitable by customers. The concern here is that the business's return rate has jumped up in quarter 2 and is now well above the average for the industry. In other words, performance is worsening and below that of the competitors. If the business is under pressure on delivery (as shown by the lateness of delivery) it could be that errors are being made. If wrong goods are sent out then they will be returned by disappointed customers.

The alternative view is that the quality of the product is not what is suggested by the website. If the quality is poor then the products could well be returned by unhappy customers.

This is clearly concerning and an investigation is needed.

System down time

System down time is to be avoided by internet based sellers as much as possible. If the system is down then customers cannot access the site. This could easily lead to lost sales at that time and cause customers not to try again at later dates. Downtime could be caused by insufficient investment at the development stage (we are told that the server was built to a high specification) or when the site is under pressure due to peaking volumes. This second explanation is more likely in this case.

The down time percentage has risen alarmingly and this is concerning. Ideally, we would need figures for the average percentage down time achieved by comparable systems to be able to comment further.

The owners are likely to be disappointed given the level of initial investment they have already made. A discussion with the website developers may well be warranted.

Summary

This new business is doing well. It is growing rapidly and ignoring non-recurring costs is profitable. It needs to focus on delivery accuracy, speed and quality of product. It also needs to focus on a remedy for the falling gross profit margin.

Workings

(W1) **Gross profit**

Quarter 1:

$$\frac{218,400}{420,000} = 52\%$$

Quarter 2:

$$\frac{339,320}{680,000} = 50\%$$

(W2) **Website conversion rates**

Quarter 1:

$$\frac{27,631}{690,789} = 4\%$$

Quarter 2:

$$\frac{38,857}{863,492} = 4.5\%$$

(W3) **Website hits growth**

Between quarter 1 and quarter 2 the growth in website hits has been:

$$\frac{863,492}{690,789} = 1.25 = 25\%$$

ACCA marking scheme		
		Marks
(a)	Sales	2
	Gross profit	3
	Website development	2
	Administration	2
	Distribution	1
	Launch marketing	2
	Overall comment	2
		——
	maximum	8
		——
(b)	Future profits comment	4
		——
(c)	Website hits	2
	Number of tie sales	1
	Tie price calculation	2
	On time delivery	2
	Returns	2
	System down time	1
	Summary comment	1
		——
	maximum	8
		——
Total		20
		——

Examiner's comments (extract)

I wanted some attempt at a qualitative assessment of the financial in part (a) and non-financial performance in part (c). Calculating a ratio without real comment did not gain full marks. For example in part (a) the sales were up 61% from quarter 1 to quarter 2. This calculation gained a half mark only. Saying that this growth was 'impressive' scored a mark! Saying that growth rates such as this are hard to maintain or that market share was probably increasing impressed the markers for more marks. Far too often candidates did little more than calculate a ratio. This is not good enough to pass.

Part (b) was done reasonably with most scoring at least 2 marks. Of the failing candidates it was clear that a deeper understanding of what simple financial data tells you was not present. If this business continued to grow, maintained the same gross profit and controlled its administration and other costs then it would make profit. It would also benefit from the inevitable reduction in 'launch' marketing and website 'development'. These last two short sentences would have scored full marks.

The problem was not as acute in part (c) where candidates seemed more willing to give a qualitative assessment of the non-financial data. Linking the problems of poor delivery times and the rapid growth of the business was not uncommon and gained good credit. However, failing candidates did little more than repeat the data I had given them or calculated a % change in them without any qualitative comment at all.

For the record, increasing sales returns proportion is not a good thing, as a substantial minority thought.

The qualitative comments required were not too difficult. For example I gave data suggesting that the web system was down more often in quarter 2 than in quarter 1. Marks were awarded for comments such as:

- The website was a critical aspect of the business
- The increased amount of time was significant
- Sales could be lost
- That it was disappointing, given the high level of investment

Markers were given flexibility in this area to give credit for any reasonable comments.

It might be worth pointing out here that I did not ask for suggestions as to what should be done by the business to correct the apparent problem (e.g. raise more finance for the rapid growth) and so these type of comments did not earn marks.

I see this type of question (the interpretation type) as central to performance management. It is what separates F2 from F5. Candidates need to be better prepared for future questions of this type. The Pilot paper had a similar question to Ties Only in it, which also gave financial and non financial data for a business. If you look at both these questions you should get a clear idea of how future questions will be set.

65   NON-FINANCIAL MEASURES

Key answer tips

This question tests your knowledge of non-financial measures (NFMs) of performance.

Parts (a) and (b) are standard bookwork. In part (c) ensure you discuss the problems with using NFMs. In part (d) make sure you explain each of your measures.

(a)   **Arguments in favour of using the profit measure** in evaluating the performance of a business

- Profit (however calculated) is a generally accepted measure to evaluate a business both internally and externally. Internal users of financial information identify profit as the reward for the skills of being a successful entrepreneur. This measure is still a major determinant of the reward systems of managers of decentralised units. If they meet certain quantified performance targets they obtain the financial rewards that recognise their entrepreneurial skills.

- External users of accounts recognise profit as a measure for identifying the success or failure of the policies of the directors who, as stewards of the assets, are entrusted with the task of increasing the wealth of shareholders. Why do an investors invest? Generally to improve their financial position over time. How do investors improve their financial position over time? Hopefully the stock market's system of intelligence identifies the important factors in the performance of a business and this is reflected in the share price. How do market analysts identify performance? Certainly the measure of 'earnings' is a major determinant in the influential commentaries that can influence investor behaviour.

- The concept of profit is intuitive. A street trader buys inventory at $100 and sells it at the end of the day for $500. He makes a gain of $400 out of which he replenishes his inventory, pays his living expenses and has a surplus to demonstrate that his wealth has increased after meeting all necessary expenditure.

- 'Profit' is the maximum amount that the company can distribute during the year and still expect to be as well off at the end of the year as at the beginning. Consequently profit-based measures such as return on capital employed and earnings per share recognise this all encompassing need to measure how wealth (or capital) grows or is maintained.

(b)   **Limitations of the profit measure**

Managers may focus on profitability to the expense of such important factors as good cash flow management, which is so essential for long and short run survival. The following issues are relevant to the argument that profit measurement approaches to evaluation suffer from considerable limitations.

- **Subjectivity of accounting bases**: No single universally accepted measure for profit can ever be defined. Exchange rate problems can inflate or deflate profits. Depreciation policies can also manipulate the measurement of profit depending on the age and current values of depreciable assets.

- **Profit is a short term measure**: Profit is often a bar to taking risks in ventures that may be slow to mature and do not generate an accounting profit in the early years of their lives. It is always possible to find situations where a project makes losses in year 1 and year 2 and therefore runs the risk of being rejected by management. If however, the project was evaluated on a basis that recognised long run costs and benefits (such as the calculation of Net Present Value) the worthwhile nature of the project would become apparent. The business might therefore reject potential sources of wealth because of an indifferent performance in the short term.

- **Profit can be manipulated**: The profit measure can be manipulated by the preparers of accounts by the following methods:

    - Deferring expenditure to later periods either by accounting adjustments or by delaying the incidence of transactions

    - Changing accounting policies so that a more favourable result is obtained. This can be done by judgmental differences on the valuation of inventories, for example

    - Recognition of income by imprudent methods or by highly subjective accounting treatments.

(c)   Problems in the use of **non-financial measures** (NFMs) for long and short term control.

Many businesses recognise the imperfections of financial measures oriented on the profit measure and may wish to devise NFMs for performance evaluation. NFMs fall into two categories, qualitative and quantitative. For example, it would be relatively easy to define quantitative measures in certain areas of management. Schemes of total quality management often define measures for such issues as customer care by accumulating data on:

- Complaints
- Rejections
- Disputes
- Errors in charging.

However, developing qualitative measures is difficult and often subjective. What is a satisfactory measure of customer care? What constitutes an effective service to the public in a non profit making entity such as a local authority? For example, a well known grocery chain has publicised its intention to concentrate on performance measures that provide competitive advantage and to spend less time on pure 'number crunching' of accounting data. They perceive that identifying problems at operating unit level (where the customer is served) is far more significant for strategic (long term) aims as well as for short term control.

Most systems involving the use of NFMs fail because staff are insufficiently educated about the aims of the organisation or are not sufficiently aware of the purpose of the measures.

In conclusion, the success or failure of NFMs is attributable to top management's ability to define the aims or mission of the organisation and direct the employees towards the achievement of that essential mission.

(d)   **Financial perspective**

- Meeting a key financial target such as ROCE.
- Sales growth. Insurance companies are concerned with market share and would like to see strong sales growth.

Customer perspective

- Customer retention. This is the proportion of customers who renew their policies from one year to the next. If the proportion is high, then it would imply that the insurance company is keeping its customers happy; if low, it would seem that the company is doing something wrong.
- Number of complaints. This measure could be used for just about any organisation. A high level of complaints would indicate where the company's customers are not pleased with the service that they are receiving.

Learning and growth perspective or innovation and learning perspective

- Labour turnover. Labour measures come within this perspective. A high labour turnover would indicate that the workforce is not happy, which may then lead to problems with their performance. It also means that those workers who leave will have to be replaced and that their replacements will need training, leading to extra cost and possibly initially poor performance.
- The number of new types of policies issued each year. This would be a good indication of innovation.

Internal business process perspective

- The percentage of policies issued or claims processed with the target time. This is an indication of how well the company performs its core functions.
- Unit cost. The cost per policy issued, or per claim processed, would be an indication of how well the business is performing its internal functions. Care must be taken that if the cost is reducing so then the service to the customer is not getting worse.

Note: Only ONE measure is required for each perspective.

66 PUBLIC SECTOR ORGANISATION

Budget preparation

It would be in line with the principles of modern management if the department manager was encouraged to participate more in setting the budget. In this way, he would be more likely to show commitment to the organisational goals in general and the budget in particular. He is closer to the activity for which the budget is prepared, and so the relevance and accuracy of the budget should be improved. This involvement should extend also to discussion of the form and frequency of the reporting which is to take place for his/her department.

Activity volume

The volume of visits undertaken is 20% greater than that budgeted. It is inappropriate to compare the actual costs of visiting 12,000 clients with a budget for 10,000 clients. Costs such as wages, travel expenses and consumables would be expected to be higher than the fixed budget in these circumstances.

One way to deal with this is to adjust, or flex, the budget to acknowledge the cost implications of the higher number of visits, or to be aware of it when making any comparison. If a factor of 1.20 is applied to the overall wages budget for permanent and casual staff (i.e. on the assumption that it is a variable cost), the flexed budget $5,040 ($4,200 × 1.2) is greater than the actual cost of $4,900. Taking a similar approach to travel expenses and consumables expenses:

- actual travel expenses are exactly in line with the flexed budget (1,500 × 1.20), but

- the consumables costs seem to be highly overspent compared to the flexed budget (4,000 × 1.2).

To circulate a report as originally constructed seems to highlight and publicise some invalid comparisons from which inappropriate conclusions may be drawn. It is recommended that for cost control purposes, a report is prepared which compares actual spending with a flexed budget based on the actual activity. This would require an estimate of the variable, fixed and semi-variable nature of the cost items.

Controllability

It is possible to question whether all the costs shown need to feature in the report. For example, the allocated administrative costs and equipment depreciation are book entries that do not directly affect the department and are not likely to be controllable by employees of the department. There are, therefore, adverse variances on the report contributing to the overall overspend that are not the responsibility of the departmental manager. The difference between actual and budgeted cost of administration serves no useful purpose in this report, because the manager can take no action to influence this directly. The only justification to include this is if the manager can bring about some pressure to reduce this spending by someone else.

It may be unwise to adopt the guide of a 5% deviation to judge variances. The key is whether a cost is out of control and can be corrected by managerial action. Also, 5% of some values can be significant whilst on others 5% of the total cost might be of little consequence.

Funding allocation

The Director is correct in pointing out that 'the department must live within its funding allocation'. However, it is not like a commercial organisation where more output can result in more revenue and hence more money to spend. Increased funding will only be achieved if this organisation and the department is allocated more funds as a result of national or local government decisions to support an increase in services.

It would be appropriate for the funding allocation to be compared with the flexible budget (based on actual activity) to encourage the managers to be aware of and live within the budget allocation. Ways can always be found to spend more money, and so authority structures must be in place to ensure that requests to spend have been budgeted and appropriately funded. Hence the organisational arrangements which authorised the increased visits would be examined.

The nature of the activity for which the budget is being developed should not be lost sight of. It is more complex to deal with budget decisions related to the welfare needs of society than those for a typical manufacturing firm. There are no clear input-output relationships in the former, and hence it is difficult to judge what is justifiable spending for the department compared with other departments and public sector organisations.

Other aspects

One possible outcome from discussion over the appropriate form of report would be the use of non-financial measures. The total staff hours worked, client satisfaction and size of the potential client population are all examples of extensions to the reporting procedure which would help to place the results in context.

The style of the approach adopted by the Director may show some lack of behavioural insight. The despatch of a memo to deal with a prototype report may result in lower staff morale and increased tension in the Homecare department. This may lead to inappropriate future decisions on spending and budget 'game playing' within the department. It may, of course, be a conscious decision of the Director to place the manager in the position of having to reduce spending to the allocated level.

Although this is the first month's report, in the future it may be helpful to use an additional column of the report to show the year-to-date figures. This would help to identify trends and assist discussion of whether costs are being controlled over the longer term. To show future results for only one month may be insufficient; for example, the repairs to equipment may not follow a regular pattern and this would be revealed if cumulative data existed.

67   WOODSIDE CHARITY (JUNE 07 EXAM)

(a)   **Discussion of performance of Woodside Charity**

In a year which saw fundraising fall $80,000 short of the target level, costs were over budget in all areas of activity except overnight shelter provision. The budget provided for a surplus of $98,750, but the actual figures for the year show a shortfall of $16,980.

Free meals provision cost $12,750 (14%) more than budgeted. Most of the variance (69%) was due to providing 1,750 more meals than budgeted, although $4,000 of it was due to an increase of 20p in the average cost per meal.

Variable cost of overnight shelter provision was $26,620 (11%) less than budgeted. $31,000 was saved because usage of the service was 1,240 bed-nights below budget, but an adverse variance of $4,380 arose because of an increase of 50p in the average unit cost of provision.

Variable advice centre costs were $16,600 (37%) above budget. This was due to increased usage of the service, which was 17% up on budget from 3,000 to 3,500 sessions, and to an increase in the average cost of provision, which rose by 17% from $15 to $17.60 per session.

Fixed costs of administration and centre maintenance were $18,000 (28%) above budget and the costs of campaigning and advertising were $15,000 (10%) above budget.

While investigation of some of the variances in the reconciliation statement below may be useful in controlling further cost increases, the Woodside charity appears to have more than achieved its objectives in terms of providing free meals and advice. The lower usage of overnight shelter could lead to transfer of resources from this area in the next budget to the services that are more in demand. The reasons for the lower usage of overnight shelter are not known, but the relationship between the provision of effective advice and the usage of overnight shelter could be investigated.

Operating statement

	$	$	$
Budgeted surplus (W1)			98,750
Funding shortfall (W3)			(80,000)
			18,750

	Favourable	Adverse	
Free meals (W4)			
Price variance		4,000	
Usage variance		8,750	
Overnight shelter (W5)			
Price variance		4,380	
Usage variance	31,000		
Advice centre (W6)			
Price variance		9,100	
Usage variance		7,500	
Campaigning and advertising (W7)			
Expenditure variance		15,000	
Fixed cost (W8)			
Expenditure variance		18,000	
	31,000	66,730	(35,730)
Actual shortfall (W2)			(16,980)

Workings

(W1) **Budgeted figures**

	$	
Free meals provision	91,250	(18,250 meals at $5 per meal)
Overnight shelter (variable)	250,000	(10,000 bed-nights at $30 – $5 per night)
Advice centre (variable)	45,000	(3,000 sessions at $20 – $5 per session)
Fixed costs	65,000	(10,000 × $5) + (3,000 × $5)
Campaigning and advertising	150,000	
	601,250	
Surplus for unexpected costs	98,750	
Fundraising target	700,000	

(W2) **Actual figures**

	$	
Free meals provision	104,000	(20,000 meals at $5.20 per meal)
Overnight shelter	223,380	(8,760 bed-nights $25.50 per night)
Advice centre	61,600	(3,500 sessions at $17.60 per session)
Fixed costs	83,000	
Campaigning and advertising	165,000	
	636,980	
Shortfall	16,980	
Funds raised	620,000	

(W3) Funding shortfall – 700,000 – 620,000 = $80,000 (A)

(W4) Free meals price variance = (5.00 – 5.20) × 20,000 = $4,000 (A)

Free meals usage variance = (18,250 – 20,000) × 5.00 = $8,750 (A)

(W5) Overnight shelter price variance = (25.00 – 25.50) × 8,760 = $4,380 (A)

Overnight shelter usage variance – (10,000 – 8,760) × 25 = $31,000 (F)

(W6) Advice centre price variance = (17.60 – 15.00) × 3,500 = $9,100 (A)

Advice centre usage variance = (3,000 – 3,500) × 15.00 = $7,500 (A)

(W7) Campaigning and advertising expenditure variance = 150,000 – 165,000 = $15,000 (A)

(W8) Fixed cost expenditure variance = 65,000 – 83,000 = $18,000 (A)

(b)   Financial management and control in a not-for-profit organisation (NFPO) such as the Woodside charity must recognise that the primary objectives of these organisations are essentially non-financial. Here, these objectives relate to helping the homeless and because the charity has no profit-related objective, financial management and control must focus on providing value for money. This means that resources must be found economically in order to keep input costs as low as possible; that these resources must be used as efficiently as possible in providing the services offered by the charity; and that the charity must devise and use effective methods to meet its objectives. Financial objectives could relate to the need to obtain funding for offered services and to the need to control costs in providing these services.

Preparing budgets

The nature of the activities of a NFPO can make it difficult to forecast levels of activity. In the case of the Woodside charity, homeless people seeking free meals would be given them, and more food would be prepared if necessary, regardless of the budgeted provision for a given week or month. The level of activity is driven here by the needs of the homeless, and although financial planning may produce weekly or monthly budgets that consider seasonal trends, a high degree of flexibility may be needed to respond to unpredictable demand. This was recognised by the charity by budgeting for a fundraising surplus for unexpected costs.

It is likely that forecasting cost per unit of service in a NFPO can be done with more precision if the unit of service is small and the service is repetitive or routine, and this is true for the Woodside charity. It is unlikely, though, that a detailed analysis of costs has been carried out along these lines, and more likely that an incremental budget approach has been used on a total basis for each service provided. It depends on the financial skills and knowledge available to the charity from its three full-time staff and team of volunteers.

Controlling costs

Because of the need for economy and efficiency, this is a key area of financial management and control for a NFPO. The costs of some inputs can be minimised at the point of buying, for example the Woodside charity can be economical when buying food, drink, crockery, blankets, cleaning materials and so on. The costs of other inputs can be minimised at the point of use, for example the Woodside charity can encourage economy in the use of heating, lighting, water consumption, telephone usage and postage. In an organisation staffed mainly by volunteers with an unpredictable clientele, cost control is going to depend to a large extent on the way in which responsibility and authority are delegated.

Collecting information

Cost control is not possible without collecting regularly information on costs incurred, as well as storing and processing this information. In the Woodside charity, provision has been made in the budget for fixed administration costs and the administration duties must hopefully relate in part to this collecting of costing information. Without it, budgeting and financial reporting would not be possible. Annual accounts would be needed in order to retain charitable status and to show providers of funds that their donations were being used to their best effect.

Meeting objectives

A NFPO organisation must be able to determine and demonstrate whether it is meeting its declared objectives and so needs to develop measures to do this. This can be far from easy. The analysis of the performance of the Woodside charity over the last year shows that it may be possible to measure objective attainment quantitatively, i.e. in terms of number of free meals served, number of bed-nights used and number of advice sessions given. Presumably, objectives are being met to a greater extent if more units of service are being provided, and so the adverse usage variances for free meals and advice sessions can in fact be used to show that the charity is meeting a growing need.

The meaning of quantitative measures of service provision may not be clear, however. For example, the lower usage of bed-nights could be attributed to the effective provision of advice to the homeless on finding housing and financial aid, and so may also be seen as a success. It could also be due to dissatisfaction amongst the homeless with the accommodation offered by the shelter. In a similar vein, the higher than budget number of advice sessions may be due to repeat visits by homeless people who were not given adequate advice on their first visit, rather than to an increase in the number of people needing advice. Qualitative measures of objective attainment will therefore be needed in addition to, or to supplement, quantitative ones.

Section 3

2007 PILOT PAPER EXAM QUESTIONS

Note: The pilot paper was written when the exam structure was based on four 25 mark questions. Given that the new structure is five 20 mark questions, we have re-written the pilot questions as indicated below. You are advised to still look at all the elements of the original questions as they still reflect the examiner's emphasis and expectations.

1   TRIPLE LIMITED

Triple Limited makes three types of gold watch – the Diva (D), the Classic (C) and the Poser (P). A traditional product costing system is used at present; although an activity based costing (ABC) system is being considered. Details of the three products for a typical period are:

| | Hours per unit | | Materials | Production |
	Labour hours	Machine hours	Cost per unit ($)	Units
Product D	½	1½	20	750
Product C	1½	1	12	1,250
Product P	1	3	25	7,000

Direct labour costs $6 per hour and production overheads are absorbed on a machine hour basis. The overhead absorption rate for the period is $28 per machine hour.

Required:

(a)   Calculate the cost per unit for each product using traditional methods, absorbing overheads on the basis of machine hours.   (3 marks)

Total production overheads are $654,500 and further analysis shows that the total production overheads can be divided as follows:

	%
Costs relating to set-ups	35
Costs relating to machinery	20
Costs relating to materials handling	15
Costs relating to inspection	30
Total production overhead	100

The following total activity volumes are associated with each product line for the period as a whole:

	Number of set-ups	Number of movements of materials	Number of inspections
Product D	75	12	150
Product C	115	21	180
Product P	480	87	670
	670	120	1,000

Required:

(b) **Using ABC principles the revised overhead costs per unit are as follows**

Product	D	C	P
Overhead cost per unit ($)	94.95	79.07	69.21

Show how the revised overhead cost per unit for each Diva has been determined (work to two decimal places). **(7 marks)**

Note: The original pilot question asked you to calculate the cost per unit under ABC for all three products for a total of 12 marks)

(c) **Explain why costs per unit calculated under ABC are often very different to costs per unit calculated under more traditional methods. Use the information from Triple Limited to illustrate.** **(4 marks)**

(d) **Discuss the implications of a switch to ABC on pricing and profitability.** **(6 marks)**

(Total: 20 marks)

2 SIMPLY SOUP LIMITED

Simply Soup Limited manufactures and sells soups in a JIT environment. Soup is made in a manufacturing process by mixing liquidised vegetables, melted butter and stock (stock in this context is a liquid used in making soups). They operate a standard costing and variances system to control its manufacturing processes. At the beginning of the current financial year they employed a new production manager to oversee the manufacturing process and to work alongside the purchasing manager. The production manager will be rewarded by a salary and a bonus based on the directly attributable variances involved in the manufacturing process.

After three months of work there is doubt about the performance of the new production manager. On the one hand, the cost variances look on the whole favourable, but the sales director has indicated that sales are significantly down and the overall profitability is decreasing.

The table overleaf shows the variance analysis results for the first three months of the manager's work.

Table 1

F = Favourable. A = Adverse

	Month 1	Month 2	Month 3
Material price variance	$300 (F)	$900 (A)	$2,200 (A)
Material mix variance	$1,800 (F)	$2,253 (F)	$2,800 (F)
Material yield variance	$2,126 (F)	$5,844 (F)	$9,752 (F)
Total variance	$4,226 (F)	$7,197 (F)	$10,352 (F)

The actual level of activity was broadly the same in each month and the standard monthly material total cost was approximately $145,000.

The standard cost card is as follows for the period under review.

	$
0.90 litres of liquidised vegetables @ $0.80/ltr =	0.72
0.05 litres of melted butter @$4/ltr	0.20
1.10 litres of stock @ $0.50/ltr	0.55
Total cost to produce 1 litre of soup	1.47

Required:

(a)   **Using the information in table 1:**

(i)   **Explain the meaning of each type of variance above (price, mix and yield but excluding the total variance) and briefly discuss to what extent each type of variance is controllable by the production manager.** **(6 marks)**

(ii)   **Evaluate the performance of the production manager considering both the cost variance results above and the sales director's comments.** **(5 marks)**

(b)   The board has asked that the variances be calculated for Month 4. In Month 4 the production department data is as follows:

Actual results for Month 4

Liquidised vegetables:	Bought	82,000 litres	costing $69,700
Melted butter:	Bought	4,900 litres	costing $21,070
Stock:	Bought	122,000 litres	costing $58,560

Actual production was 112,000 litres of soup.

Calculate the material price, mix and yield variances for Month 4. You are not required to comment on the performance that the calculations imply. Round variances to the nearest $. **(9 marks)**

(Total: 20 marks)

Note: The original question also had a requirement (a) part (iii) for 4 marks:

Outline two suggestions how the performance management system might be changed to better reflect the performance of the production manager.

---

3   BFG LIMITED

BFG Limited is investigating the financial viability of a new product the S-pro. The S-pro is a short-life product for which a market has been identified at an agreed design specification. The product will only have a life of 12 months.

The following estimated information is available in respect of S-pro:

(1)   Sales should be 120,000 in the year in batches of 100 units. An average selling price of $1,050 per batch of 100 units is expected. All sales are for cash.

(2)   An 80% learning curve will apply for the first 700 batches after which a steady state production time will apply, with the labour time per batch after the first 700 batches being equal to the time for the 700th batch. The cost of the first batch was measured at $2,500. This was for 500 hours at $5 per hour.

(3)   Variable overhead is estimated at $2 per labour hour.

(4)   Direct material will be $500 per batch of S-pro for the first 200 batches produced. The second 200 batches will cost 90% of the cost per batch of the first 200 batches. All batches from then on will cost 90% of the batch cost for each of the second 200 batches. All purchases are made for cash.

(5)   S-pro will require additional space to be rented. These directly attributable fixed costs will be $15,000 per month.

A target net cash flow of $130,000 is required in order for this project to be acceptable.

Note: The learning curve formula is given on the formulae sheet. At the learning rate of 0.8 (80%), the learning factor (b) is equal to −0.3219.

Required:

(a)   **Prepare detailed calculations to show whether product S-pro will provide the target net cash flow.**   **(12 marks)**

(b)   **Calculate what length of time then second batch will take if the actual rate of learning is:**

    (i)   **80%;**

    (ii)   **90%.**

    Explain which rate shows the faster learning.   **(5 marks)**

(c)   **Outline specific actions that BFG could take to improve the net cash flow calculated above.**   **(3 marks)**

(Total: 20 marks)

> *Note:* The original question gave 8 marks for part (c), thus expecting a more in-depth discussion than needed for the revised version here

4   PRESTON FINANCIAL SERVICES

The following information relates to Preston Financial Services, an accounting practice. The business specialises in providing accounting and taxation work for dentists and doctors. In the main the clients are wealthy, self-employed and have an average age of 52.

The business was founded by and is wholly owned by Richard Preston, a dominant and aggressive sole practitioner. He feels that promotion of new products to his clients would be likely to upset the conservative nature of his dentists and doctors and, as a result, the business has been managed with similar products year on year.

You have been provided with financial information relating to the practice in appendix 1. In appendix 2, you have been provided with non-financial information which is based on the balanced scorecard format.

Appendix 1: Financial information

	Current year	Previous year
Turnover ($000)	945	900
Net profit ($000)	187	180
Average cash balances ($000)	21	20
Average debtor/trade receivables days (industry average 30 days)	18 days	22 days
Inflation rate (%)	3	3

Appendix 2: Balanced Scorecard (extract)

Internal business processes

	Current year	Previous year
Error rates in jobs done	16%	10%
Average job completion time	7 weeks	10 weeks

Customer knowledge

	Current year	Previous year
Number of customers	1,220	1,500
Average fee levels ($)	775	600
Market share	14%	20%

Learning and growth

	Current year	Previous year
Percentage of revenue from non-core work	4%	5%
Industry average of the proportion of revenue from non-core work in accounting practices	30%	25%
Employee retention rate	60%	80%

Notes

(1)   Error rates measure the number of jobs with mistakes made by staff as a proportion of the number of clients serviced.

(2)   Core work is defined as being accountancy and taxation. Non-core work is defined primarily as pension advice and business consultancy. Non core work is traditionally high margin work.

Required:

(a) Using the information in appendix 1 only, comment on the financial performance of the business (briefly consider growth, profitability, liquidity and credit management). **(8 marks)**

(b) Using the data given in appendix 2 comment on the performance of the business. Include comments on internal business processes, customer knowledge and learning/growth, separately, and provide a concluding comment on the overall performance of the business. **(12 marks)**

(Total: 20 marks)

Note: The original question also included the following requirement for 5 marks:

Explain why non financial information, such as the type shown in appendix 2, is likely to give a better indication of the likely future success of the business than the financial information given in appendix 1.

Section 4

ANSWERS TO 2007 PILOT PAPER EXAM QUESTIONS

1 TRIPLE LIMITED

(a) Traditional cost per unit

	D	C	P
	$	$	$
Material	20	12	25
Labour ($6/hour)	3	9	6
Direct costs	23	21	31
Production overhead ($28/machine hour)	42	28	84
Total production cost/unit	65	49	115

(b) ABC cost per unit

> **Examiner's comments (extract)**
>
> Each step required has been given its own sub-heading to make the procedure clear. The basic principle is to find an overhead cost per unit of activity for each element of overhead cost. In some cases it might then be possible to find an overhead cost per unit directly, like we have shown in the alternative answer; here it is probably easier to split overheads between each product type first and then find a cost per unit as shown.

(i) Total overheads: These were given at $654,500

(ii) Total machine hours (needed as the driver for machining overhead)

	Hours/unit	Production units	Total hours
D	1½	750	1,125
C	1	1,250	1,250
P	3	7,000	21,000
Total machine hours			23,375

(iii)   Analysis of total overheads and cost per unit of activity

Overhead and Driver	%	Total overhead $	Level of driver activity	Cost/driver
Set ups: Number of set ups	35	229,075	670	341.90
Machining: Machine hours	20	130,900	23,375	5.60
Materials handling: Material movements	15	98,175	120	818.13
Inspection: Number of inspections	30	196,350	1,000	196.35
	100	**654,500**		

(iv)   Total overheads by product and per unit

> **Note:** With the revised form of the question, only the figures for product D are required from this point onwards

	Product D $ Cost	Product C $ Cost	Product P $ Cost	Total $ Cost
Overhead:				
Set-ups	25,643	39,319	164,113	229,075
Machining	6,300	7,000	117,600	130,900
Material handling	9,817	17,181	71,177	98,175
Inspection	29,453	35,343	131,554	196,350
Total O/H cost	71,213	98,843	484,444	654,500
Units produced	750	1,250	7,000	
Costs per unit	$94.95	$79.07	$69.21	

(v)   Cost per unit

	D $	C $	P $
Direct costs (from (a))	23.00	21.00	31.00
Overheads (from (iv))	94.95	79.07	69.21
	117.95	100.07	100.21

Alternative Answer for b)

Overhead per unit:

	D
	$
Set up (W1)	34.19
Machinery (W2)	8.40
Material handling (W3)	13.09
Inspection (W4)	39.27
	94.95

(W1) Cost pool = set up

Cost driver = number of set ups

$$\text{Cost driver rate (CDR)} = \frac{0.35 \times 654{,}500}{75 + 115 + 480} = \$341.90 \text{ per set up}$$

D: 341.90 x 75 setups / 750 units = 34.19

(W2) Cost pool = machinery

Cost driver = machine hours

$$\text{CDR} = \frac{0.20 \times 654{,}500}{(1.5 \times 750) + (1 \times 1250) + (3 \times 7000)} = \$5.60 \text{ per machine hour}$$

D: 5.6 x 1.5 machine hours per unit = 8.40

(W3) Cost pool = materials handling

Cost driver = number of movements of material

$$\text{CDR} = \frac{0.15 \times 654{,}500}{12 + 21 + 87} = \$818.13 \text{ per movement of material}$$

D: 818.13 x 12 material movements / 750 units = 13.09

(W4) Cost pool = inspection

Cost driver = number of inspections

$$\text{CDR} = \frac{0.3 \times 654{,}500}{150 + 180 + 670} = \$196.35 \text{ per inspection}$$

D: 196.35 x 150 inspections / 750 units = 39.27

(c)   **Comment**

The overhead costs per unit are summarised below together with volume of production.

Product	D	C	P
Volume	750	1,250	7,000
Conventional overheads	$42	$28	$84
ABC overheads	$95	$79	$69

The result of the change to Activity Based Costing is clear, the overhead cost of D and C have risen whilst that of P has fallen.

This is in line with the comments of many who feel that ABC provides a fairer unit cost better reflecting the effort required to make different products.   This is illustrated here with product P which may take longer to make than D or C, but once production has started the process is simple to administer.   This may be due to having much longer production lines.

Products D and C are relatively minor volume products but still require a fair amount of administrative time by the production department; i.e. they involve a fair amount of 'hassle'. This is explained by the following table of 'activities per 1,000 units produced'.

	Set-ups	Materials movements	Inspections
D	100	16	200
C	92	17	144
P	69	12	96

This table highlights the problem.

–   Product P has fewer set-ups, material movements and inspections per 1,000 units than or C.

–   As a consequence product P's overhead cost per unit for these three elements has fallen.

–   The machining overhead cost per unit for P is still two or three times greater than for products D or C, but because this overhead only accounts for 20% of the total overhead this has a small effect on total cost.

–   The overall result is P's fall in production overhead cost per unit and the rise in those figures for D and C.

(d)   **Pricing and profitability**

Switching to ABC can, as in this case, substantially change the costs per unit calculations. Consequently if an organisation's selling prices are determined by a version of cost-plus pricing then the selling prices would alter.

In this case the selling price of D and C would rise significantly, and the selling price of P would fall. This, at first glance may be appealing however:

–   Will the markets for D and C tolerate a price rise? There could be competition to consider. Will customers be willing to pay more for a product simply because Triple Ltd has changed its cost allocation methods?

– Product P is a high volume product. Reducing its selling price will have a dramatic effect on revenue and contribution. One would have to question whether such a reduction would be compensated for by increased volumes.

Alternatively, one could take the view that prices are determined by the market and therefore if Triple Ltd switches to ABC, it is not the price that would change but the profit or margin per unit that would change.

This can change attitudes within the business. Previously high margin products (under a traditional overhead absorption system) would be shown as less profitable. Salesmen (possibly profit motivated) can begin to push the sales of different products seeking higher personal rewards. (Assuming commission based on profits per unit sold).

It must always be remembered that if overheads are essentially fixed then they should be ignored in business decision making. Switching to ABC can change reported profits per unit but it is contribution per unit that is perhaps more important.

ACCA marking scheme		
		Marks
(a)	1 mark for each product	3
(b)	Total machine hours	1
	Cost per driver calculation	3
	Overheads split by product table	2
	Cost per unit calculation	1
	Maximum	6
(c)	Explanation	4
(d)	Comment on pricing, markets, customers and profitability	6
Total		20

2   SIMPLY SOUP LIMITED

(a)   Simply Soup Limited

(i)   Meaning and controllability of the variances

Material price variance

Indicates whether Simply Soup has paid more (adverse) or less (favourable) for its input materials than the standard prices set for the period. For example, if a new supplier had to be found and the price paid was more than the standard price then Simply Soup would incur an extra cost. This extra cost is the price variance.

Price variances are controllable to the extent that Simply Soup can choose its suppliers. On the other hand, vegetables are a seasonal and weather dependent crop and therefore factors outside Simply Soups control can influence prices in the market. The key issue is that the production manager will not control the price paid that is the job of the Purchasing Manager.

Material mix variance

Considers the cost of a change in the mix of the ingredients to make soup . For example adding less butter (which is expensive) and more stock (which is cheaper) will be a cheaper mix than the standard mix. A cheaper mix will result in a favourable variance.

The recipe determines the mix. The recipe is entirely under the control of the production manager.

Material yield variance

This shows the productivity of the manufacturing process. If the process produces more soup than expected then the yield will be good (favourable). At the moment 2.05 litres of input produces 1 litre of soup, if 2.05 litres of input produces more than 1 litre of soup then the yield is favourable. Greater yield than expected can be a result of operational efficiency or a change in mix.

The production manager controls the operational process so should be able to control the yield. Poor quality ingredients can damage yield but the production manager should be in control of quality and reject dubious ingredients. The production manager is also responsible for things like spillage. Higher spillage can also reduce yield.

(ii)   **Production manager's performance**

Cost efficiency

The production manager has produced significant favourable cost variances. The total favourable variance has risen from $4,226 to $10,352 in the first three months. This last figure represents approximately 7.1% of the standard monthly spend.

The prices for materials have been rising but are probably outside the control of the production manager. The rising prices may have put pressure on the production manager to cheapen the mix.

The mix has become cheaper. This could be seen as a cost efficient step. However, Simply Soup must question the quality implications of this (see later).

The yield results are the most significant. The manager is getting far more out of the process than is usual. The new mix is clearly far more productive than before. This could easily be seen as an indicator of good performance as long as the quality is maintained.

Quality

The concern is that the production manager has sacrificed quality for lower cost and greater quantity. The sales director has indicated that sales are falling, perhaps an indication that the customers are unhappy with the product when compared to competitor offers. The greater yield and cheaper mix may well have produced a tasteless soup.

Overall

Overall there has to be concern about the production manager's performance. Cost control and efficiency are important but not at the expense of customer satisfaction and quality. We do not have figures for the extent to which sales have been damaged and small reductions may be acceptable.

(iii)   **Changes to the performance management system**

> **Note:** this element is not required in the revised version of the question. The solution is left here so you can see how the examiner may ask for changes to the system.

The performance management system needs to take account of the quality of the soup being produced and the overall impact a decision has on the business.

Quality targets need to be agreed with the manager. These are difficult to quantify but not impossible. For example soup consistency (thickness) is measurable. Regular tasting will indicate a fall in quality; tasters could give the soup a mark out of 10 on taste, colour, smell etc.

The production manager should not be rewarded for producing lots of cheap soup that cannot be sold. The performance management system should reflect the overall effect that decisions have. If the production manager's actions have reduced sales then sales volume variances should be allocated to the production manager as part of the performance assessment.

(b)   **Variance calculations**

Material price variance

Mixed vegetables: $\dfrac{\$69,700}{82,000} - 0.80 \times 82,000 = \$4,100 \text{ (A)}$

Butter: $\dfrac{\$21,070}{4,900} - 4 \times 4\ 4,900 = \$1,470 \text{ (A)}$

Stock: $\dfrac{\$58,560}{122,000} - 0.50 \times 122,000 = \$2,440 \text{ (F)}$

Material mix variance

Mixed vegetables: $(82,000 - 91,712.2^*) \times 0.80$	=	$7,770 (F)
Butter: $(4,900 - 5,095.1) \times 4$	=	$780 (F)
Stock: $(122,000 - 112,092.7) \times 0.50$	=	$4,954 (A)
Total mix variance		$3,596 (F)

Note: it is only the total mix variance that is a valid variance here

Total input volume = $(82,000 + 4,900 + 122,000) = 208,900$

*Standard mix for mixed vegetables is = $91,712.2

Note: alternate approaches are acceptable.

Material yield variance

$[112,000 - 101,902.4] \times 1.47$ = $14,843(F)

The standard inputs add up to 2.05 units (0.9 + 0.5 + 1.1). This produces 1ltr of soup. The actual inputs were 208,900 litres and therefore the standard expected output should be

$208,900\ \dfrac{1}{2.05} = 101,902.4$ litres.

Alternative answer

Vegetables

	AQ		AP	
		=	69,700	

4,100 A Material Price Variance

	AQ		SP		
	82,000 litres	x	$0.8/ltr	=	65,600

Butter

	AQ		AP	
		=	21,070	

1,470 A Material Price Variance

	AQ		SP		
	4,900 litres	x	$4/ltr	=	19,600

Stock

	AQ		AP	
		=	58,560	

2,440 F Material Price Variance

	AQ		SP		
	122,000 litres	x	$0.5/ltr	=	61,000

	Veg litres	Butter litres	Stock litres	Total litres
(1) AQAM	82,000	4,900	122,000	208,900
(2) AQSM (W1)	91,712	5,095	112,093	208,900
(3) SQapSM (W1)	100,800	5,600	123,200	229,600 (W2)

Mix Variance:				
(2) – (1)	9,712	195	–9,907	
x SP	x 0.8	x 4	x 0.5	
	7,770F	780F	4,954A	3,596F

Yield Variance:

(3) – (2)	9,088	505	11,107	
x SP	x 0.8	x 4	x 0.5	
	7,270F	2,020F	5,554F	14,844F

(W1)
From Std cost card:

	litres					
Veg	0.9	43.9%	x	208,900	=	91,712
Butter	0.05	2.4%	x	208,900	=	5,095
Stock	1.1	53.7%	x	208,900	=	112,093
	2.05					

43.9%	x	229,600	=	100,800
2.4%	x	229,600	=	5,600
53.7%	x	229,600	=	123,200

(W2)

$$\text{\textbf{SQap}} = \frac{\text{Actual Output in total (ltr)}}{\text{Std Output per cost card (ltr)}} \times \text{Standard input per cost card (ltr)}$$

$$= \frac{112,000}{1} \times 2.05$$

$$= 229,600$$

	ACCA marking scheme		Marks
(a)(i)	For each variance		
	Explanation of meaning of variance		1
	Brief discussion of controllability		1
		Maximum	6
(a)(ii)	Comment on cost variance		
	Price:		
	Outside production managers control		1
	Rising prices pressures		1
	Mix		
	Cheaper mix and comment		1
	Yield		
	High yield results and comment		1
	Quality		
	Comment on quality implications		1
	Overall summary		1
		Maximum	5
(b)	Variance calculations		
	Price: 1 mark for each ingredient		3
	Mix:		3
	Yield:		3
	Method marks should be awarded as appropriate		
		Maximum	9
Total			20

3   BFG LIMITED

(a)

Sales	120,000 units	
Sales revenue	$1,260,000	
Costs:		
Direct materials (W1)	$514,000	
Direct labour (W2)	$315,423	
Variable overhead	$126,169	
Rent	$180,000	
Net cash flow	$124,408	
Target cash flow	$130,000	

The target cash flow will not be achieved.

Workings

(W1) Direct material: Batches

		$
First 200 @ $500		100,000
Second 200 @$450		90,000
Remaining 800 @$405		324,000
Total		514,000

(W2) Direct labour

For first seven hundred batches $y = ax^b$

$y = 2{,}500 \times 700^{-0.3219}$

$y = \$303.461045$

Total cost for first 700 batches $= \$303.461045 \times 700 = \$212{,}423$

All batches after the first 700 will have the same cost as the 700th batch. To calculate the cost of the 700th batch we need to take the cost of 699 batches from the cost of 700 batches.

For 699 batches $y = ax^b$

$y = 2{,}500 \times 699^{-0.3219}$

$y = \$303.600726$

Total cost for first 699 batches $= \$303.600726 \times 699 = \$212{,}217$

Cost of 700th batch is $212,423 – $212,217 = $206

Total cost for the 12 months of production

$212,423 + ($206 $\times$ 500) = $315,423

(W3) Variable overhead is $2 per hour or 40% of direct labour

(b)   To calculate the learning factor BFG will have had to measure the time taken to make the first batch (500 hours) and then the time taken to make the second batch. The learning rate measures the relationship between the average time taken between two points as production doubles. The easiest way to measure the learning rate is when the production doubles between the first and second batches.

At 80%

Time for first batch			500
Average time for two batches @80%	500 x 0.8	=	400
Total time for two batches	2 x 400	=	800
Time for second batch	800 – 500	=	300

At 90%

Time for first batch			500
Average time for two batches @90%	500 x 0.9	=	450
Total time for two batches	2 x 450	=	900
Time for second batch	900 – 500	=	400

The 80% learning rate reduces the time taken for the two successive batches above by a greater amount (or faster). Hence the 80% learning rate is the faster learning.

(c)   Possible actions to improve the net cash flows are:

– Increase the price charged. The question states that an agreed specification has been reached, however further research may reveal that a higher price could be tolerated by the market. Equally a form of price skimming may be possible to improve short term net cash flow.

– Reduce the labour cost per batch by removing unnecessary operations or processes. It may be possible to simplify the design without damaging the ability to achieve the price stated.

– Improve the learning rate. This may involve improving the training or the quality of people involved in the production process. This does takes time and costs money in the short run.

– Consider substitute materials (without damaging the product specification). Also look for new suppliers to reduce the input cost.

– Consider ways to reduce the level of variable overhead incurred by the product.

– Investigate whether the production of product X could take place in existing space and hence avoid the extra rent charge. Re-negotiate the rent charge with the landlord.

> **Note:** you are not expected to explain ideas in this depth given the mark allocation for the requirement has been changed

	ACCA marking scheme		
			Marks
(a)	Sales		1
	Direct material		2
	Direct labour	first seven months	3
		last five months	2
	Variable overhead		1
	Rent		1
	Decision		1
	Total for part (a)		1
			—
		Maximum	12
			—
(b)	Second batch times	80%	2
		90%	2
	Comment on faster learning		1
			—
		Maximum	5
			—
(c)	Actions to improve net cash flow		
	(1 mark per idea)		
		Maximum	3
			—
Total			20
			—

4   PRESTON FINANCIAL SERVICES

(a)   **Financial analysis**

There are various financial observations that can be made from the data.

–   Turnover is up 5% – this is not very high but is at least higher than the rate of inflation indicating real growth. This is encouraging and a sign of a growing business.

–   The main weakness identified in the financial results is that the net profit margin has fallen from 20% to 19.8% suggesting that cost control may be getting worse or fee levels are being competed away.

–   Profit is up 3.9%. In absolute terms profits are impressive given that Richard Preston is the sole partner owning 100% of the business.

–   Average cash balances are up 5% – indicating improved liquidity. Positive cash balances are always welcome in a business.

–   Average debtors days are down by 3 days – indicating improved efficiency in chasing up outstanding debts. It is noticeable that Preston's days are lower than the industry average indicating strong working capital management. The only possible concern may be that Richard is being particularly aggressive in chasing up outstanding debts.

Overall, with a possible concern about margins and low growth, the business looks in good shape and would appear to have a healthy future.

(b)   The extra non-financial information gives much greater insight into key operational issues within the business and paints a bleaker picture for the future.

Internal business processes

Error rates

Error rates for jobs done are up from 10% to 16%, probably a result of reducing turnaround times to improve delivery on time percentages. This is critical as users expect the accounts to be correct. Errors could lead to problems for clients with the Inland Revenue, bankers, etc. What is worse, Richard could be sued if clients lose out because of such errors. One could say that errors are unlikely to be revealed to clients. Businesses rarely advertise mistakes that have been made. They should of course put mistakes right immediately.

Customer knowledge

Client retention

The number of clients has fallen dramatically – this is alarming and indicates a high level of customer dissatisfaction. In an accountancy practice one would normally expect a high level of repeat work – for example, tax computations will need to be done every year. Clearly existing clients are not happy with the service provided.

Average fees

It would appear that the increase in revenue is thus due to a large increase in average fees rather than extra clients – average fee is up from $600 to $775, an increase of 29%! This could explain the loss of clients in itself, however there could be other reasons.

Market share

The result of the above two factors is a fall in market share from 20% to 14%. Looking at revenue figures one can estimate the size of the market as having grown from $4.5m to $6.75m, an increase of 50%. Compared to this, Preston's figures are particularly worrying. The firm should be doing much better and looks to being left behind by competitors.

Learning and growth

Non-core services

The main weakness of the firm seems to be is its lack of non-core services offered. The industry average revenue from non-core work has increased from 25% to 30% but Richard's figures have dropped from 5% to 4%. It would appear that most clients are looking for their accountants to provide a wider range of products but Richard is ignoring this trend.

Employee retention

Employee turnover is up indicating that the staff are dissatisfied. Continuity of staff at a client is important to ensure a quality product. Conservative clients may resent revealing personal financial details to a variety of different people each year. Staff turnover is possibly a result of extra pressure to complete jobs more quickly without the satisfaction of a job well done. Also staff may realise that the lack of range of services offered by the firm will limit their own experience and career paths

Conclusion

In conclusion, the financial results do not show the full picture. The firm has fundamental weaknesses that need to be addressed if it is to grow into the future. At present it is being left behind by a changing industry and changing competition. It is vital that Richard reassesses his attitude and ensures that the firm has a better fit with its business environment.

In particular he should seek to develop complementary services and reduce errors on existing work.

Note: The answer to the additional requirement in the original question is as follows:

Financial performance indicators will generally only give a measure of the past success of a business. There is no guarantee that a good past financial performance will lead to a good future financial performance. Clients may leave and costs may escalate turning past profits to losses in what can be a very short time period.

Non financial measures are often termed 'indicators of future performance'. Good results in these measures can lead to a good financial performance. For example if a business delivers good quality to its customers then this could lead to more custom at higher prices in the future.

Specifically the information is appendix 2 relates to the non financial measures within the balanced scorecard.

Internal business processes are a measure of internal efficiency. Interestingly these measures can indicate current cost efficiency as much as any future result

---

Customer knowledge measure how well the business is dealing with its external customers. A good performance here is very likely to lead to more custom in the future.

Innovation and learning measures that way the business develops. New products would be reflected here along with indicators of staff retention. Again this is much more focused on the future than the present.

Measuring performance by way of non-financial means is much more likely to give an indication of the future success of a business.

	ACCA marking scheme		
			Marks
(a)	Financial commentary		
	Turnover growth		2
	Profitability		2
	Cash position		2
	Debtor management		2
			—
	Maximum		8
			—
(b)	Assessment of future prospects		
	Internal business processes		
	Error rates		3
	Not revealed to clients		1
	Customer knowledge		
	Retention		1
	Fee levels		2
	Market share/size		1
	Learning and growth		
	Lack of product range		2
	Employee retention		2
			—
		Maximum	12
			—
Total			20
			—